Literacy for All Students

The Culturally Responsive Instruction Observation Protocol (CRIOP) presented in this book is a framework for implementing culturally relevant literacy instruction and classroom observation. Drawing on research and theory reflecting a range of perspectives—multicultural instruction, literacy theory, equity pedagogy, language and discourse models, sheltered instruction, critical pedagogy—it provides a means for assessing the many variables of classroom literacy instruction and for guiding practitioners in their development as multicultural educators.

Literacy for All Students

- Discusses issues in multicultural literacy instruction within the context of various essential instructional components (such as assessment, curriculum, parent collaboration);
- Provides a protocol for observing features of literacy instruction for culturally and linguistically diverse students;
- Presents vignettes from real classrooms, written by elementary and middle school teachers, showing their victories and struggles as they attempt to implement a pedagogy that is culturally responsive within a climate of high stakes testing.

Illuminating the importance of balanced literacy instruction while also examining the weaknesses of such approaches, this book makes the case that culturally relevant instruction needs to evolve from the literacy uses and cultural practices of the communities being served, and that teachers must be intentional in creating literacy experiences that are affirming and that empower students to take charge of their own learning. A highly effective instrument for assessing culturally responsive literacy instruction in schools, the CRIOP serves as a model for realizing a literacy that is both relevant and transformative.

Rebecca Powell is Marjorie Bauer Stafford Endowed Professor of Education at Georgetown College, Kentucky.

Elizabeth Campbell Rightmyer is an Education/Research Consultant. She directs the statewide Read to Achieve research project from which this book evolved.

Literacy for All Students

An Instructional Framework for Closing the Gap

Edited by
Rebecca Powell and
Elizabeth C. Rightmyer

Routledge
Taylor & Francis Group

NEW YORK AND LONDON

First published 2011
by Routledge
711 Third Avenue, New York, NY 10017

Simultaneously published in the UK
by Routledge
2 Park Square, Milton Park, Abingdon, Oxon OX14 4RN

Routledge is an imprint of the Taylor & Francis Group, an informa business

© 2011 Taylor & Francis

Library of Congress Cataloging in Publication Data
Literacy for all students: an instructional framework for closing the gap / [edited by] Rebecca Powell, Elizabeth Rightmyer.
       p. cm.
   1. Language arts—Social aspects—United States. 2. Literacy—Social aspects—United States. 3. Multicultural education—United States. 4. Language arts teachers—Rating of—United States. I. Powell, Rebecca, 1949– II. Rightmyer, Elizabeth.
   LB1576.L555 2011
   428.0071–dc22   2010049070

ISBN 13: 978–0–415–88586–7 (hbk)
ISBN 13: 978–0–415–88587–4 (pbk)
ISBN 13: 978–0–203–83873–0 (ebk)

Typeset in Perpetual and Bell Gothic
by Keystroke, Station Road, Wolverhampton

To teachers everywhere who are passionate about their craft and who believe in the potential of every child.

Contents

Preface   xi

Acknowledgments   xv

1   Introduction   1
    REBECCA POWELL

Part I The Sociocultural Context of Literacy Instruction   11

2   Classroom Caring and Teacher Dispositions: The Heart to
    Teach All Students   13
    ELIZABETH CAMPBELL RIGHTMYER

    Teachers' Voices: Paper Airplanes 17
    AMY BAKER

    Reflective Activities 31

3   Classroom Climate/Physical Environment: Creating an Inclusive
    Community   35
    REBECCA POWELL

    Teachers' Voices: The Kindergarten Star 48
    HEIDI HAMLYN

    Reflective Activities 53

CONTENTS

4   Parent Collaboration: Developing Partnerships with Families
    and Caregivers   57
    KELLY A. SEITZ

    Teachers' Voices: Welcoming Family Collaboration 71
    DEBBIE CARTER

    Reflective Activities 81

Part II Core Instructional Practices   87

5   Culturally Responsive Assessment: Creating a Culture of
    Learning   89
    REBECCA POWELL

    Teachers' Voices: Kindergarten Voices 102
    LAURA HAMPTON

    Reflective Activities 114

6   Curriculum and Planned Experiences: Bridging the Classroom
    with Students' Worlds   119
    ANGELA COX

    Teachers' Voices: Pop Culture 135
    VICTOR MALO-JUVERA

    Teachers' Voices: Using Native Dance to Teach Writing 139
    SALLY SAMSON

    Reflective Activities 148

7   Pedagogy/Instruction: Beyond "Best Practices"   152
    SUSAN CHAMBERS CANTRELL AND TIFFANY WHEELER

    Teachers' Voices: Vocabulary Instruction in Diverse Classrooms 173
    VICTOR MALO-JUVERA

    Reflective Activities 182

8   Discourse/Instructional Conversation: Connecting School and
    Personal Discourses   190
    SHERRY WILSON POWERS

Teachers' Voices: Our Favorite Discourse Protocols 215
DARELL RICKMERS, AMY BAKER, REBEKAH PASCUCCI,
MEGAN BECHARD, ANGELIA HOWARD, LAURA HAMPTON,
SUE ELLIS, AND MADELINE TODD

Reflective Activities 224

Part III Becoming Critical   231

9   Sociopolitical Consciousness and Multiple Perspectives:
     Empowering Students to Read the World   233
     YOLANDA GALLARDO CARTER

     Teachers' Voices: "This Land Is Your Land" 245
     DARELL RICKMERS, KARA RUBY, SARAH CAREY,
     LAUREN CORNELE, MADELINE TODD, HEIDI HAMLYN,
     AND LESLIE BUSCH

     Reflective Activities 254

Notes on Contributors   258
Index   260

Preface

The aim of this text is to provide guidance for teachers and other school personnel who find the achievement gap to be a problem in their schools. The authors of this book, having worked together for several years in both teacher education and literacy program evaluation, have taught and observed hundreds of classroom literacy activities. Over time, we have become aware that traditional reform efforts such as "research-based" literacy programs and school-wide literacy initiatives have been ineffective in closing the gap. What does seem to make a difference is for teachers to learn about students and their families, and to use this knowledge to provide *culturally responsive instruction*.

To measure culturally responsive instruction, the authors developed the *Culturally Responsive Instruction Observation Protocol (CRIOP)*. The CRIOP is a field-tested instrument that is primarily a tool for *analyzing* teacher instruction. As we became more interested in guiding teachers to become more sensitive to cultural strengths and cultural differences, we expanded our research base and gathered practical strategies and reflective activities to help teachers start on a journey of cultural understanding and successful teaching of historically marginalized students. This book is the result of that search.

This text is designed to serve as a bridge between theory and practice. Each chapter is grounded in sociocultural theory and in research that describes effective teaching practices for underserved students. We believe that all students (and their families) come to school with strengths and motivation that can be tapped by teachers who are willing to confront and work through the ethnocentric biases and ideologies of their own social and cultural identities.

The book is divided into three Parts. Part I, "The Sociocultural Context of Literacy Instruction," describes the background and setting for culturally responsive instruction. In Chapters 2–4, we suggest that learning is at its roots a *human endeavor* and that children and adults in school must be treated *humanely* if they are to perform at high levels. Culturally responsive teachers establish a classroom that radiates care, concern, and respect to students and families and invites them to collaborate with the teacher and with one another to embellish and enrich the education effort. The hallmarks of a warm, demanding teacher; a collaborative classroom climate; and reciprocal partnerships with families are explained with supporting literature and practical applications.

Part II, "Core Instructional Practices," describes a literacy teacher's core practices including assessment, curriculum, instruction, and classroom discourse; explains how current practices create achievement gaps; and suggests how culturally responsive teachers can adjust their daily work in order to better educate all students. Many of these "adjusted" practices are consistently taught in teacher education programs but are largely unused once teachers are acculturated into the typical American school. The authors show how research-based curricula and instructional practices, standardized achievement measures, and traditional classroom discourse structures tend to marginalize students from underrepresented groups. Culturally responsive teachers instruct students in ways that open the curricula to all learners, use a variety of discourse patterns that enable all learners to develop linguistic competence, and measure achievement with multiple assessments during authentic literacy activities.

Part III, "Becoming Critical," enunciates the need for teachers to recognize and grapple with the hegemonic culture of American schools and society that priveleges the language, culture, and history of White, middle-class families. Within the education establishment, multiple perspectives are often avoided in order to maintain efficiency and to reinforce dominant views. However, to become critical consumers and thoughtful citizens, students must be shown how to "read the world" and to question the ideological perspectives embedded in texts. To do this, the culturally responsive educator finds ways to make multiple voices heard and understood and fights for school and community practices that serve everyone.

The reader will see that the CRIOP components overlap and influence each other. For instance, unless teachers believe all students can succeed, they will not be motivated to alter their teaching practices. Culturally responsive instruction is an attitude, work style, or set of values more than it is a set of instructional strategies. In fact, we believe that teachers who want to grow into successful educators for all students must first do the sometimes excruciating work of recognizing their own cultural roots and try to expand their understanding of cultural difference before the instructional strategies will "work."

To that end, each chapter contains three activities for the reader's contemplation. First, each chapter includes at least one vignette written by a practicing teacher in a K-8 classroom that illustrates the CRIOP component. These *Teachers' Voices* can serve to inspire the reader and to understand that practical solutions do not have to be revolutionary to bring success to historically underserved students.

Next, there is a *Summary Table* which outlines the signs of a culturally responsive classroom as well as the indicators of a classroom that is not culturally responsive. Readers might use the summary tables to assess their own classrooms and use the indicators as guides for improving their practice. Alternately, summary tables might be used as discussion starters at faculty meetings or in teacher education classes.

Finally, at the end of each chapter are suggested *Reflective Activities* which require either philosophical or practical questioning of one's own practice. These can be addressed by individual teachers, teacher research groups, or teacher education classes in search of improving instruction so that all learners can succeed.

We invite you to join in our quest to become culturally responsive educators who wish to teach, know, and challenge all of America's schoolchildren. We hope that this text will help to guide you on this journey.

Acknowledgments

The chapters in this book are written by a research team consisting of teacher educators and graduate students from colleges and universities in Kentucky. Through many sessions of research design and data analysis, we gradually became aware of the need for schools, curricula, and teachers to honor and cultivate during instruction the cultural and family backgrounds of students. This work would not have been accomplished without the vision and the generous support of the Collaborative Center for Literacy Development (CCLD) at the University of Kentucky and its Director of Research, Susan Chambers Cantrell. We are also indebted to the CCLD researchers, especially Ellen McIntyre and Dee Jones, who came before us and who helped us craft our grounded theory of culturally responsive instruction and the research methodology to assess it. We also thank Yvonne Greenwalt, program manager for the Read to Achieve research, and Rachel Aiello, University of Kentucky doctoral student, whose attention to detail and field work were key to our collection and analysis of these data.

The work reported in this book was also made possible through a grant from the U.S. Department of Education, Office of English Language Acquisition. Funding from this grant was used to establish the Center for Culturally Relevant Pedagogy at Georgetown College, which for the past three years has implemented a professional development project in culturally responsive instruction with K-8 teachers that uses the instructional framework outlined in this book. We are particularly grateful to the teachers who participated in the grant project. Many of these teachers provided valuable insights on the usefulness of the model for the professional growth of practicing educators, and several also provided vignettes for this volume. We have been particularly impressed by their passion for the teaching profession and by their commitment to educating all students.

We owe a debt of thanks to the reviewers of the prospectus, whose suggestions helped to guide our thinking as we began to shape this volume. We also gratefully acknowledge the work of Naomi Silverman and the excellent staff at Routledge, who provided continuous support from the initial conceptualization of the manuscript to its final production.

Finally, we gratefully acknowledge the hundreds of Kentucky teachers who, while implementing new grant-funded programs, graciously allowed us to study them and their students. We hope that teachers and students around the globe will benefit from this work.

Chapter 1

Introduction

Rebecca Powell

Recently I received an invitation to an expensive meal, compliments of a company that was aiming to sell its products to our institution. Upon exploring the company on the internet, I discovered that the "products" they sell are actually college and graduate-level courses. For a certain price, you can pick your course and they will "deliver" it to you. College classes have now become a commodity to be bought and sold on the open market.

What does this have to do with literacy instruction, and more specifically, with culturally responsive literacy instruction? Consider that literacy, too, has become a commodity. If your students aren't achieving, there's sure to be a "new" program right around the corner that will "fix" the problem. The thinking goes something like this: If we only had enough research, and if we could design a program that precisely matched that research, we could discover that elusive panacea that would lead to reading proficiency for all students.

The problem with this perspective is that learning is more than receiving the delivery of a prepackaged program. Rather, learning occurs through entering into dialogue with others. It is a social activity. As Vygotsky (1978) pointed out in his seminal theory of learning, learning is innately social; that is, it is a socially mediated activity whereby the teacher supports and guides the meaning-making process within the learner's "zone of proximal development." Because learning is fundamentally social, teaching and learning are completely tied to the social context within which they occur.

The commodification of literacy and learning ignores this social context. In so doing, it also ignores the critical importance of the learning environment. Relationships between teachers and students, teachers and families, students and students can either support or hinder the social dynamics of the classroom and the quality of learning that takes place there. Conceptualizing literacy as a set of seemingly neutral "skills" that can be packaged and delivered using research-based "best practices" denies the vital importance of the social dimension of literacy learning and the role that the teacher plays in creating and sustaining the social environment in which learning transpires.

In this book, we present a decidedly different view of literacy instruction. Because literacy is fundamentally a social process, we believe that teachers, students and their families are the most important variables in instruction. We must begin with what students and families know, and what teachers bring in terms of their understanding of literacy, learning, and their role as educators. In this framework, our ideological perspectives matter. As teachers, we must begin the difficult process of questioning who we are, how we view our task, and the lenses through which we view the students and families that we serve.

These lenses are shaped by who we are—our race, social class, gender, age, religion, sexual orientation. The semiotic space within which learning occurs requires that we break down barriers created through human differences and enter into a relationship with "the Other." Teaching is fundamentally about relationship; indeed, we suggest that learning is sabotaged in classrooms that are not characterized by care and mutual respect. Trusting and supportive relationships are essential for learning to occur.

Thus, we begin this book with a fundamental principle: relationships matter. Far too often educators perceive students from underrepresented populations as deficient, thereby undermining the teacher–student relationship. Students who live in poverty or who speak a language or vernacular that differs from Standard English are often viewed as "difficult to teach," coming from families who simply "don't value education." What is important here is that the way we view students and their families makes a huge difference in students' learning, for our pedagogical practices largely emerge from our ideas about teaching and the assumptions that we have of our students and their families/communities (Kagan, 1992; McKown & Weinstein, 2008; Monzó & Rueda, 2001; Tenenbaum & Ruck, 2007). Research shows that teachers' negative beliefs about students have resulted in lowered expectations and decreased opportunities for learning (Crawford, 2007; Harry & Klingner, 2006; Rubie-Davis, Hattie, & Hamilton, 2006; Waxman & Tellez, 2002).

I invite you to think about the assumptions that you have about the students that you teach. Which of your students might you predict to be a potential heart surgeon? Scientist? College professor? Author? President of the United States? For most of us, if we are honest, the students we have in mind would typically be White (or perhaps Asian—particularly in the area of science), middle- to upper-class, and from "professional" homes. How would our teaching change if we saw each one of our students as future surgeons, famous poets, or CEOs of major corporations? If you believe this to be an impossible scenario for the students that you teach, then consider that in all of these categories, persons from disadvantaged homes and communities have excelled, and oftentimes it was *their teachers* that made a difference—teachers who believed that despite the odds, their students would succeed. In essence, they saw their students as capable learners, and they worked hard to make learning meaningful and relevant and to establish a culture of learning in their classrooms.

Unfortunately, however, far too often we hear teachers make comments such as the following:

I'm really worried about next year, because they're closing XYZ school [in a high poverty neighborhood] and they'll all be coming to our school.

The problem is that so many parents just don't care about their child's education. —I've said this

It's just impossible to control these kids. I can't imagine what their homes must be like.

When I first began teaching at this school, students were more disciplined. Our demographics have changed, and the students we have now just don't care about learning. RACIST

Most of my students know that they'll be able to make more money on the streets selling drugs, so they're not really motivated to learn.

While there may, indeed, be a few genuinely unmotivated students and parents, the vast majority of our students do want to learn, and they want their teachers *to treat them as learners*. We contend that the essence of culturally responsive instruction is validating our students as learners. This requires that we sincerely believe that they can think critically and creatively, and that they have valuable resources that they bring to learning that can be leveraged to mediate their understanding. In other words, it requires eliminating the deficit thinking that so often colors our perspectives of our students and their families.

In fact, we would go so far as to suggest that if you hold a deficit perspective toward the students and families you serve, you will be unable to respond in culturally appropriate ways and thus you will undoubtedly perpetuate the achievement gap, despite using "best instructional practices." Ladson-Billings (1994) notes that "culturally relevant teaching is a pedagogy that empowers students intellectually, socially, emotionally, and politically by using cultural referents to impart knowledge, skills, and attitudes" (pp. 17–18). A basic premise of culturally responsive instruction (CRI) is that we must learn from our students and discover the resources they bring to the classroom so that we can provide supportive environments and guide their learning. A second premise is that CRI can only occur in a democratic environment in which teachers, families, and students become partners and work together to promote students' academic, social, and emotional development.

Developing relationships with students and their families allows us to unveil their intellectual, social, linguistic and emotional assets. Teachers find that when they get to know students and parents/caregivers on a personal basis, their perspectives change. They learn about families' hopes and visions for the future, and discover that they have rich experiences that can be used as a foundation for learning. Such discoveries dispel previously held negative stereotypes grounded in deficit thinking (Compton-Lilly, 2003; González et al., 2005).

One of my favorite "teacher stories" is shared by Richard Meyer (1996) in his book entitled, *Stories from the Heart*. He tells of Tami, an 8-year-old student who was totally disengaged and would periodically "disappear" in the classroom. One day, Meyer decided to visit her farm to learn about the new bull that the family had purchased. During the visit, he learned that Tami had "pulled a calf" and knew a great deal about farming. He writes:

> I realized how little I knew about where I was teaching . . . So I started to ask Tami lots of questions about farming. I asked her about manure and how it gets taken out of the barn, and if she ate the animals she raised (she did). I asked her about growing corn and also learned about bulk tanks and electric fences. ("Don't ever pee on one, Mr. Meyer"). Tami and I formed a relationship.
>
> She still went under the desk to suck her fingers, and occasionally to work. But I became a visitor she could tolerate under there. I visited her there and at home and she taught me a lot. I thanked her a lot. I thanked her for every bit of information she gave me. She helped me talk to the other parents of the children in my class and to the other children, too . . . She never became a lover of school, but she did become a credible and reliable resource. It was a role that made her important to me, through me, to others. I think she sensed her importance.
>
> School became okay for Tami. I became okay for Tami. And she became okay for me . . . I was finding myself—finding that, in spite of my own education, I was a learner. The rural context in which I was teaching brought with it an urgency to learn in order to teach. I was inventing myself as a teacher in a context that was new to me in many ways. I was learning the children's ways with words.
>
> (pp. 50–51)

As teachers, we possess important pedagogical knowledge. We have been educated in "best practices" in curriculum, instruction, assessment, classroom management. What can be missing, however, is how to connect those practices to students' lives. As Meyer suggests, to become truly effective educators, we must "re-invent" ourselves as teachers. We must value the cultural knowledge of our students and families, and learn from those we serve.

ABOUT THE BOOK

Each chapter examines a specific component of the Culturally Responsive Instruction Observation Protocol (CRIOP), which was designed as a classroom observation tool to guide and assess teachers' growth in implementing culturally responsive practices. Acknowledging that literacy instruction is inherently social, we have chosen to begin this book on culturally responsive literacy practices with a discussion of relationships, both within and outside the classroom. Chapter 2 by Elizabeth Campbell Rightmyer examines the critical importance of trusting and caring student–teacher relationships in literacy learning. A great deal of research supports the notion that students must believe that teachers truly care about them as learners, and that their teachers believe that they can learn. This theme is woven throughout several other chapters in the book, as it drives the decisions we make in terms of curriculum, pedagogy, and assessment.

Rebecca Powell in Chapter 3 addresses the classroom environment and the ways in which we can structure our classrooms to support the learning of every student. A culturally responsive environment is one that affirms students' cultural identities and nurtures a climate of collaboration and mutual respect. In Chapter 4, Kelly A. Seitz builds on these ideas by examining the ways in which we can invite parents to become true partners in teaching their children. Culturally responsive literacy practices are embedded in an environment that values the resources that students and families bring to learning, and that uses these resources to mediate the language and literacy growth of students.

The next four chapters target specific aspects of instruction. In Chapter 5, Rebecca Powell examines assessment practices. In this chapter, we argue that because literacy is a social practice, valid literacy assessment must occur as students are engaged in meaningful uses of written and oral language. We also suggest that our assessment practices ought to create a culture of learning versus a culture of evaluation, in that assessment should tap into students' potential for learning, versus merely measuring what they already know.

Chapters 6 and 7 examine curriculum and instruction. In these chapters, Angela Cox and Susan Chambers Cantrell and Tiffany Wheeler make the point that culturally responsive literacy instruction is grounded in "best practices." However, while best practices are necessary, they are not sufficient for closing the achievement gap. Rather, for optimal learning to occur, teachers must use instructional materials and practices that provide the necessary support for students within their "zone of proximal development"—materials and practices that use students' "cultural data sets" (Lee, 2007) and families' "funds of knowledge" (González, Moll, & Amanti, 2005) to scaffold students' learning. Hence, no prepackaged instructional program can be culturally responsive. Uncovering the resources of our students and families and planning instruction that utilizes those resources ought to be an important part of the assessment/instruction cycle.

In Chapter 8, Sherry Wilson Powers examines the conversational patterns (discourse structures) that we use in our classrooms. Classroom discourse practices can reveal much about how we perceive our students and their linguistic competence, and our preferences for a more democratic or authoritarian environment. In this chapter, we examine the basic tenets of language acquisition and use and suggest that, to develop language proficiency, students must be given opportunities to use both oral and written language in a variety of social contexts. Language is power; it is also an integral part of our identities. Thus, it is important to affirm students' native languages and give them a voice while simultaneously teaching the "language of power."

The final chapter by Yolanda Gallardo Carter examines literacy from a critical perspective. Critical literacy suggests that no text is neutral; rather, every text can be deconstructed to illuminate its ideological perspective. "Text," in this sense, is anything that can be "read" for its inherent meaning: films, bumper stickers, billboards, toys, websites, video games, and so on, as well as more conventional written texts. Critical literacy brings together all of the elements of culturally responsive literacy instruction, in that it both builds on and extends the world of our students. The ultimate goal of critical literacy is "reconstruction"—re-figuring the text to encourage social transformation.

To assist the reader, the chapters are similarly structured. Each begins with a brief introduction, followed by a review of the professional literature and a discussion of how the ideas can be applied in practice. Within each chapter, we have included vignettes from teachers that serve to illustrate the particular component of the CRIOP. Finally, every chapter includes reflective activities that are designed to extend the concepts presented, as well as a table that summarizes the essential elements of the CRIOP component.

ABOUT THE CRIOP

This volume evolved from a statewide research study that examined literacy practices in schools that participated in a state-funded reading intervention initiative in primary classrooms. Student achievement data gathered over a three-year period revealed that, while early intervention led to positive student achievement gains in literacy for all students, the achievement gap persisted between middle-/upper-class White students and their historically marginalized peers (e.g., students of color and those from a lower socioeconomic class). Coupled with this finding was the fact that the researchers were able to identify very few instances of culturally responsive instructional practices in the classrooms that were observed.

Similar results have been found in national investigations. As we write this book, a national research study has recently been published that reveals the disappointing results of the federally funded program, Reading First. Reading First was launched in 2002 and was primarily targeted at raising the reading achievement of students in high-poverty schools. By promoting "scientifically-based" literacy practices, Reading First was heralded as a means to close the literacy achievement gap. Yet the Reading First Impact Study, contracted by the U.S. Department of Education and published in 2008, found that the reading scores of children in schools receiving Reading First funding were not significantly higher than the scores of children who attended schools that did not receive funding.

For those of us who have been involved in multicultural/equity education for a number of years, such results are not surprising. Absent in the popular educational rhetoric is the recognition that learning is as much social as it is cognitive. Students are cultural, linguistic, and emotional beings. As noted previously, how educators interact with students, the assumptions that they bring to the learning task, how they view the families and communities they serve—all have a profound impact on student achievement. Teachers, too, see the world through their own cultural experiences—experiences that often are in contrast to those of their students. Thus, while the "best practices" of such programs are necessary, we maintain that they are not sufficient to assure success for every student.

CRI—also known as culturally relevant instruction or culturally responsive/relevant pedagogy—can be defined as instruction that is grounded in the lives of students. That is, CRI is instruction that considers the language, experiences, social identities, cultural resources, and "funds of knowledge" (González, Moll, & Amanti, 2005; Moll, Amanti, Neff, & González, 1992) of the students and families we serve. Given the diversity of today's classrooms, it is clear that no instructional package can meet the learning needs of all students. Beyond this, however, by assuming that literacy can be "neutral" and reducing it to a series of disembedded skills, we fail to acknowledge the social, cultural, and political contexts within which literacy is learned and practiced. Literacy learning—and indeed, all learning—occurs within a social and cultural space that can either affirm or diminish students' social and cultural identities.

In order to be able to capture and measure the various elements of culturally responsive instruction, our research team embarked on a project that eventually led to this book. The Culturally Responsive Instruction Observation Protocol (CRIOP) draws from the research base on culturally relevant pedagogy. After a comprehensive review of the published literature in culturally responsive instruction (CRI), the team categorized its findings under eight themes, which led to the eight components that comprise the CRIOP: Classroom Caring/Teacher Dispositions; Classroom Climate/Physical Environment; Parent Collaboration; Assessment; Curriculum/Planned Experiences; Pedagogy/Instructional Practices; Discourse/Instructional Conversation; and Sociopolitical Consciousness/Multiple Perspectives. The instrument was subsequently developed, field tested, and refined over a two-year period. The CRIOP has been used as an instrument for coding classroom observations as well as a framework for the professional development of teachers.

We are continuing to field-test and refine the CRIOP instrument, and it is currently undergoing even further revision in order to include the most up-to-date research on culturally relevant instruction. The CRIOP framework that is presented in this book reflects our latest understanding of the research on culturally responsive literacy practices, and is designed to be a tool for guiding practitioners in their development as multicultural educators. A summary of the CRI features for each component can be found in the table at the end of each chapter.

Throughout this text, we suggest that our narrow conceptualization of literacy has contributed to the achievement gap between White, middle-/upper-class students and those from historically marginalized populations. A focus on discrete skills and the commodification of instruction obscures the social dimension of literacy and the sociocultural and political contexts in which it is used. It also denies the cultural knowledge and linguistic competence that students possess that can be used to scaffold learning. All students have resources that can be leveraged for instruction; all students are, in some sense, "literate." A reductionist perspective of literacy, however, restricts our understanding of how students' communicative competence, knowledge, and experiences can be used to build bridges to new knowledge. Even more unfortunate, however, is that students' cultural knowledge is generally perceived as being outside the domain of schooling, and is often even viewed as inhibiting students' access to "real literacy."

The CRIOP framework attempts to close this cultural divide by examining the essential elements of culturally responsive literacy instruction. The framework includes "best practices," but does not privilege them; rather, the focus is on the cultural identities of students and teachers, and how these identities can serve as resources or hindrances to students' literacy achievement. Learning does not occur in a vacuum. By acknowledging the sociopolitical context of schooling, schools and educators can create learning communities that nurture a respect for all students, thereby creating the necessary conditions for supporting student learning. They can assure that all dimensions of learning—from the classroom environment, to the instructional resources they use, to their pedagogical and assessment practices—affirm students' cultural and linguistic identities and allow students to demonstrate competence.

It is important to point out, as Ladson-Billings (1995) does, that CRI is ultimately just "good teaching." The practices espoused in this book are appropriate for *all* students. Indeed, as will be discussed throughout this volume, research-based "best practices" are the foundation for culturally responsive literacy instruction. What differentiates traditional practices from those that are culturally responsive, however, is that culturally congruent practices evolve from students' lives. Culturally responsive instruction cannot be codified and packaged, but rather emerges from the "ways with words" of the populations being served. As Ladson-Billings suggests, in culturally responsive classrooms, "[K]nowledge is continuously recreated, recycled, and shared by the teachers and the students" (p. 163).

Ultimately, culturally responsive instruction is about honoring who students are and what they bring to learning. In honoring students, we send the message that we believe in them as learners. They come to us with knowledge about language and literacy that they have acquired within the rich social contexts of their families and communities. As culturally responsive educators, we value those communities and affirm students as learners by acknowledging that they have been immersed in literacy since the day that they were born.

When we honor the cultural knowledge of our students by making it an integral part of the curriculum, we change the social dynamics within the classroom. That is, when we discover and legitimize students' areas of expertise outside the world of the classroom and adapt our instructional practices to meet their needs, we begin to view our students in a new way. *Honoring students' knowledge changes us as teachers*. We see our students differently. We value who they are, and what they know. Similarly, students begin to value one another. And in the process, we discover the genuine rewards of teaching in a way that makes a difference in students' lives. It is our hope that this book will assist teachers in realizing this goal.

REFERENCES

Compton-Lilly, C. (2003). *Reading families: The literate lives of urban children*. New York: Teachers College.

Crawford, F. A. (2007). Why bother? They are not capable of this level of work: Manifestations of teacher attitudes in an urban high school self-contained special education classroom with majority Blacks and Latinos. *2007 E-Yearbook of Urban Learning, Teaching, and Research, 2007*, 12–24.

González, N., Moll, L. C., & Amanti, C. (Eds.). (2005). *Funds of knowledge: Theorizing practices in households, communities, and classrooms*. Mahwah, NJ: Lawrence Erlbaum.

González, N., Moll, L., Tenery, M. F., Rivera, A., Rendón, P., Gonzales, R., & Amanti, C. (2005). Funds of knowledge for teaching in Latino households. In N. González, L. C. Moll, & C. Amanti (Eds.), *Funds of knowledge: Theorizing practices in households, communities, and classrooms* (pp. 89–111). Mahwah, NJ: Lawrence Erlbaum.

Harry, B., & Klingner, J. (2006). *Why are so many minority students in special education? Understanding race and disability in schools*. New York: Teachers College.

Kagan, D. M. (1992). Implications of research on teacher belief. *Educational Psychologist, 27*, 65–90.

Ladson-Billings, G. (1994). *The dreamkeepers: Successful teachers of African American children*. San Francisco: Jossey-Bass.

Ladson-Billings, G. (1995). But that's just good teaching! The case for culturally relevant pedagogy. *Theory into Practice, 34*(3), 159–165.

Lee, C. D. (2007). *Culture, literacy, and learning: Taking bloom in the midst of the whirlwind*. New York: Teachers College.

McKown, C., & Weinstein, R. S. (2008). Teacher expectations, classroom context, and the achievement gap. *Journal of School Psychology, 46*(3), 235–261.

Meyer, R. J. (1996). *Stories from the heart: Teachers and students researching their literacy lives*. Mahwah, NJ: Lawrence Erlbaum.

Moll, L. C., Amanti, C., Neff, D., & González, N. (1992). Funds of knowledge for teaching: Using qualitative research to connect homes and communities. *Theory and Practice, 31*, 132–141.

Monzó, L. D., & Rueda, R. S. (2001). *Sociocultural factors in social relationships: Examining Latino teachers' and paraeducators' interactions with Latino students*. Research Report 9. Washington, DC: U.S. Department of Education, Office of Educational Research and Improvement.

Rubie-Davis, C., Hattie, J., & Hamilton, R. (2006). Expecting the best for students: Teacher expectations and academic outcomes. *British Journal of Educational Psychology, 76*, 429–444.

Tenenbaum, H. R., & Ruck, M. D. (2007). Are teachers' expectations different for racial minorities than for European American students? A meta-analysis. *Journal of Educational Psychology, 99*(2), 253–273.

Vygotsky, L. S. (1978). *Mind in society: The development of higher psychological processes* (M. Cole, V. John-Steiner, S. Scribner, and E. Souberman, eds.). Cambridge, MA: Harvard University Press.

Waxman, H. C., & Tellez, K. (2002). *Research synthesis on effective teaching practices for English language learners*. The Mid-Atlantic Regional Educational Laboratory at Temple University, Center for Research in Human Development and Education. Retrieved from ERIC database. (ED474821).

Part I

The Sociocultural Context of Literacy Instruction

Chapter 2

Classroom Caring and Teacher Dispositions: The Heart to Teach All Students

Elizabeth Campbell Rightmyer

I don't have nothing to write today—maybe never. Hammer in my heart now, beating me, I feel like my blood a giant river swell up inside me and I'm drowning. My head all dark inside. Feel like giant river I never cross in front me now. Ms Rain say, You not writing Precious. I say I'm drownin' in river. She don't look me like I'm crazy but say, If you just sit there the river gonna rise up drown you! Writing could be the boat carry you to the other side. One time in your journal you told me you have never really told your story. I think telling your story git you over that river Precious.

(Sapphire, 1996, pp. 96–97)

Writing is a powerful tool. It captures the heart. It touches the soul. It can be the "boat" that carries us to the "other side." Yet too often, literacy is taught as if it didn't really matter. It becomes a mere skill—one that is mechanical and disconnected from students' lives outside the classroom. Taught in this way, literacy fails to become a medium for understanding one another and ourselves, for capturing reality, for demonstrating our humanity. To teach literacy as more than a mechanical skill, the teacher must show she *cares about her students and their abilities* for using language.

When I was involved in teaching undergraduate students to build on children's natural inclinations to read and write, there were always many questions about why a teacher should use engaging, personal strategies instead of more direct, authoritarian ones. To help them understand, each semester we adopted a primary classroom and collected reading and writing samples from children, inspected these artifacts to detect the children's interests, assessed the students' literacy development, and designed lessons that attracted students' attention. The undergrads often asked why I asked them to "figure out" what children knew and what they liked to do, why we had to drive across town to study children, and why I refused to teach them to follow an adopted reading series step-by-step. One year a student answered that question: "Because she *cares.*"

It's true. I care. I care that many elementary students come to school eager to learn but within a few years become demoralized and disengaged. I care that preservice teachers are likely to find their first job in schools that are labeled "underperforming" and where there are many children "whose nightmares come both day and night" (Irvine, 1999, p. 245) so that the teachers begin to feel like adversaries of the children in their own classrooms. I care that in our country, based on democratic principles, the tax-funded public schools educate some children better than others. I wanted children to be able to express their lives through their writing and to connect their lives to their reading. I wanted *my* students to see the importance of writing for getting to know *their* students and to discover connections between their lives through their writing and reading, just as Ms Rain connected to her student Precious.

"Do you know the movie *Jerry Maguire?*" the brave undergrad continued. "You should rent it. You'd like it." She was right. The young and virile Tom Cruise dressed in a crisp white shirt with a glint in his eye and an appealing, crooked smile, Jerry Maguire realizes that his career as a flashy, fast-talking broker for his client's commercial endorsements is not what he expected it to be:

> I couldn't escape one simple thought: I hated myself. No, no, no, here's what it was: I hated my place in the world . . . I was remembering even the words of the original sports agent, my mentor, the late great Dickey Fox, who said, "The key to this business is personal relationships." . . . Suddenly it was all pretty clear. The answer was fewer clients. Less money. More attention. Caring for them, caring for ourselves.
>
> (Transcribed from Brooks & Crowe, 1996)

This chapter, indeed, this book, is written for each teacher we have met in schools in the past 25 years who came to their career full of hope that their students would learn and enjoy learning. It is for the students who might love and admire them because they were the teachers who cared. It is for the reader who wants to understand why a *caring personal relationship* is the foundation for reaching all children and for closing the achievement gap. The tendrils of personal relationship are many, and they are grounded in the concept of care. Ms Rain, Precious' teacher, knows the power of writing for developing a caring personal relationship with students (Sapphire, 1996). Throughout the novel, she communicates with her students through dialogue journals. Writing becomes the medium for establishing a relationship grounded in trust and care.

Yet too often, the very process of schooling militates against our ability to care for our students. Sonia Nieto, who devotes her career to understanding the development of successful teachers for children of color, describes how the "official discourse" of education and its themes of accountability, standards, and testing have obscured the essential work of the teacher who cares (Nieto, 2005). Instead of assessing children's literacy in terms of "the light in their eyes" (Nieto, 2009), we are asked instead to measure their reading speed and accuracy. Literacy instruction that focuses only on skills that are easily quantifiable conflicts with our current knowledge of reading instruction (National Institute of Child Health and Human Development, 2000), child development (Vygotsky, 1934/1978), and human learning (American Psychological Association, 1997) which suggests that learning occurs within a social context and that academic skills and learning dispositions co-develop during instruction. Unfortunately, the official discourse convinces teachers that student performance on tests is the goal and that practicing on tests is an integral part of the daily education of students. Classroom teachers with whom we have recently worked, for example, discussed the assessments in their school this way:

> I think that with third grade they are starting to become "intermediate" so they have to take assessments that the primary students have to take *and* they take the assessments that the fourth and fifth graders are taking also. And I think it would be more beneficial for them to focus on what the [state] test is going to be like.
>
> (Third grade teacher, 5/12/09)

> With the [fluency test] . . . it is pretty much a weekly assessment. If you get to your oral reading test, you are going to hit those at least once a week, maybe once every other week, but it is immediate feedback . . . We can get on the [fluency test web] site now, they have got that free trial going where you have got your entire class just categorized and here, these are the lessons you can do with your kids, every lesson is step by step. This is what your child needs to work on.
>
> (First grade teacher, 5/12/09)

The official school discourse so bombards the teacher with the importance of multiple, periodic assessments and a focus on disembedded skills that it obscures the building of personal relationships. Instead of viewing the child holistically, as a young mind eager to grow and to learn, it portrays the child as a one-dimensional raw material to be shaped to fit the expectations of the school. We

15

have seen this dehumanizing ritual played out in many classrooms. Further, often the more different the students are from ourselves, the more we rely on rigid, authoritarian methods to control and measure them.

Just as the achievement and progress of students are defined by standard-ized procedures in the official discourse, so also is the competence of the "highly qualified" teacher assessed. Measurements of teacher quality such as scores on standardized tests, college grade point averages, and advanced degrees and credentials set by national accrediting agencies are primary in the licensing of America's teachers (Nieto, 2005). Once released to the classroom, teachers are further evaluated by their school's aggregated scores on mandated, standardized tests. Just as Cruise's success was evaluated by the size of his client's contracts and endorsements while the client suffered life-threatening injuries on the field, teachers' success is gauged by aggregated increases in standardized test scores while their students struggle with language and cultural differences.

Students of color often view this official discourse as unwelcoming and impenetrable. They characterize their apathy and frustration for school with phrases such as "It don't make no sense to give us all these tests," and their opinion of teachers with comments such as "You can tell if they care. You can tell if they like teaching" (Thompson, 2007, p. 24). These students (who compose almost one-third of all American students, and are disproportionately non-White and economically disadvantaged) often drop out of school as soon as they can. With few prospects for employment, they sometimes resort to crimi-nal activity to stay afloat (Bridgeland, Ballenz, Moore, & Friant, 2010). When Shobe (2003) asked incarcerated adults to describe their favorite teacher, 37% replied that she was "willing to help," 31% reported that she "worked with me to make sure I understood," and others declared that this teacher was con-siderate, open-minded, and "didn't give up on me." These adults remembered that their favorite teacher "liked" them and treated them the same as everyone else—decently, with concern, respect, and caring.

Consider that schooling in America could be different. It could, for example, be conducted in an atmosphere of care and in which caring was taught as an essential skill for human success. Noddings (1992) suggests six themes of care than can frame the K-12 curriculum, including caring for the self; for the inner circle; for strangers and distant others; for animals, plants, and the Earth; for the human-made world; and for the world of ideas. A curriculum centered on care can be rigorous academically as well as focused socially (Noddings, 1992). Noddings states:

> Teachers can be very special people in the lives of children, and it should be
> legitimate for them to spend time developing relations of trust, talking with

students about problems that are central to their lives, and guiding them toward greater sensitivity and competence across all the domains of care.

(1995, p. 677)

In our experience, there are many teachers who care in the current education system, but their affection and stamina for teaching and learning are not described in the official discourse. Yet, they are described elsewhere, in what Nieto (2005) calls "the discourse of possibility" (p. 28) in which positive, proactive adults arrange their instructional settings to communicate to students *you can do it, you can learn this, you can achieve. I, as your teacher, am successful when you achieve, and as I like to feel successful, you WILL achieve*. These teachers are not held back by the damaging climate in American education today; instead, they work with a vision of what is possible: that all students in America can and will succeed.

This chapter looks at the pivotal and foundational concept of *teacher care*, the desire to reach out to students, to connect with them:

[C]aring is not just a warm, fuzzy feeling that makes people kind and likable. Caring implies a continuous search for competence. When we care, we want to do our very best for the objects of our care. To have as our educational goal the production of caring, competent, loving, and lovable people is not anti-intellectual. Rather, it demonstrates respect for the full range of human talents.

(Noddings, 1995, p. 679)

Care is the personal energy to listen to all students and to hear what they think. Care is the impetus for communicating, "This may be hard for you, but I know you can do it. Try. I'm here to help." Care is characterized by respect, under-standing, help, and commitment to teach all students in ways that show them they are valued, worthy, accepted, and appreciated and that leads them to academic proficiency.

TEACHERS' VOICES

Paper Airplanes

Amy Baker

THIRD GRADE TEACHER, WESTERN ELEMENTARY, GEORGETOWN, KY

In 2008, I stepped into my classroom of 27 kids. Of those 27 students, all but two were in our ESL program and five were of Hispanic descent. As I scanned my classroom, my eyes stopped at Emanuel. Cute kid, but I had already heard about

17

him. He was the one who never turned his papers in. Good luck getting him to participate in the classroom; he will just sit there and do nothing. Over and over I heard these things, so I knew I had my work cut out for me. As any teacher would, I stood over him and watched to make sure he turned in his class work. I cleaned out his desk to find work that he shoved into his desk, unfinished. I asked the ESL teacher to talk to his parents about turning in the homework. I encouraged him when he completed something, but there still wasn't that internal motivation on his part—incentive was still external and the learning process was still run by me. Emanuel was making some progress, but I did not have a connection with this child. I had already done what every good teacher does, hadn't I?

As the first few weeks passed, Emanuel did his work, as long as I checked for everything and stood above him watching his every move. When I did step away from him to work with others, I started noticing he liked to make paper airplanes. Over and over he made these planes, and when I cleaned out his desk, guess what I found? Airplanes made out of plain paper, airplanes made out of notebook paper, airplanes made out of incomplete work pages. I didn't show my interest in his planes because Emanuel did not like to have attention drawn to him. But why won't he do what I ask of him? I am nice and encouraging to him. Why? Why? Why? Then the light bulb went off.

I was sitting at home one night and my husband had just come back from a big conference. He had these posters of military helicopters and airplanes. There was a whole calendar full of them. Airplanes . . . Emanuel . . . Could they really go together? I grabbed them up for the next day.

When I saw Emanuel the next morning, I pulled him aside and showed him what I had. His eyes lit up like it was Christmas. I gave them to him. No stipulation involved—I just told him that I noticed he liked planes and that my husband worked with planes and thought he may like these. I told him it was our secret so the others wouldn't get jealous.

Then a funny thing happened. Papers started getting completed. Homework was turned in. There wasn't as much "stuff" stuffed into his desk. He started talking to a table mate more and more.

As the year progressed, Emanuel continued to work hard. Of course there were days that the worksheets did not get done, or homework wasn't turned in, but for the most part, he did what was asked of him. He even started working with partners other than his Hispanic friends. He made a best friend that year too—he and Chris were like two peas in a pod. I even let them sit together a lot because it really helped Emanuel to come out of his shell even more.

Emanuel and I also talked at different times throughout the year about his life and what he did and didn't like to do. I had finally realized that he needed *that* connection, too. I also talked to the ESL teacher about the parts of his home life that Emanuel did not divulge. I found that his parents were very hard workers. Dad worked on a horse farm and mom stayed at home with the kids. He had an older high-school sister and a pre-school brother. He didn't get to see dad much because of his hours and dad did extra work on the side at night to make ends meet.

One of the highlights of the year was when we, the class, were reading a story about a Hispanic grandfather and grandson looking for work. There were many Spanish terms in the book that I couldn't pronounce and really had no idea what they were. I gathered my five Hispanic students and asked for their help. You would have thought I had given them the moon. They helped me and the class to pronounce the words and explained to us what the different items were. There was also a question/ answer session at the end of the presentation and the kids asked the Hispanic kids about their life and their culture. Many in this group remembered life in Mexico or visits that they had taken there. One of the girls' families was building a house and getting ready to move back. Another's uncle had died and the aunt and cousins were moving up here to live with them. The little group really enjoyed sharing their lives, but the best part for me was when the class asked Emanuel a question and he responded. He wanted to tell them about himself and his life. In front of the whole class! Oh, what a wonderful day to see him want to work and share in front of his peers. He wasn't trying to hide so hard anymore.

A couple of weeks after this presentation, near the end of school, I noticed the airplanes coming back out again. Right on the heels of the airplanes being made, the papers started disappearing in the desk and homework wasn't being completed. This time, it was a very clear signal to me that something was wrong. I did the usual teacher things. I got the ESL teacher involved and she let the parents know that homework wasn't being done. But I did something different this time. I pulled him aside one morning and asked him straight out what was wrong. He told me! (I had tried this at the beginning of the year to no avail.) Apparently his mom had gotten a part-time job at night and she wasn't home, so dad took care of them, plus he was still working his extra jobs at night. Emanuel felt like he had been on his own and it was really bothering him. So of course we worked together and made a plan to get his homework done at school with our help, and then he didn't have to worry about it at night. The airplane making slowed down again.

Throughout the year, Emanuel and I worked to build a relationship. I learned how to make that connection with him and showed him and the others that their lives and cultures were important to us and the class, especially when it came to another language. How incredibly lucky they were to know two languages instead of one like me! You could tell Emanuel was proud to know these things that I, the teacher, didn't know and it turned him into a teacher himself. I know all teachers look for those connections in every one of their students, but with him, it was *my learning what was important to him and his culture* that told him I cared. Who would have thought it would start with a paper airplane?

CARE AS RESPECT FOR ALL

"This is your journal," Miz Rain say. "You're going to write in it every day." Jo Ann look disgusted, like yeah right! One minute we doin' ABCs, next minute we spozed to be writing. Miz Rain give her look like f—you bitch. I can tell Miz Rain don't like her but she don't say nothin'. She jus' tell us we gonna write in our journals for fifteen minutes every day . . . Miz Rain say, "Write what's on your mind, push yourself to see the letters that represent the words you're thinking."

(Sapphire, 1996, pp. 60–61)

The teacher is the force behind the classroom (Au and Kawakami, 1991). She sets the tone with her demeanor and her insight into student activity. Many students follow along with an assertive teacher and participate in learning without disrupting. Others may act in disrespectful ways towards the teacher's authority. A culturally responsive teacher coaches these disengaged students back into the fold by acting in respectful ways towards them and demanding that they act in respectful ways towards her and others in the classroom community. Instead of entering into power struggles with students by invoking controls and punishments, the teacher puts the focus of her communication and relationship with students on the schoolwork itself. "We are here to learn" becomes the overarching message of the classroom.

The caring attitude of the culturally responsive teacher is grounded in a concern for the whole child and a respect for the child's every effort to learn. Gay (2000) writes that:

Teachers demonstrate caring for children as *students* and as *people*. This is expressed in concern for their psychoemotional well-being and academic success; personal morality and social actions; obligations and celebrations; communality and individuality; and unique cultural connections and universal human bonds. In other words, teachers who really care about students honor their humanity, hold them in high esteem, expect high performance from them, and use strategies to fulfill their expectations.

(pp. 45–46)

One hallmark of a respectful teacher is her ability to act with fairness towards all students. In a diverse classroom, fairness means that every student has the same rights as well as the same responsibilities. Classrooms in which a White (for example) teacher has greater rapport with her White students than with her African American students is acting unfairly. Culturally responsive teachers work consistently to overcome their own assumptions about diversity, care when their students do not participate, and look for avenues to equalize student contributions to class activities. Unfair teachers give privileges and make exceptions for students that they like, and give students the impression that teachers must always be pleased in order to be considered respectful. Such unfair treatment can lead to psychological disengagement (Norguera, in Cartledge & Kourea, 2000, p. 9) and helplessness—the idea that no matter what one does, it is not affirmed, so it is not worth the effort to engage.

The inner compass of the respectful teacher adjusts for time, place, and task at hand. Not every student can respond with interest and vigor to every assigned activity, transition, discussion, or exam. In any group of children or adults, there is diversity of response. A culturally responsive teacher expects diversity in student behavior and respects students' attempts to join the class activity. The teacher shows respect when she guides students with predictable routines and offers school work that is interesting and challenging. She shows respect when she makes an effort to incorporate students' "ways of knowing" in classroom routines and the curriculum. She shows respect by thinking ahead to how students might respond and, when students do not engage, she redirects them with courteous reminders.

Another marker of respect is the teacher's ability to include every student in the affairs of the classroom and the school. Just as playing favorites is a way of disrespecting students, exclusion is a way of insulting and injuring them (Kohl, 1994, p. 21). A culturally responsive teacher is dedicated to the task of teaching all children (Shade, 1994) and cares enough about each student to keep working with each and every one of them. The teacher's stamina for inclusion is viewed by the students as a cue for their own engagement. Teachers who connect with every student every day model an acceptance of difference that students can emulate. When a teacher shows both inclusiveness and respect, she affirms the students in the class, and that affirmation fuels the students' energy to stay engaged. Such teachers are known as *warm demanders*. Warm demanders communicate "a non-negotiable demand for student effort and mutual respect" (Bondy & Ross, 2008, p. 54). Such teachers not only promote high student achievement, but also cultivate better classroom behavior from under-represented students.

Brown (2004) interviewed 13 urban teachers regarding their culturally responsive practices and learned that one of the ways teachers showed they care was to create a "business-like atmosphere" (p. 276) in their classroom. An elementary teacher in this study expressed her approach this way:

You have to be real. I cannot pretend that I am from Harlem or Washington Heights. Their experience is not my experience. I think convincing them that what I have to say is important is the key. That happens through consistency—

through just being honest. Trying to fit in to be one of them never works. I always follow up and keep my promises to them. Doing exactly what you say you'll do means something to students. They experience so many empty promises.

(Brown, 2004, p. 277)

Using language that shows this mutual respect is non-negotiable in culturally responsive classrooms. The language of respect is *encouraging* and *dialogic* (Larrivee, 2002). Culturally responsive teachers use hopeful words with students that convince students to try and to persevere.

Children build on their strengths, not on their weaknesses . . . it's as important for us to see and name what children are doing well as to identify how they can improve. This is true whether we're teaching academic or social skills.

(Denton, 2007, p. 91)

Culturally responsive classrooms are filled with discussions and critical conversations that are enacted with respectful dialogue and that create a climate of tolerance and acceptance. The teacher values student autonomy and teaches students how to use self-acceptance to put forward their own ideas while building other-acceptance in listening to and challenging others. The teacher's use of praise is limited to the acknowledgement of effort (e.g., "Keep trying; I know you can get it") and to the prompting of student self-evaluation ("You've really been focused on your book. What's so interesting?") (Denton, 2007, p. 87).

A diverse classroom can be a tricky place to demonstrate respect, as *respect* is a cultural concept and the style of respectful interaction varies with cultural norms. Earning students' respect is sometimes a matter of acting in a manner that they perceive as an authority (Au, 1993). For example, Cynthia Ballenger (1992), talking about the Haitian 4-year-olds in her class, says:

[They] ran me ragged. In the friendliest, most cheerful, and affectionate manner imaginable, my class followed their own inclinations rather than my directions in almost everything. Though I claim to be a person who does not need to have a great deal of control, in this case I had very little—and I did not like it.

(pp. 50–51)

Ballenger then notes, to her frustration, that the other teachers (all Haitian women) "had orderly classrooms of children who, in an equally affectionate and

22

cheerful manner, *did* follow directions" (p. 51). Through the auspices of a teacher–researcher seminar, Ballenger studied the disciplinary language of her Haitian colleagues and learned that the Haitian children were more responsive to instructions such as "Does your mother let you bite? . . . Does your father let you punch kids? . . . You are taking the good ways you learn at home and not bringing them to school . . . Do you want your parents to be ashamed of you?" (p. 52), than to the more analytical method of Euro-American teachers (e.g., "If you need to find a seat in the group, don't hit, use your words"). When Ballenger tried out this "Haitian way" (p. 55), the children's behavior improved significantly.

Because teachers need to learn what students respect, the language of respect also includes *listening*. Just as Ballenger listened carefully to the Haitian teachers in her school, each classroom teacher can learn to modify her discourse to communicate caring and acceptance.

> Through careful listening, I learn that Trisha cares perhaps more than most children her age about appearing capable. This tells me that it might be best to give her any needed redirections in private. Listening to Ben's sharing about his weekend, I gather that he likes having choices of activities to do. I make a mental note that the classroom strategy of giving students some choices in their learning might be especially effective with him.
>
> (Denton, 2007, p. 7)

Listening lets us know the child and it also lets the child know that we care what they say. Active listening (rephrasing what someone says) and questioning (delving deeper into the student's comment or activity) lengthen the conversation in ways that extend the student's learning. When the teacher recapitulates a student's idea, she shows the class that she values students' opinions and that listening is a form of thinking. Also, the student's idea opens a window into that student's identity, so that other classmates can see him; this helps build classroom community. Bondy and Davis (2000) found that attentive, respectful listening was a successful strategy for unseasoned teachers to build relationships with their students:

> I'm learning to respect who he is by listening to him. Listening to how beautiful he is. Listening to how good he is at speaking, and about how much he understands. When I listen to him, I see his possibilities, and I respect him . . . I listen to him, and I'm open to what he has to say and to what he really feels. I try not to put my beliefs into what he might be feeling because I have no idea what he's truly experiencing.
>
> (Preservice teacher, in Bondy & Davis, 2000, p. 60)

23

CARE AS UNDERSTANDING, COMPASSION, AND EMPATHY

Dear Precious,

Don't forget to put the year, '88, on your journal entries.

Precious, you are not a dog. You are a wonderful young woman who is trying to make something of her life. I have some questions for you:

Where was your grandmother when your father was abusing you?
Where is Little Mongo now?
What is going to be the best thing for you in this situation?

Ms Rain

(Sapphire, 1996, p. 71)

Caring teachers are advocates for their students. When Precious wrote in her journal that her grandmother told her she was no better than a dog—"only a dog will drop a baby and walk off" (p. 68)—Ms. Rain responded to Precious as a writer and as a person. It can be difficult for teachers to empathize with students when their experiences differ in many ways. Vivian Gussin Paley, for example, describes in each of her 13 books a different aspect of children's active learning, the caring community in which they play and work, and her experience as a teacher in the diverse kindergarten classroom at the University of Chicago Laboratory Schools. Being a white, Jewish teacher is the explicit subject of one of these narratives (1979), in which she reflects that school is essentially a "white environment" (p. xvii) and realizes, when making a list of the students she "couldn't handle" (p. 8), that the list named mostly African American children in her class. She made a goal for herself that year to learn to study her own inability to confront discrimination among the children's playgroups and to evaluate her judgment in her child guidance strategies. Her overarching question became "Am I fair to the black children?"

Many researchers document the "whiteness" of school's official discourse. For example, the typical patterns of interaction include students sitting passively while the teacher delivers instruction; students raising their hands and waiting for the teacher to acknowledge their turn to speak; students speaking and writing in ways logical to Whites; and the many assignments and assessments designed using White cultural norms (Au, 1993; Delpit, 1988; Ginsberg & Wlodowksi, 2000; Weinstein, Curran, & Tomlinson-Clarke, 2003). Banks (1992) writes that "Our schools were designed for a different population at a time when immigrant and low-income youths did not need to be literate or have basic skills to get jobs and to become self-supporting citizens" (p. 15).

It is no wonder, then, that children from underserved populations can find school to be a difficult and uncaring place. What these students need is what all students need—a teacher who strives to understand them. Understanding is a deep form of learning; it requires study and reflection:

> I have developed special "antennae" that help me to see my students as individuals, some of whom attend school against great personal odds. There is nothing magical about my antennae. I have developed them by carefully constructing an environment in which my students are comfortable sharing with me things they might not even be able to share with others—even their own family members.
>
> (Marshall, 2003, n.p.)

The caring teacher empathizes with her students. She celebrates with them when they succeed and she digs in to work harder when they do not. She understands that each individual student is constructing knowledge in his own way and that some children may initially refuse to learn. Kohl (1994) reminds us that students can make a choice whether to learn; they have "free will" (p. 10) and sometimes it may be safer for a student to refuse to learn than to try.

Our own work in early reading instruction uncovered the sad finding that many students choose to avoid reading in their classrooms, especially when they were assigned more "closed" tasks (Powell, McIntyre, & Rightmyer, 2006)—those that lack choice, challenge, student control, collaboration, constructing meaning, and consequences (Turner & Paris,1995). When students feel that they lack control in the learning environment—when they are treated as *objects* instead of subjects—they may refuse to learn. This is one way of gaining control. One teacher we interviewed, confronting the apathy and refusal of her elementary school students, blamed the students' families instead of the school:

> There are just so many things going on [in this school] to really, really help these kids. But if they are not getting the practice and if they have no motivation of their own, whether it's just because they don't have much confidence or whether nobody else cares, so why should they care, I don't really know where that lack of motivation comes from, but that's a really hard bridge to cross when they just don't seem to care a lot.
>
> (Third grade teacher, 5/26/09)

The empathetic teacher looks for the reasons, including those in her own environment, that encourage students not to learn, and she structures the classroom to allow for many divergent responses, including ones that are critical of her work. She continues to perceive the students as capable and assumes that

25

student behavior is inherently logical (Au, 1993). Empathy—attempting to see the school the way the student sees it—diminishes the possibility that the teacher will misunderstand and therefore misdirect the students (Shade, 1994).

In order to understand the diversity of students in our classrooms, it is necessary to know students' cultural identities. Often teachers emphasize content and diminish the importance of getting to know their students as individuals. In diverse classrooms, where there may be a cultural mismatch between the teacher and her students, this can be particularly problematic. It is important to acknowledge that we teach students, not content. Students value teachers who care and want the teacher to get to know them personally (Ford, Howard, Harris, & Tyson, 2000). Just as the respectful teacher is aware that there are multiple ways for children to learn and show respect, the compassionate teacher learns the values of children's families and indigenous cultures and the power of those values to motivate learning (Ballenger, 1992). Much of this information can be obtained from students' families as well as observing students within their ethnic peer group.

Similarly, all families have important "funds of knowledge" that can be leveraged for learning (Moll, 2007). More will be said about families' funds of knowledge in the following chapters, but here it is important to note that teachers who can learn their students' family ways will be more successful in developing the safe place that all children need to learn. The compassionate teacher acknowledges that students will participate in class in ways that they have been socialized at home. She appreciates that students participate and finds ways to accommodate students' "ways of knowing" so that she and her students can learn through everyone's participation. For example, she demonstrates working collaboratively and using respectful words, then allows students to work collaboratively with each other and requires that they use respectful words. She makes adjustments to routines and redirects when she sees that students do not participate. She steps in when children misinterpret her and their fellow students and brokers understanding between her and the students and between students and their peers.

CARE AS AN ETHIC OF HELPING

Jermaine say, "Where we gonna begin?"

Miz Rain say, "At the beginning," and pick a piece of chalk out her purse and walk to the board. She write A on the board, she hand the chalk to Jermaine. Jermaine write B. Jermaine hand it to Consuelo, she write C. Consuelo hand it to Rhonda she write D. Rhonda hand it to Rita. Rita take a step and start to cry. Miz. Rain say we all in this together. All us say E real loud, Rita go up 'n write E, hand me chalk 'n I write F and so it go. Then we sits back down all at once, that makes us laff, and Miz Rain say this is the beginning.

(Sapphire, 1996, p. 48)

Helping is a quality that many students cite as an indicator that teachers care (Berry, 2006; Gay, 2002; Ford et al., 2000; McDermott & Rothenberg, 1999). Ms. Rain's helpful nature and collaborative methods (such as allowing high school age students to help each other write the alphabet on the board) transformed an untenable situation (teaching the alphabet) into a joyful one. All students need help—that's why they're in school—and appreciate the assistance of others when it is given with care. Culturally responsive, collaborative classrooms (as described in Chapter 3) are ones in which students and teachers help each other. For example, one primary teacher we observed in our former work described her students as "junior teachers" who were authorized to help anyone else in the class understand the material and complete the work. In diverse classrooms where students of many backgrounds and abilities coexist, helping becomes an important medium for bridging differences. "The group functions somewhat like a 'mutual aid society' in which all members are responsible for helping each other perform and ensuring that everyone contributes to the collective task" (Gay, 2002, p. 110).

The building of a helping, caring community takes time and attention. One teacher and her class created a visual web of interdependence by tossing a ball of yarn from person to person across the circle of students:

"I feel the whole web shake when someone else moves" . . . "because we are all connected" . . . "Yeah, just like we're connected to our class. When we do something mean, we all feel it." . . . We agreed that we must pay attention to how our actions affect those around us, just as we'd had to mind the yarn to ensure we didn't pull too hard on someone's fingers. We agreed to pledge to take care of one another.

(Collins, 2009, p. 82)

In the official discourse of schooling, helping is characterized as harmful to student independence and students work solo on much of their schoolwork. If a student asks for help out of turn, he is considered weak-minded or behavior-challenged. Because students are to work alone, teachers in the official discourse school spend a great deal of time controlling the students to be quiet, take turns, bring their own materials, stay on task and participate when asked. Students of all backgrounds find this sort of control disrespectful and demeaning, especially when they need help.

27

Within the discourse of possibility, teachers identify the range of skill that a child can accomplish independently and provide mental and emotional scaffolding for the student to practice a new skill (Vygotsky, 1934/1978). Teachers monitor students as they complete their assignments and often provide supportive comments and strategies to challenge and extend individual student thinking and to encourage perseverance. Likewise, students are also resources for one another. *They help each other with their work.* The Center for Research on Education, Diversity, and Excellence (CREDE) cites *joint productive activity* as a primary principle of culturally responsive instruction (CREDE, 2002). More will be said about the importance of a "helping" classroom environment in Chapter 3.

CARE AS THE COMMITMENT TO TEACH ALL CHILDREN

"I think I understand you, Precious. But for now, I want you to try, push yourself, Precious, go for it."

I reach out my hand for book.

"Just do the best you can, if you don't know a word skip—" She stop.

"Just look at the page and say the words you do know."

I look at the page, it's some people at the beach. Some is white, some is orange and gray (I guess thas spozed to be colored).

"What do you think the story is about Precious?"

"Peoples at the beach."

"That's right." Miz Rain point to a letter, ask me what is it. I say,

"A."

(Sapphire, 1996, p. 52)

The diverse, multi-ability classroom is a complex arena for teaching every student well; however, this is what culturally responsive teachers do. Through communicating high expectations, the friendly, warm demander sees to it that all students excel. "Excuses for not doing one's best are not accepted in culturally responsive classrooms. Failure, of this or any other type, is not an option" (Ford et al., 2000, p. 420). High expectations are beneficial to all students in several ways: motivationally, aspirationally, academically, and socially. An uncaring environment is characterized by "impatience, intolerance, dictations, and control . . . A most effective way to be uncaring and unconcerned is to tolerate and/or facilitate academic apathy, disengagement, and failure" (Gay, 2000, pp. 47–48).

In the familiar Pygmalion studies (Rosenthal & Jacobsen, 1968), teachers were informed that one group of students (which was actually randomly selected by the experimenters) was capable of advanced academic performance. After instruction, this "advanced" group showed higher achievement than their randomly-selected counterparts. The teachers' expectations during instruction "caused" some students to outperform others. Extending the Pygmalion effect to racial and ethnic groups, teacher Jane Elliot taught her own third graders (in 1968) a lesson in discrimination by telling them that today, the blue-eyed people in the class were better than the brown-eyed people, and thereby giving the blue-eyed people privileges such as second helpings at lunch and five minutes of extra recess. The brown-eyed people wore special collars so they could be identified from a distance as the "inferior persons" they were. By the end of the day, among other things, one brown-eyed boy had punched a blue-eyed boy who called him "brown eyes." In discussing the incident, Elliot asked the students why that was a problem: the boy did have brown eyes and he had brown eyes yesterday but there was no name-calling or punching. The third graders realized it was because they had learned the practice of social discrimination and marginalization (Peters, 1985).

Teachers are social beings who have lived a number of years in a milieu that enacts a set of values. Other persons who hold membership in the teacher's setting and context are similar to the teacher and she feels comfortable with them. Her attitudes and beliefs are shaped by that background and those people; she feels that they are "right." When that teacher is a White, middle-class person (as are over 80% of American teachers), those values include the attitude of White privilege, expectation of college completion and upward mobility, and a strong sense of the importance of school and teacher authority. Thus, an American teacher is likely to come to believe that the White, middle-class students in her class are superior, simply because they act in and aspire to the same things she does.

Thus, before we can care, we must recognize ourselves (in addition to our students) as cultural beings (Weinstein, Curran, & Tomlinson-Clarke, 2003). Because American schools were established by Whites and Whites continue to be the dominant voice in the process of schooling, our schools are drenched in White values. These values can create what several authors have called "a cultural mismatch" between the teacher and (some of) her students (Delpit, 2006; Diller & Moule, 2005; Ford et al., 2000; Weinstein, Curran, & Tomlinson-Clarke, 2003). Cultural mismatch can lead to marginalization of students who seem to be "others" who are not like "us." Like Ballenger (1992), whose work with young Haitian children led her to learn from the students and families she served, we must recognize our own ethnocentrism and acknowledge the value in our students' cultural "ways of knowing."

Ms. Rain cared for Precious and her other students and used literacy, especially dialogic journal writing, to learn about their lives. Despite the fact that they came from horrific environments, she accepted them and validated their knowledge—even though they barely knew the alphabet. Teacher care brought Precious out of the abyss. Literacy was the medium for doing this. Rather than denigrating her students and seeing them as "culturally deficient," Ms. Rain became their advocate. Culturally responsive teachers remind themselves that they teach in classrooms of multiple perspectives. A caring teacher recognizes that we all see the world through a particular cultural lens, and questions her own beliefs and attitudes. Throughout this book, we encourage teachers to broaden their sociopolitical consciousness in order to challenge the attitude of middle-class superiority and the bias of White privilege.

Caring grows exponentially in culturally responsive classrooms. "When a teacher cares enough to keep polishing, the shiny luster that all children have comes shining through" (Collins, 1992, p. 186). We believe that it is the teacher's job to lead students to literacy and also to lead them to self-control and self-respect. The caring teacher sets the tone for the inclusive diverse classroom and moves every student forward in both academic achievement as well as personal development.

Table 2.1 *Summary of CRIOP Component: Teacher Dispositions and Care*

Element	What you would expect to see in a classroom where CRI practices are occurring	What you would expect to see in a classroom where CRI practices are not occurring
Students and teacher show respect for themselves and others.	Teacher sets the tone for respect by treating students as *people*. Students' attempts to join in the learning are recognized and nurtured. Teacher uses culturally responsive ways for showing respect and care.	Teacher treats students as objects that need to be honed and improved. Teacher focuses on teaching content versus teaching students.
Students and teacher show compassion and empathy.	Teacher and students see each other as individuals. They celebrate each other's achievements. They work to understand each other's perspectives.	Teacher shows impatience and intolerance for student behavior. Teacher blames students and families for "poor motivation."
Teacher and students are helpful to each other.	Teacher supplies many scaffolds that assist students to perform well. Children are encouraged to help one another so that all can experience success. There are many joint productive activities.	Students work on solitary, prescribed assignments. Student collaboration is discouraged.

Table 2.1 *Continued*

Element	What you would expect to see in a classroom where CRI practices are occurring	What you would expect to see in a classroom where CRI practices are not occurring
Teacher shows a commitment to teach all students.	Teacher is a warm demander who insists that all students put forth their best effort every day. Teacher insists that students do the work. Everyone is included in activities and discussions.	Some students are allowed not to work or to just "get by." It's clear that the teacher has lower expectations for some students.

REFLECTIVE ACTIVITIES

1 During the first six weeks of school, ask students to share their hopes and dreams for the school year (Northeast Foundation for Children, 2001). Post them in the classroom via sentence strips or artwork to remind students of their goals and celebrate as students approach and achieve them.

2 Spend a few of your opening literacy activities learning about your students and their lives. Develop with the class an inventory of the games, sports, pastimes that children enjoy inside and outside of class. Allow students to interview each other (or respond in small groups to your interview questions). Ask students to report to the whole class two interesting things they learned during the interview. Record these "interesting things" for use in other activities.

3 Discuss with your school librarian the key information you learned from the interview activity above. Ask him/her to select a text set of high-quality picture books that address these topics. From time to time, introduce each book in the collection to the class with a short talk that refers to particular students' interests. Read some of these books aloud and encourage children to read them in order to learn more about each other and the world around them.

4 Begin a dialogue journal with each student. Set aside five uninterrupted minutes each day for writing in the journal and make it your practice to respond to five student journals each day. Once students learn the routine of uninterrupted writing, invite them to trade journals and respond to each other.

5   Develop a Friday sharing time in which two or three students can talk for a few minutes about one of their own or their family's interests or special events (these can vary widely from pet grooming and toy collections to family events and holidays). In preparation for this, ask students to brainstorm topics that they know a lot about and another list of topics they would like to know more about. Post these lists in a prominent place and allow students to self-select their topics (on or off the lists). Ask students periodically if they have ideas to add to the list. When the curriculum touches on one of these topics, point out to the class that this is what someone wanted to learn this year.

REFERENCES

American Psychological Association (APA). (1997). *Learner-centered psychological principles: A framework for school reform and redesign.* Retrieved June 23, 2010, from http://www.apa.org/ed/governance/bea/learner-centered.pdf.

Au, K. H. (1993). *Literacy instruction in multicultural settings.* New York: Harcourt Brace.

Au, K. H., & Carroll, J. H. (1997). Improving literacy achievement through a constructivist approach. *Elementary School Journal, 97,* 203–221.

Au, K. H., & Kawakami, A. J. (1991). Culture and ownership: Schooling of minority students. *Childhood Education, 67,* 280–284.

Ballenger, C. (1992). Because you like us: The language of control. *Harvard Educational Review, 62,* 199–208.

Banks, J. A. (1992). Creating multi-cultural learner-centered schools. In J. A. Banks, L. Darling-Hammond, & M. Greene, *Building learner centered schools: Three perspectives.* New York: Teachers College National Center for Restructuring Education, Schools, and Teaching. (ERIC Document Reproduction Service No. ED357480).

Berry, R. A. W. (2006). Inclusion, power and community: Teachers and students interpret the language of community in an inclusion classroom. *American Education Research Journal, 43,* 489–529.

Bridgeland, J. M., Ballanz, R., Moore, L. A., & Friant, R. S. (2010). *Raising their voices: Engaging students, teachers, and parents to help end the high school dropout epidemic.* Retrieved June 23, 2010 from http://www.civicenterprises.net/pdfs/raisingtheirvoices.pdf.

Bondy, E., & Davis, S. (2000). The caring of strangers: Insights from a field experience in a culturally unfamiliar community. *Action in Teacher Education, 22,* 54–66.

Bondy, E., & Ross, D. D. (2008). The teacher as warm demander. *Educational Leadership, 66,* 54–58.

Brooks, J. L., (Producer) & Crowe, C. (Director). (1996). *Jerry Maguire* [Motion picture]. United States: TriStar Pictures.

Brown, D. F. (2004). Urban teachers' professed classroom management strategies: Reflections of culturally responsive teaching. *Urban Education. 39,* 266–289.

Cartledge, G., & Kourea, L. (2000). Culturally responsive classrooms for culturally diverse students with and at risk for disabilities. *Exceptional Children, 74,* 351–371.

Center for Research on Education, Diversity, and Excellence (CREDE). (2002). *The five standards for effective pedagogy.* Retrieved June 30, 2010 from http://gse.berkeley.edu/research/credearchive/standards/standards.html.

Collins, M. (1992). *Ordinary children, extraordinary teachers.* Charlottesville, VA: Hampton Roads Publishing.

Collins, R. R. (2009). Taking care of one another. *Educational Leadership, 66,* 81–82.

Delpit, L. (1988). The silenced dialogue: Power and pedagogy in educating other people's children. *Harvard Educational Review, 58,* 280–298.

Delpit, L. (1996). *Other people's children: Cultural conflict in the classroom.* New York: New Press.

Delpit, L. (2006). Lessons from teachers. *Journal of Teacher Education, 57,* 220–231.

Denton, P. (2007). *The power of our words: Teacher language that helps children learn.* Turners Falls, MA: Northeast Foundation for Children.

Diller, J. V., & Moule, J. (2005). *Cultural competence: A primer for educators.* Belmont, CA: Thomson Wadsworth.

Ford, D. Y., Howard, T. C., Harris III, J. J., & Tyson, C. A. (2000). Creating culturally responsive classrooms for gifted African American students. *Journal for the Education of the Gifted, 23,* 397–427.

Gay, G. (2000). *Culturally responsive teaching: Theory, research, and practice.* New York: Teachers College Press.

Gay, G. (2002). Preparing for culturally responsive teaching. *Journal of Teacher Education, 53,* 106–116.

Ginsberg, M. B., & Wlodowski, R. J. (2000). *Creating highly motivating classrooms for all learners: A schoolwide approach to powerful teaching with diverse learners.* Hoboken, NJ: Wiley.

Irvine, J. J. (1999). The education of children whose nightmares come both day and night. *Journal of Negro Education, 68*(3), 244–253.

Kohl, H. (1994). *I won't learn from you.* New York: New Press.

Larrivee, B. (2002). The potential perils of praise in a democratic interactive classroom. *Action in Teacher Education, 23,* 77–88.

Marshall, K. (2003). *Teachers' "antennae" help them better understand at-risk students.* Retrieved February 26, 2010 from http://www.educationworld.com/a_curr/voice/voice096.shtml.

McDermott, P., & Rothenberg, J. J. (1999). Teaching in high-poverty, urban schools: Learning from practitioners and students. Paper presented at the annual meeting of the American Educational Research Association. Montreal, QC, April. Retrieved from ERIC database (ED431058).

Moll, L. (2007). Reflections and possibilities. In N. González, L. C. Moll, & C. Amanti (Eds.), *Funds of knowledge: Theorizing practices in households, communities, and classrooms* (pp. 275–298). Mahwah, NJ: Lawrence Erlbaum Associates.

National Institute of Child Health and Human Development (NICHD). (2000). *Report of the National Reading Panel. Teaching children to read: An evidence-based assessment of the scientific research literature on reading and its implications for reading instruction.* Retrieved June 22, 2010, from http://www.nichd.nih.gov/publications/nrp/upload/smallbook_pdf.

Nieto, S. (2005). Schools for a new majority: The role of teacher education in hard times. *New Educator, 1*, 27–43.

Nieto, S. (2009). *The light in their eyes* (2nd ed.). New York: Teachers College Press.

Noddings, N. (1992). *The challenge to care in schools.* New York: Teachers College Press.

Noddings, N. (1995). Teaching themes of care. *Phi Delta Kappan, 76,* 675–679.

Northeast Foundation for Children. (2001). Our hopes and dreams for school. *Responsive Classroom Newsletter, 13*(3). Retrieved September 12, 2010 from http://www.responsive classroom.org/newsletter/13_3nl_1.html.

Paley, V. G. (1979). *White teacher.* Cambridge, MA: Harvard University Press.

Peters, W. (Producer & Director). (1985). *A class divided* [Motion picture]. USA: Yale University Films for Frontline.

Powell, R., McIntyre, E., & Rightmyer, E. C. (2006). Johnny won't read, and Susie won't either: Reading instruction and student resistance. *Journal of Early Childhood Literacy, 6,* 5–31.

Rosenthal, R., & Jacobsen, L. (1968). *Pygmalion in the classroom.* New York: Holt, Rinehart, and Winston.

Sapphire. (1996). *Push.* New York: Knopf.

Shade, B. (1994). Understanding the African American learner. In E. Hollins, J. E. King, & W. C. Hayman, *Teaching diverse populations: Formulating a knowledge base* (pp. 175–189). Albany, NY: SUNY Press.

Shobe, R. (2003). Respecting diversity: A classroom management technique – A survey of incarcerated adult students. *Journal of Correctional Education, 54*(2), 60–64.

Thompson, G. L. (2007). *Up where we belong: Helping African American and Latino students rise in school and in life.* Indianapolis, IN: Jossey-Bass.

Turner, J. C. & Paris, S. G. (1995). How literacy tasks motivate children's literacy. *Reading Teacher, 48,* 662–673.

Vygotsky, L. (1934/1978). *Mind in society.* Boston, MA: Harvard University Press.

Weinstein, C. S., Curran, M., & Tomlinson-Clarke, S. (2003). Culturally responsive classroom management: Awareness into action. *Theory into Practice, 42,* 269–276.

Chapter 3

Classroom Climate/ Physical Environment: Creating an Inclusive Community

Rebecca Powell

> To teach in a manner that respects and cares for the souls of our students is essential if we are to provide the necessary conditions where learning can most deeply and intimately begin.
>
> (hooks, 1994, p. 13)

A few years ago, a colleague and I had the privilege of visiting the Culture and Language Academy for Success (CLAS) in Los Angeles. CLAS is a K-8 charter school that serves an African American inner-city population. When we arrived, children and staff were assembled outside for opening activities—singing, recitations, and celebrations of students' accomplishments.

Upon entering the building, we were immediately struck by the way that the school reflected the population being served. There was a display of the symbolic representation of Ma'at, with a list of seven principles that were used throughout the school as a framework for student behavior: justice, righteousness, truth, harmony, balance, order, reciprocity. These principles evolve from ancient Egyptian sources of moral and spiritual instruction and are used to guide students' character development. Accompanying this display were charts that noted various ways that the children could demonstrate these principles, e.g., "how we show righteousness." Children were expected to show respect to others in the community and to demonstrate a solid work ethic, and they were tangibly rewarded when they displayed these principles in their daily actions.

Throughout the building and in all of the classrooms, there was affirmation of the African American community. Pictures on walls reflected their culture and community. In one hallway, we saw a chart that compared Ebonics structures with Standard English structures, clearly the result of a lesson (or perhaps even a series of lessons) that validated students' language while comparing it to the language of power. In a first grade classroom we visited, the class had developed brainstorm webs of "My Community Place" that examined students' special places in the community. The classrooms had what we would call a "print-rich" environment, with hundreds of books of various genres, all of which had Black protagonists.

The children in this school were excited about literacy, and about learning in general. In a fourth grade classroom we visited, every student was actively engaged in a discussion of a literary text; in fact, they were so eager to participate that they were literally "jumping out of their seats." In one of the first grade classrooms, a young boy came up to me as I was leafing through a library book and said, "I can recite the poem in that book." (He did, word for word.) In essence, there seemed to be an "ethos of learning" in this school, where students viewed themselves as learners, were encouraged to support one another in their pursuit of literacy, and celebrated the accomplishments of their peers.

On the CLAS website, one finds the following statement: "Schools are communities and should at all times seek to reinforce their identity as a community through deliberate practices" (http://www.cultureandlanguage. org/learncomm_a.html). Since our visit to CLAS, I have tended to refer to this school as a model of the ways that the environment of a school can show respect for—or alternately, can marginalize—the identity of the population being served. Far too often, schools fail to capitalize on the ways that space and activity can be used to affirm students and their families. For instance, I was recently in a middle school classroom where the teacher had placed pictures on the wall that demonstrated a particular concept she was teaching. The students—most of whom were African American and Latino/a—were asked to circulate around the room and note various features in the pictures. This activity included many culturally responsive features in that it involved active learning, allowed for student collaboration, and asked students to apply what they were learning to popular texts (magazines). At the same time, it fell short of being truly culturally responsive, because every picture they were required to deconstruct displayed White, upper-/middle-class individuals.

While this may seem like a minor point, especially if the reader is one of the White majority of teachers, consider the message that we send to our students when none of our classroom displays contain images of individuals who look like them, or show examples of their language or community practices. Pictures, charts, and other visual images are a form of literacy, and individuals "read" them through their own cultural lenses. Our classroom displays can reinforce the notion of White privilege by marginalizing other racial and ethnic groups, and by inadvertently associating "White" with academic achievement and success.

The physical environment is a reflection of the overall climate of the school, which can either be one that welcomes diversity and portrays a multicultural community of learners, or one that largely ignores diversity, thereby dismissing the unique contributions and funds of knowledge of students and their families. An African American colleague of mine recounted a powerful story of her experience with desegregation. She recalls entering the White school and being escorted to her classroom by "the whitest man she had ever seen"—a tall principal with a white coat and white beard. As she was seated in the back of the classroom, he informed her that this was "his" school, and she had better not make trouble. When her mother tried to participate in her child's education, she was told that she was not allowed in the classroom, and if she wanted to meet with the teacher she would have to do so in the main office. This experience was contrasted with her previous schooling in a Rosenwald school, where the parents literally "owned" the institution. They cooked the meals and did the custodial work, and were integrally involved in their children's education. All of the resources of the community were leveraged to assure that their children learned.

Unfortunately, we still have vestiges of desegregation in our schools. Many schools take a color-blind stance, assuming that by implementing best instructional practices, all students will learn. Throughout this text, we emphasize the idea that best practices are necessary, but not sufficient, to realize high levels of achievement for all students. As a foundation for student learning, schools must be inclusive communities in which every child and every family feels valued. Inclusive educational settings welcome diversity and honor it by validating the experiences of those being served.

In discussing a culturally responsive school and classroom climate, it is important to note that schools historically have endorsed a White, middle-class orientation of individual achievement and advancement, which is characteristic of individualistic, Euro-centric cultures (Delpit, 1995; Deyle, 1995; Valenzuela, 1999; Weinstein, Curran, & Tomlinson-Clarke, 2003). This orientation contrasts with the collectivist cultures of many non-European populations, which value group collaboration and support. Thus, in establishing an inclusive school and classroom community, the cultural orientation of the group must also be an important consideration. That is, it is not enough to validate students' cultural experiences; rather, schools must be "oriented" to embrace the preferred ways of "being in the world" of the populations being served. This may mean promoting the accomplishments of the group over individual achievement, for instance, or encouraging students to assist one another with challenging tasks. We turn now to the research literature in this area.

SUPPORTING RESEARCH

The literature supporting this particular domain of the CRIOP suggests that a caring and inclusive classroom environment can have a profound effect on students' academic achievement (Edelsky, Draper, & Smith, 1983; Finnan, Schnepel, & Anderson, 2003; Nunnery, Butler, & Bhaireddy, 1993). Such environments are characterized by positive social interactions that create a sense of community within the classroom. Within these learning communities, there is a norm of interdependence, where students take responsibility for the learning of their peers. Berry (2006) suggests that such classrooms can be distinguished by a "helping ethic," where students assist others in their learning. Similarly, the knowledge that students bring to the learning task is valued and is viewed as a useful resource for others in the community. Within a community of learners, peer collaboration is the norm, and students and their families are respected for who they are and for the cultural and linguistic knowledge that they contribute.

Research suggests that a communal learning environment can be particularly beneficial for students of color (Au, 1993: Fordham, 1991; Ladson-Billings, 1994; Reyes, Scribner, & Scribner, 1999). At the same time, it should be emphasized that it is not merely the use of group work that is beneficial. Rather, it is an emphasis on the achievement of the group versus the individual. Reflecting a collectivist versus an individualistic orientation, the achievement of the group, and not individual students, is primary.

In her book, *The Dreamkeepers: Successful Teachers of African American Children*, Ladson-Billings (1994) compares the social relations in culturally congruent classrooms with those that are more assimilationist. In culturally responsive classrooms, the teacher demonstrates a connectedness with all students and encourages students to learn collaboratively. Students are expected to support the learning of others and to take responsibility for the collective learning of the group. She explains:

> Each of the teachers who participated in my study uses some form of co-operative learning techniques in their teaching. However, the underlying ideology that informs their use of these strategies is to prepare their students for collective growth and liberation. Rather than elevate the importance of individual achievement, the teachers encourage their students to work within a collective structure and reward group efforts more often than individual ones. Even in discussions of heroes or role models, several of the teachers expose the underlying group structure and support that boosted the individuals to excellence.
>
> (p. 60)

Ladson-Billings goes on to state that these highly effective classrooms are like family units, where students form "extended family groups." Within these groups, students take responsibility for monitoring and supporting the learning of others to assure that all are achieving at high levels. "Although testing is individual, test results reflect on the whole family" (p. 62). Thus, culturally relevant cooperation can be contrasted with more traditional "group work," in that students assume mutual responsibility for one another's learning.

Research on effective schools for Hispanic students shows similar findings. In their study of eight border schools, Reyes, Scribner, and Scribner (1999) found that successful schools are those that have a shared vision of success for all students. Teachers and staff view their students and their families as valuable resources who have knowledge and expertise that can enhance the learning of the group. Students are given a voice in their own learning, and they are encouraged to work together to solve problems and discover new insights. In effective learning communities, the researchers found that students "experience the personal satisfaction gained from constructing their own knowledge in a social environment or contributing to another's knowledge base and understanding" (Scribner & Reyes, 1999, p. 201). Students are empowered as learners because they come to recognize that their knowledge is central in the instructional process:

> Because students realize they are indispensable resources to each other, they replace previously held assumptions about who can teach and what constitutes knowledge and understanding. They are armed with the powerful realization that they are the most important participants in the teaching and learning process!
>
> (p. 201)

Students in these highly effective classrooms and schools receive messages that reinforce the idea that they are competent learners who have knowledge and resources that can contribute to the learning of others.

In addition to empowering students as learners, however, effective teachers of all children acknowledge that one of their primary responsibilities is to empower students to work for change. Particularly for students of color and those who live in poverty, this empowerment involves the capacity to bring about social change within the larger community. Hence, culturally responsive teachers recognize that one of their responsibilities is to teach students how to build social networks that can be leveraged for social action. Collaborative work environments, therefore, are important not only for realizing high levels of student achievement; rather, students learn "skills needed to engage in social and political reform action," and "students practice them in helping each other through the learning process" (Gay, 2002, p. 623). Indeed, in her research of highly effective teachers, Ladson-Billings (1994) found that such teachers sought to "help students see community-building as a lifelong practice that extends beyond the classroom" (p. 73).

Most schools, however, tend to perpetuate White, middle-/upper-class norms that promote individual advancement and upward mobility. Further, the cultural experiences of students of color and those living in poverty are rarely found in the formal school curriculum. In response to their resulting marginalization, there is some evidence that suggests that students of color and those of lower socioeconomic status may develop an oppositional identity that impedes their academic achievement (Fordham & Ogbu, 1986; MacLeod, 1995; Ogbu, 1987, 2003). In his research in Shaker Heights, a high socioeconomic school district in Cleveland, Ogbu (2003) found that Blacks do not oppose high educational achievement *per se*, but rather reject those attitudes and behaviors "that they perceived or interpreted as White, but that were conducive to making good grades" (p. 198). Those behaviors included speaking Standard English, enrolling in honors classes, and acting "smart" by always completing homework and raising their hands in class. Dressing like White students and having a predominantly White peer group also were perceived as "acting White." Ogbu writes that "Black friends did not study together; instead, some influenced one another to do poorly in school" (p. 191). While the adverse effects of peer pressure tended to be more prevalent in middle and high school, Ogbu found that this pressure began at the elementary school, where students might be teased by their peers for either being "good students" or for attending remedial classes. In her book, *Why Are All the Black Kids Sitting Together in the Cafeteria?* Tatum (1997) puts it, "Being smart becomes the opposite of being cool" (p. 62).

While Ogbu's oppositional identity theory has been criticized on a number of grounds (e.g., Ainesworth-Darnell & Downey, 1998; Foster, 2004; Trueba, 1988), it nevertheless can be viewed as an indictment of the educational institution—an institution that often fails to validate the cultural norms and experiences of students from historically oppressed populations. Schools tend to be "assimilationist" in that they expect students to conform to White, middle-/upper-class norms. Indeed, student resistance to traditional schooling has been well documented in the research literature (see, for example, Foley, 1990; MacLeod, 1995; Willis, 1977).

Given these dynamics, it is clear why classroom environments that are distinguished by an ethos of collective group achievement can have a positive impact on student learning. Such environments reinforce the notion that every student is a capable learner, and studying together and encouraging one's peers to do well become the expected standard. A notable example of an effective program based upon collaborative learning principles can be found in the work of Treisman (1992), who restructured his math classes to build on the benefits of peer support. Treisman noted that the Chinese students tended to excel in his courses, whereas the Black students tended to do poorly. When he compared the study habits of these two groups, he found that the Chinese students studied together and had developed a highly effective academic support network. The Black students, on the other hand, tended to study in isolation. Treisman subsequently restructured his math classes by forming heterogeneous study groups. Students were provided with challenging math problems and were required to develop problem-solving strategies together. Because the problems were difficult, students took on the role of teacher by assisting one another in arriving at solutions, and they had a sense of accomplishment when they were successful. Establishing "learning communities" within his math classes resulted in higher levels of student achievement for his Black and Hispanic students.

In addition to using students as resources for promoting group achievement, a supportive learning community affirms students' racial and ethnic identities. Such environments are characterized by the explicit valuing of human differences. Research on racial identity formation suggests that individuals go through various stages in the development of a positive racial identity (Cross, 1995; Diller & Moule, 2005; Helms, 1993; Tatum, 1997). To overcome negative stereotypes and to develop a positive identity, students must be provided with positive images and messages about their race or ethnicity. Because students, particularly those in adolescence, tend to seek an understanding of what it means to be a member of a particular group, in reference to one another and to the popular culture, it is critical that schools provide alternative images that portray a more accurate and holistic portrait of various racial and ethnic groups.

As noted previously, investigations of the processes of schooling teach us that schools tend to marginalize students' racial, ethnic, and linguistic identities and reinforce a homogenized, Eurocentric cultural perspective. Valenzuela's (1999) research in a high school that largely services youth of Mexican descent is instructive as to how such schooling practices affect recent and second- and third-generation immigrants. Like Ogbu's work with Black students, Valenzuela found that schools tend to "subtract" students' cultural identities, which contributes to their academic failure. Subtractive schooling is manifested in several ways, including labeling students as "limited English proficient" versus as potentially bilingual, ignoring their history and culture, and viewing their families and communities through a deficit lens. Rather than seeing students and their families as resources—which is characteristic of high-performing schools—the more typical pattern was to alienate students and their families. Additionally, in contrast to those highly effective teachers in Ladson-Billings' study, who saw student collaboration as central to the development of skills required for community organization and change, the teachers in Valenzuela's

41

investigation tended to emphasize individual upward mobility and to value traditional pedagogy and curriculum. In describing one underachieving Hispanic youth ("Frank"), Valenzuela writes:

> Success in school means consenting to the school's project of cultural disparagement and de-identification. Frank is not unwilling to become a productive member of society; he is simply at odds with a definition of productivity that is divorced from the social and economic interests of the broader Mexican community.

(pp. 94–95)

Valenzuela is particularly critical of the school's lack of attention to the difficult identity issues that students face through the process of assimilation. Ideally, schools should be "additive," e.g., they should affirm the language and cultural experiences of immigrant populations while enhancing students' identities through new cultural experiences. Such additive policies would do much to lessen the tensions in families and communities that result from students' emerging, often contrasting, identities.

More recently, Li (2008) reports on students' experiences with schooling in a low-income community in Buffalo. Examining the lives and literacy practices of Vietnamese, Sudanese, and working-class White families, she documents the "psycho-social stress" of their children who are "torn between the contradictory values of school and home" (p. 161). Like Valenzuela, Li argues that schools need to provide experiences that assist students in negotiating their identities as they transverse a "hybrid cultural space" between "the past and the present and between the individual and the collective" (p. 164). One of the more revealing findings of Li's investigation is that many teachers had little knowledge of students' language and cultural backgrounds, which led to serious consequences such as sending a student to an Arabic-speaking teacher for assistance when, in fact, the child did not speak Arabic. Not only does such ignorance undermine relationships of trust and respect, but it is quite difficult to utilize students' cultural knowledge as a resource when teachers fail to learn about their students' out-of-school lives.

To summarize the research on effective classroom environments for under-represented populations, the literature supports an environment that puts the student at the center. Teachers who implement effective learning environments for all students view students and their families holistically and value the resources that they bring to learning. Such environments are characterized by a collectivist orientation in which students contribute to the learning of the whole group and the success of the group is salient. Such learning environments also affirm students' racial, ethnic, and linguistic identities and provide support, through both the formal and informal curricula, for developing a positive sense of self.

This section on research findings would be incomplete without a discussion of the physical attributes of the classroom, which can either enhance or diminish student collaboration and cultural affirmation. For instance, research on seating arrangements in classrooms indicates that dividing the room into smaller spaces increases student interaction (Reutzel, Morrow, & Casey, 2009). Collaborative work requires that students be able to work in pairs or small groups, and hence the physical space needs to provide for this. It is also important to acknowledge that "architectural structures and classroom arrangements carry cultural biases" that can impact students' academic performance (Wilson & Wilson, 2000, p. 11). For instance, placing students in single rows with the teacher standing at the front of the room reinforces the idea of individualism and centers on the teacher as authority. In contrast, a circular arrangement suggests equity and is consistent with the idea of a community of learners, in which all students have a voice.

In their work with indigenous students, Wilson and Wilson (2000) have experienced success in using "talking circles," which build on an important symbol of the native world-view. The talking circle consists of a circular seating pattern that represents "the holism of Mother Earth and the equality of all members" (p. 11). Each member of the group is given a chance to speak in turn. The authors report: "In our university classrooms, we began to experience changes in communication patterns as we incorporated more culturally relevant structures. In an introductory psychology class, a group of students progressed from 'F' to 'A' grades after the classroom was rearranged" (p. 12).

Research also supports the importance of a "print-rich" environment in fostering literacy achievement (Morrow, Tracey, Woo, & Pressley, 1999; Neuman, 1999). Students need access to a wide variety of reading materials to support their literacy development. In their research on the literacy preferences of boys, Smith and Wilhelm (2006) found that "no single text or kind of text appealed to all of the young men in our study" (p. 54). Rather, boys tend to enjoy texts that promote "flow experiences"—those experiences that encourage passionate engagement. The boys they studied indicated that they found their school texts to be lacking in purpose, and preferred texts that provided a sense of challenge and control, and that gave them immediate feedback (video games, instruction manuals, reading on the web).

Importantly, Smith and Wilhelm found that the boys gravitated toward literacy experiences that enhanced their social connections: the sports page in the local newspaper, game rulebooks, movies. Hansen (1998) reports similar findings in her interviews with students in grades 1–11. Interviewees discussed reading as a social activity that enhances relationships and provides the opportunity to learn with and from others.

43

In addition to having a variety of print sources in the classroom, print materials need to be available that include the experiences of diverse populations. While it may not always be necessary for students to "see themselves" in the books that they read (Mohr, 2003), it is nevertheless important to include such texts to support a positive racial/ethnic identity and to promote an effective classroom community. Au, Carroll, and Scheu (1997) suggest that multicultural literature is not only important for expanding students' background knowledge, but it "offers the additional advantage of raising students' consciousness of their own cultures and the cultures of others" (p. 55). To avoid reinforcing cultural stereotypes, it is crucial to provide students with literature that provides authentic portrayals of characters and events (Council on Interracial Books for Children, 1980).

It is also important to recognize that print is not just found in books, but can encompass a variety of media, e.g., pictures, posters, billboards, T-shirts, bumper stickers, rap music, cartoons, film, video games. All should be considered as "texts" that communicate particular messages to the "reader" (Powell, 2009). Culturally responsive teachers consider such familiar texts as valuable resources that can be leveraged to scaffold new learning (Lee, 2007). They also recognize that all texts contain ideological messages that can either affirm or negate students' cultural identities, and can subsequently be deconstructed and critiqued (Cortés, 2000; Spring, 2003; Tobin, 2000). This topic will be addressed in greater depth in Chapter 9.

PRACTICAL APPLICATIONS

Culturally responsive educators are advocates for their students. They value the students and families they serve, and they work hard to affirm their students' identities as individuals and as learners so that they will have a positive sense of self. They recognize and appreciate the unique talents and resources of students and their families, and they use these resources in instruction. They encourage students to appreciate one another as learners and the contributions that they bring to the collective learning of the group.

Additionally, culturally responsive teachers use physical space to showcase the culture of their students and families, to promote respect, and to encourage collaboration. Books, classroom displays, and learning activities all reflect and validate students' diverse cultures and experiences and contribute to a positive racial identity. In this section, I provide practical suggestions for implementing a school and classroom climate that is culturally responsive.

ENCOURAGING COLLABORATION AND GROUP ACHIEVEMENT

As noted in the research, many cultural groups respond positively to a group orientation that is more collectivist, as opposed to individualistic. With the current school climate of standardized testing, it is more challenging to implement practices that allow for group achievement and peer support. Nevertheless, while teachers must prepare students to work within the dominant structure, they can also design classroom structures that are consistent with student preferences and that support group achievement goals.

For instance, a local fifth grade classroom teacher has her students graph the mean scores of their social studies tests throughout the year. The class goal is to increase the class's average score with each test. Students assist one another as they prepare for the test, with the aim of advancing the collective score of the class. At one point in the year, the teacher intentionally chose to ignore this goal and gave a test without discussing the group score. The students' scores went down. Whether this decrease was a result of the teacher's actions cannot be determined; it could have been related to many factors. Interestingly, however, the students all attributed the decline to the fact that they did not discuss a class goal. In this case, whether valid or not, the students *perceived* that setting a group goal helped their performance and encouraged them to succeed.

When I give final exams in my college classroom, my students are assigned to heterogeneous groups. They are given the essay questions a week before the exam is scheduled and are instructed to review the material and take notes. They are also encouraged to work together in preparing for the exam. On the day of the exam, students work in their group and submit a single product for a group grade. They also submit their notes for an individual grade. Thus, students who work harder are rewarded, while all have an equal opportunity to succeed through submitting a collective set of responses. The two grades are combined for a single final exam grade. Students report that they like this exam format because it requires them to review the material and allows them to work together, while diminishing the stress associated with a final exam.

Teachers who provide challenging tasks for students to solve together, who encourage students to study together, and who assign collaborative projects are supporting the norms of more collectivist cultures. In literacy classrooms, students can engage in peer writing conferences, literature discussion groups, and paired reading. Teaching students the social skills required for such peer- and group-collaborative activities will help to assure student success.

Classroom seating arrangements, therefore, need to provide for peer collaboration. The traditional arrangement of desks in single rows reflects an individualistic orientation where students work alone and peer interaction is

45

discouraged. A paradigm shift occurs when desks are arranged in a semi-circle; an even greater shift occurs with a full circle, when the teacher becomes a learner with her students. A circle implies that all are learners and reflects a democratic environment where sharing is encouraged.

Chairs can be arranged for "talking partners," which can be highly effective for formative assessment (see Chapter 5) as well as for reinforcing important concepts ("Turn to your partner and talk about this idea"). Desks can be pushed together in clusters for small group dialogue and shared space. In her book, *On Solid Ground*, teacher Sharon Taberski (2000) discusses how she uses short tables with no chairs in her primary classroom, and her young students sit on the floor. This plan eliminates the noise that comes with pushing chairs under tables. Her classroom makes great use of floor space; in the videos that correspond with the text, it is clear that the teacher also does a great deal of instruction "on their level." Students cluster on the floor for small and whole group instruction. There are also couches and other comfortable chairs for encouraging students to "curl up with a good book" or to converse with one another.

I recall visiting one second grade classroom where students were allowed to use every available space for reading. On one particular occasion, three young boys were lying together in the closet, enthralled by a particular information book. Consistent with research (Hansen, 1998; Smith & Wilhelm, 2006), the children enjoyed the socialization they experienced in conversing about a shared text. When reading time was up, they carefully hid the book on the book rack so that no one else would choose it and they could return to it later. In this classroom, children were reading under tables, on the rocking chair, under the teacher's desk—any place they could find a space to enjoy a good book. This classroom contained a variety of books, including books that reflected students' cultural experiences and lots of information books, in order to address a variety of student interests. It is important to note that this classroom also promoted shared ownership in that students were provided with the choice of what and where to read.

ESTABLISHING A SUPPORTIVE COMMUNITY

For peer collaboration to be effective, students need to learn how to work effectively in groups. That is, working productively with peers requires social skills that must be explicitly taught and nurtured. Culturally responsive educators often take time to teach appropriate interaction skills by modeling appropriate behaviors and asking students to role-play various scenarios. They also practice positive discipline by encouraging respect and appreciation for one another's needs. A classroom that is characterized by bullying, prejudice, and discriminatory behavior will not be conducive to collaborative work. These behaviors need direct intervention and also need to be addressed in the formal curriculum.

A few years ago, I volunteered frequently at an elementary school in an impoverished area of a nearby city. Many of the classrooms were quite chaotic; students were unruly and often resistant, and the frustration level of teachers was high. One class, however, stood out as an oasis in the midst of such chaos. The teacher never raised her voice, and her students were always productively engaged in their work. She happened to be a graduate student of mine, and I asked her to share how she managed to have a calm and inviting classroom when so many of the other teachers struggled just to maintain a certain level of control. She told me that at the beginning of the year, she intentionally instructs students on how to show respectful behavior to one another. Additionally, a cornerstone of her management plan was classroom meetings. These occurred frequently at the start of the year, and less frequently as the year progressed. Students were invited to add to the meeting agenda whenever they had a problem that required resolution. These frequent classroom discussions taught children how to resolve their differences and also affirmed the right of every child to have a safe and supportive learning environment.

Teachers, too, can model positive relationships in the way that they respond to student disruptions. One highly effective primary teacher I know continuously reinforces a positive classroom climate by helping her students think of the needs of others and their responsibilities as learners. For instance, when her students get noisy, she reminds them to "think of your neighbors, who are struggling to finish their work." On one of my visits to her classroom, she allowed students to make the decision on the acceptable noise level by asking them "How many of you want us to be quieter?" (They all decided together that they needed to lower their voices in order to be respectful of those who were still working.) This same teacher changes students' seats when they are disruptive rather than doling out punishment, and tells them "I think you'll do better over here." Note that *the focus is on a concern for their learning and the learning of others, rather than on controlling students' behavior*. A positive and productive classroom climate is one that is centered on student learning and that continually sends the message to students that they are competent learners.

All of these practices help to establish a respectful and safe classroom climate. A primary goal of the classroom should be to build community—to establish an environment where every student feels that he or she is a vital part of the class. Teachers can also accomplish this by actively confronting instances of discrimination and by making racism, classism, and other potential biases a formal part of the literacy curriculum (Derman-Sparks & Ramsey, 2008). For example, in early primary classrooms, teachers can guide discussions about skin color and other human differences, with the aim of establishing a positive social climate that affirms difference. Carefully selected multicultural literature can be effective in helping students to respect their differences and develop empathy.

Beyond this, however, teachers can provide space for students to tell their stories, allowing students to get to know one another on a more personal level. Inviting students to share their lives can have a profound effect on the learning environment of the classroom. An interesting testament to the power of stories for building community can be found in the work of Campano (2007), who encouraged his fifth grade immigrant students to document their lives through narrative. Students wrote about difficult and compelling topics: their families' struggles with survival, the problems they faced in their neighborhoods, the experience of death. Campano shares that "[a]s we became acquainted with one another's family groups, an idiom of kinship developed in our class. I observed my students engaging in acts of empathetic displacement that drew attention away from the self to the other" (p. 82). Teachers who invite students to share their personal narratives and to write from their hearts are establishing a classroom climate that engenders respect and care.

TEACHERS' VOICES

The Kindergarten Star

Heidi Hamlyn

Kindergarten teacher, Sandersville Elementary, Lexington, KY

Marcus, Tariq, Ariel, Liam, Adolfo, Estrella, Elena, Jacqueline, and Miguel. After meeting these students and their families, I knew without a doubt that this year was going to be challenging. Where do I start? What do I do first? Do I pull out the reading "program" and start on day one with this group of children? No way! But how in the world am I going to meet the needs of all of these students?

After "putting on my thinking cap," I decided to celebrate every student, a different one each day. I began by labeling wooden sticks shaped like a boy or a girl with the name of each of my students and placing them in a cup. The next step was to set up the excitement, eagerness, respect and discovery of the children. We gathered on the carpet and I launched our "Star Student of the Day" learning experience. We discussed and brainstormed a list of questions that we could use in interviews that would let us know details about each student. I then explained the protocol for this experience. A stick would be pulled out of the cup, and that student would come up to the front of the carpet and sit in the teacher's chair. The Star

Student would call on one student at a time for them to ask a question. They could ask a question from the brainstormed list or could ask one of their own that would give us information about the Star Student of the Day. We would then do a cheer using the letters of that student's name. I would model how to write this student's name and then we would draw a picture of this student and label it with the information that we gained from the interview.

"Okay, boys and girls. Let me see your eyes on me and your body in your own space if you are ready." I continued, "Are you sure you are ready? This is going to be so exciting! I cannot wait to learn all about our friends in this classroom." As I got ready to pull out the first stick, I closed my eyes, with a smile on my face. I was so excited, I could barely contain myself. Slowly I reached into the cup, and in slow motion I retrieved the first stick out of the cup, turned it over and showed the students to see if they could read it. As I looked at the very first Star Student, the look on her face was absolutely priceless. Elena (a pseudonym) slowly stood up and made her way to the teacher chair.

Elena was in the silent period of second language acquisition, so in our first few contacts with her, she had not talked to me or any of the other students. Although her appearance indicated that she was of Asian descent, she did not speak Chinese, as was my assumption. I happened to overhear a conversation between her and her dad that sounded to me like Spanish. I was a nervous wreck as she sat down and began to point to the first child she wanted to ask a question of her. The question was, "What is your favorite thing to do on the playground?" As we all sat there in silence, I began to feel sickness creeping into my stomach. Inside my head questions were circling, "What am I going to do? How are we going to have a conversation with Elena? Are the other children going to be accepting? Are they going to continue to ask questions? What will Elena do? How will she feel?"

Then an idea burst into my head. In my prior conversations with Jacqueline, she asked me how I wanted her to talk—like her mom or her dad? It was in this conversation with her that I knew she could speak and understand Spanish. Could she translate for Elena? Would Elena talk to Jacqueline? To my delight, Jacqueline translated the question as: "What do you like to play outside?" Elena looked at me, looked at the class, and then looked at Jacqueline and whispered in her ear, "Me gusta correr." [I like to run.] At that moment, my mouth was wide open and I felt tears coming. It was as if the class had just watched a great show and they cheered in a round of applause. Wow! What an awesome moment! We continued with our interview, the name cheer, and the drawing of Elena by all of her fans. At the end of this experience, I posted her self-portrait on the wall and bound the students' drawings together in a book for her to take home to share with her family. That afternoon on the playground, there was a whole group of runners, led by none other than the Kindergarten Star of the Day, Miss Elena.

AFFIRMING STUDENTS' IDENTITIES

Many years ago, I conducted a fascinating ethnographic study of what was then known as the Eastern Kentucky Teachers' Network (Eller, 1989). One of the major findings of this study was that those teachers who identified as "Appalachian" tended to see their role differently, in that they believed it was their responsibility to reinforce and affirm the Appalachian culture. They did so by studying local history, inviting parents and grandparents to share their stories, singing native Appalachian songs, reading Appalachian tales, and encouraging students to write about their lives. These teachers acknowledged their own mountain identity in a society that denigrates that identity. They recognized that their own schooling experience reinforced the dominant culture, thereby impeding the development of their identity as Appalachians and contributing to their own negative images of the region. Consequently, they were committed to nurturing a positive sense of self in their mountain students.

The physical environment of their classrooms reflected this commitment. Many of these classrooms were distinctly "Appalachian." What follows is a description of the décor of one classroom:

> On one wall, there was a large photography display of [the county] that included 5×7 black and white photos of several local scenes: a swinging bridge, a funeral on someone's homeplace, a man in his tobacco field, the spring flood. ([The teacher] informed me that her students the previous year had taken these photographs themselves.) On another wall, there was a framed picture of Daniel Boone, who is a prominent historical figure in eastern Kentucky. In the back of the room, there was a homemade crocheted afghan on the table, which also held several Appalachian books. A bulletin board labeled "The Cumberland Gap" was decorated with a genuine deer pelt and several historical posters.
>
> (p. 240)

This particular teacher was committed to empowering her children to believe that they could do anything with their lives, and she recognized that empowerment necessitates having a positive sense of self. Consequently, her room was filled with affirming images of the region. She also invited the community into her classroom to share elements of Appalachian culture, e.g., native artists and members of the local historical society.

I have chosen to end this chapter with a story that illustrates what can happen when we provide students with concrete affirmation of their racial and social identities. In her book, *A White Teacher Talks about Race* (2001), Julie Landsman

50

recounts her experiences when she brought in an African American author ("David") to share his writing with her middle school students. He read from one of his books for 15 minutes, and then asked for questions from the audience. Landsman writes that she was "alarmed at his timing"—how would he keep their attention for the next 45 minutes? Soon, the questions from her students started flowing. She was amazed at their attentiveness.

She especially noticed Travis, who had "skin identical to David's. Travis asked lots of questions: 'What time do you get up? Do you think you had more problems because you're Black? Did all these things in these books happen to you even though it is a novel and they don't have to have happened to you?'" (p. 22). After the session, she and Travis had the following conversation:

"Hey, Travis. How you doing?" I ask.

He bursts out, "This is one of the happiest days of my life." I'm surprised. Often Travis is more withdrawn, somewhat whiny. But as I watch him settle into a seat across from David, suddenly I think I *see* why he feels the way he does.

Across from Travis sits himself. Across from Travis is a man who looks like him, who is an intellectual like him, and who is Black like him.

Travis has often been teased by other students about being "too White," about being too smart, about not being hip enough or "Black" enough. His teachers have told him that there are many Black men who look like him, who are smart and studious and who do not lose their Blackness. Now, I believe our words seem to make sense to him . . .

Perhaps his world has become resonant for just awhile here in this sun-filled classroom with the old wooden-framed windows, waxed floors, round tables, and the large poster of famous Black abolitionists on the wall. Here he is, a round young Black man with glasses, looking at a round middle-aged Black man with glasses.

(pp. 23–24)

Too often, we as teachers forget that our students need to have affirmation and a sense of belonging to a community that is bigger than themselves. In our quest to teach content and to get our students prepared for "the test," we may overlook the critical importance of the classroom environment and the learning community that is so vital for student success. Landsman's compelling story is a testament to the importance of providing opportunities for students to "see themselves" in our classrooms, from the images on our walls, to the books in our libraries, to the learning experiences that we provide.

CONCLUSION

In general, the way that we use time and space in our classrooms reflects what we value as teachers. It is also indicative of the relationships that we have with our students and families, and the types of relationships that we encourage among our students. Ultimately, genuinely equitable classrooms are those that demonstrate shared ownership and affirm our students' cultural identities. They are classrooms that are welcoming, that encourage students to take risks in their learning, and that show students in very concrete ways that we believe they are capable as learners. They are also classrooms that promote collaboration and invite students to use literacy in creative and authentic ways. Such classrooms are characterized by trust, respect, and mutual responsibility for learning.

In describing her own teaching practices, multicultural scholar Geneva Gay states that in her interactions with students, she attempts to convey the message that "we are partners in this quest for learning" (2000, p. 199). Culturally responsive educators create a shared space—a "Third Space" (Gutiérrez, 2008) —where difficult conversations can occur within a supportive environment that acknowledges that every participant has something to contribute to the learning of others. They also create a physical space that affirms students' cultural identities, that provides possibilities for their lives, and that encourages them to visualize their dreams.

Table 3.1 Summary of CRIOP Component: Classroom Climate/Physical Environment

Element	What you would expect to see in a classroom where CRI practices are occurring	What you would expect to see in a classroom where CRI practices are not occurring
The physical surroundings of the classroom reflect an appreciation for diversity.	There are books, posters, and other artifacts reflecting students' and others' cultures; there are positive and affirming messages and images about students' racial identities.	There are no or few multicultural texts; posters and displays do not show an acknowledgment and affirmation of students' cultural and racial identities.
Peer collaboration is the norm.	Students are continuously viewed as resources for one another; the emphasis is on group achievement; there is a "family-like" environment in the classroom.	There is no or very little peer collaboration; the emphasis is on individual achievement.

Table 3.1 Continued

Element	What you would expect to see in a classroom where CRI practices are occurring	What you would expect to see in a classroom where CRI practices are not occurring
The physical space supports collaborative work.	The seating arrangement is flexible and supports student collaboration and equal participation between teachers and students.	The seating arrangement is designed for individual work, with the teacher being "center stage."
Students work together productively.	The teacher implements practices that teach collaboration and respect, e.g., class meetings, modeling empathy, sharing families' histories. Students respect one another and know how to work together effectively. Biases and discrimination are addressed through the formal curriculum.	The students primarily work individually and are not expected to work collaboratively; and/or students have a difficult time collaborating. Lack of respectful interaction amongst students may be an issue. Biases and discrimination are not addressed.

REFLECTIVE ACTIVITIES

1 Make a list of the visuals that surround your room (pictures, posters, objects, etc.). What do they communicate about what you value? Whose knowledge is of most worth? Do your displays affirm or marginalize the students and families that you serve?

2 Critique your classroom seating arrangement. What messages does it convey to students?

3 Consider your instructional practices. In what ways do you promote individual success over the success of the group? In what ways do you promote group success over the success of individuals?

4 Evaluate the social ethos in your classroom. Does it reflect an "extended family group"? In what ways are students encouraged to help and support one another?

REFERENCES

Ainesworth-Darnell, J. W., & Downey, D. B. (1998). Assessing the oppositional cultural explanation for racial/ethnic differences in school performance. *American Sociological Review, 63,* 536–553.

Au, K. H. (1993). *Literacy instruction in multicultural settings.* New York: Harcourt Brace Jovanovich.

Au, K. H., Carroll, J. H., & Scheu, J. A. (1997). *Balanced literacy instruction: A teacher's resource book.* Norwood, MA: Christopher-Gordon.

Berry, R. A. W. (2006). Inclusion, power, and community: Teachers and students interpret the language of community in an inclusion classroom. *American Educational Research Journal, 43*(3), 489–529.

Campano, G. (2007). *Immigrant students and literacy: Reading, writing, and remembering.* New York: Teachers College Press.

Cortés, C. E. (2000). *The children are watching: How the media teach about diversity.* New York: Teachers College Press.

Council on Interracial Books for Children (1980). *Guidelines for selecting bias-free textbooks and storybooks.* New York: CIBC.

Cross, W. E. (1995). The psychology of Nigrescence: Revising the Cross model. In J. G. Ponterotto, J. M. Casas, L. A. Suzuki, & C. M. Alexander (Eds.), *Handbook of multicultural counseling* (pp. 93–123). Thousand Oaks, CA: Sage.

Delpit, L. (1995). *Other people's children: Cultural conflict in the classroom.* New York: The New Press.

Derman-Sparks, L., & Ramsey, P. (2008). What if all the kids are white? Anti-bias themes for teaching young children. In A. Pelo (Ed.), *Rethinking early childhood education* (pp. 43–47). Milwaukee, WI: Rethinking Schools.

Deyle, D. (1995). Navajo youth and Anglo racism: Cultural integrity and resistance. *Harvard Educational Review, 65,* 403–444.

Diller, J. V., & Moule, J. (2005). *Cultural competence: A primer for educators.* Belmont, CA: Thomson Wadsworth.

Edelsky, C., Draper, K., & Smith, K. (1983). Hookin' 'em in at the start of school in a "whole language" classroom. *Anthropology and Education Quarterly, 14*(4), 257–281.

Eller, R. G. (1989). Teacher resistance and educational change: Toward a critical theory of literacy in Appalachia. Unpublished doctoral dissertation, University of Kentucky, Lexington.

Finnan, C., Schnepel, K.C., & Anderson, L. W. (2003). Powerful learning environments: The critical link between school and classroom cultures. *Journal of Education for Students Placed at Risk, 8,* 391–418.

Foley, D. (1990). *Learning capitalist culture: Deep in the heart of Texas.* Philadelphia, PA: University of Pennsylvania Press.

Fordham, S. (1991). Peer-proofing academic competition among Black adolescents: "Acting White" Black American style. In C. E. Sleeter (Ed.), *Empowerment through multicultural education* (pp. 69–93). Albany, NY: SUNY Press.

Fordham, S., & Ogbu, J. U. (1986). Black students' school success: Coping with the burden of acting White. *The Urban Review, 18*(3), 1–31.

Foster, M. F. (2004). Coming to terms: A discussion of John Ogbu's cultural-ecological theory of minority academic achievement. *Intercultural Education, 15,* 399–412.

Gay, G. (2000). *Culturally responsive teaching.* New York: Teachers College Press.

Gay, G. (2002). Culturally responsive teaching in special education for ethnically diverse students: Setting the stage. *Qualitative Studies in Education, 15,* 613–629.

Gutiérrez, K. D. (2008). Developing a sociocritical literacy in the Third Space. *Reading Research Quarterly, 43,* 148–164.

Hansen, J. (1998). "Evaluation is all day, noticing what is happening:" Multifaceted evaluations of readers. In S. Murphy (Ed.), *Fragile evidence: A critique of reading assessment* (pp. 105–123). Mahwah, NJ: Lawrence Erlbaum.

Helms, J. E. (Ed.). (1993). *Black and White racial identity: Theory, research, and practice.* Westport, CT: Praeger.

hooks, b. (1994). *Teaching to transgress: Education as the practice of freedom.* New York: Routledge.

Ladson-Billings, G. (1994). *The dreamkeepers: Successful teachers of African American children.* San Francisco, CA: Jossey-Bass.

Landsman, J. (2001). *A white teacher talks about race.* Lanham, MD: Scarecrow Press.

Lee, C. D. (2007). *Culture, literacy, and learning: Taking bloom in the midst of the whirlwind.* New York: Teachers College Press.

Li, G. (2008). *Culturally contested literacies: America's "rainbow underclass" and urban schools.* New York: Routledge.

MacLeod, J. (1995). *Ain't no makin' it: Aspirations and attainment in a low-income neighborhood.* Boulder, CO: Westview Press.

Mohr, K. A. J. (2003). Children's choices: A comparison of book preferences between Hispanic and non-Hispanic first graders. *Reading Psychology: An International Quarterly, 24,* 163–176.

Morrow, L. M., Tracey, D. H., Woo, D. G., & Pressley, M. (1999). Characteristics of exemplary first-grade literacy instruction. *The Reading Teacher, 52,* 462–476.

Neuman, S. B. (1999). Books make a difference: A study of access to literacy. *Reading Research Quarterly, 34,* 286–311.

Nunnery, J. A., Butler, E. D., & Bhaireddy, V. N. (1993). *Relationships between classroom climate, student characteristics, and language achievement in the elementary classroom: An exploratory investigation.* Retrieved from ERIC database (ED 364325).

Ogbu, J. U. (1987). Variability in minority school performance: A problem in search of an explanation. In E. Jacob & C. Jordan (Eds.), Explaining the school performance of minority students [theme issue]. *Anthropology and Education Quarterly, 18,* 312–334.

Ogbu, J. U. (2003). *Black American students in an affluent suburb.* Mahwah, NJ: Lawrence Erlbaum.

Powell, R. (2009). The promise of critical media literacy. In L. A. Spears-Bunton & R. Powell (Eds.), *Toward a literacy of promise* (pp. 185–197). New York: Routledge.

Reyes, P., Scribner, J. D., & Scribner, A. P. (Eds.). (1999). *Lessons from high-performing Hispanic schools: Creating learning communities.* New York: Teachers College Press.

Reutzel, D. R., Morrow, L. M., & Casey, H. (2009). Meeting the needs of diverse learners: Effective management of language arts instruction. In L. M. Morrow, R. Rueda, & D. Lapp

(Eds.), *Handbook of research on literacy and diversity* (pp. 254–273). New York: The Guilford Press.

Scribner, J. D., & Reyes, P. (1999). Creating learning communities for high-performing Hispanic students: A conceptual framework. In P. Reyes, J. D. Scribner, & A. P. Scribner (Eds.), *Lessons from high-performing Hispanic schools: Creating learning communities* (pp. 188–210). New York: Teachers College Press.

Smith, M. W., & Wilhelm, J. D. (2006). *Going with the flow: How to engage boys (and girls) in their literacy learning.* Portsmouth, NH: Heinemann.

Spring, J. (2003). *Educating the consumer-citizen: A history of the marriage of schools, advertising, and media.* Mahwah, NJ: Lawrence Erlbaum.

Taberski, S. (2000). *On solid ground: Strategies for teaching reading K-3.* Portsmouth, NH: Heinemann.

Tatum, B. D. (1997). *"Why are all the Black kids sitting together in the cafeteria?" and other conversations about race.* New York: Basic Books.

Tobin, J. (2000). *"Good guys don't wear hats": Children's talk about the media.* New York: Teachers College Press.

Treisman, P. U. (1992). Studying students studying calculus: A look at the lives of minority mathematics students in college. *College Mathematics Journal, 23,* 362–372.

Trueba, H. T. (1988). Culturally based explanations of minority students' academic achievement. *Anthropology and Education Quarterly, 19,* 270–287.

Valenzuela, A. (1999). *Subtractive schooling: U.S.-Mexican youth and the politics of caring.* Albany, NY: SUNY Press.

Weinstein, C. S., Curran, M., and Tomlinson-Clarke, S. (2003). Culturally responsive classroom management: Awareness into action. *Theory into Practice, 42,* 269–276.

Willis, P. (1977). *Learning to labour.* New York: Columbia University Press.

Wilson, P., & Wilson, S. (2000). Circles in the classroom: The cultural significance of structure. *Canadian Social Studies, 34*(2), 11–12.

Chapter 4

Parent Collaboration: Developing Partnerships with Families and Caregivers

Kelly A. Seitz

Children are sensitive to the "hidden curriculum" of the school. The image they hold of their parents—already threatened in a culture whose primary value is economic success—suffers further whenever schools maintain a silent disregard . . . By encouraging communication between parents and children; by including parents' knowledge, experience, and wisdom in the curriculum; and by honoring the languages that parents speak, we further reduce children's sense of conflict.

(Ada, Campoy, & Zubizarreta, 2001, p. 171)

Most educators would agree that honoring parents as their children's first teachers is an important goal. At the same time, schools tend to maintain a system of control, whereby parents are asked to participate in predictable, limited ways. Certainly, involving parents in the educational experience is a commendable goal; rarely, however, do we seek to include "parents' knowledge, experience and wisdom"—to engage in true collaboration with the families of our students.

Consider the following scenarios:

Mrs. Thompson is a third grade teacher. She knows that she can count on a few parents to assist with classroom duties. Megan's mother is always there; in fact, Mrs. Thompson has created an "inbox" for her where she places items that she needs to have copied. Two other parents come regularly to tutor children in the classroom. Mrs. Thompson also sends home a weekly newsletter that explains the concepts the children are learning that week and provides suggestions for parents on how to help reinforce those comments. Every year, her team plans a workshop for parents in which they review various literacy concepts and share ways that parents can support the oral reading of their children.

Ms. Miller is a fifth grade teacher. Each summer she starts off the academic year with a potluck supper at the local community center. This gives her a chance to get to know her students and their families on a more informal basis. At this event, she is careful to meet every student and his/her parent. She tells a little about herself—where she grew up, her family, her hobbies, and the struggles she has faced in her life. She also shares the goals that she has for her students, and tells the parents that one of her goals is to collaborate with them so that every student can experience success. She also explains that the primary reason for this event is for all of them to get to know one another. While the families are eating together, Ms. Miller circulates from table to table, gathering any information that might help her in planning her literacy curriculum. She notes that Mr. Hernandez is a field worker. She asks him if he would be willing to come to the classroom during their science unit on plants. Mrs. Sanchez brought some wonderful burritos to the supper. Would she be willing to provide a cooking experience for the students? Through listening to their conversations, Ms. Miller also discovers that some of her families have had compelling immigration experiences. Would they be willing to share their stories with the class?

The concept of educators and parents working together for the good of the student/child is not a new one. Consider, however, that in the first scenario, the teacher "involved" parents in school-based literacy experiences, whereas in the second scenario, the parents became integral partners in literacy instruction. Both teachers focus on important literacy skills and strategies in their instruction; however, Mrs. Thompson relies on traditional texts and reading programs for instruction, whereas Ms. Miller develops storybooks, big books, and charts that are based upon the experiences of her students' families. Both teachers have frequent parent visitors to their classrooms, yet the parents' roles are very different. While family involvement is critical for the academic success of students, genuine partnerships with parents and families affirm their language and culture and help to close the "great divide" between home and school.

The aim of this chapter is to explore the relationship between educators and parents and how this relationship is so very crucial to the educational success of all children. We will use the term "parent" to mean "the person(s) who have primary care and responsibility for students at home," recognizing the many family units prevalent in today's society. Although the CRIOP (Culturally Responsive Instruction Observation Protocol) specifically draws one's attention to the need for culturally responsive and sensitive pedagogy for the culturally and linguistically diverse student/family, the message of this particular chapter is that all children benefit when educators and family members form partnerships.

SUPPORTING RESEARCH

The educational system has always, to some degree or another, sought to include parents/caregivers in the process. Historically, parent involvement has occurred in varying forms of classroom support through assisting with social events, acting as chaperones for field trips, and assisting with classroom chores. Admittedly, all of these activities are helpful and useful ways that parents have served the classroom and the school. In many circumstances, supporting the educational process through these activities is the most a parent can do given their already busy lives.

Yet education that embraces equity moves beyond simply "involving" parents, to creating true partnerships with them. In her book, *Becoming Teammates* (2008), Endrizzi suggests that parent involvement promotes a relationship of dependency, in which the teacher/school maintains control. Parents are "invited" to participate in various events, such as chaperoning field trips, assisting with homework, and reading to the class; however, "parent involvement" focuses on "sustaining the teacher's perspective of learning" (p. 11). Parents are viewed as "helpers," and the teacher is the sole decision-maker.

In contrast, partnerships lead to what Endrizzi calls "mutualism," whereby teachers engage in genuine dialogue with parents and families in order to learn from them. She writes:

[I]t is critical for teachers to have faith in family members as their child's foremost learning partners, and to discuss openly the value of this first partnership, initiate conversations with parents, and actively build connections between home and school learning experiences.

(p. 16)

Partnership is defined as *a relationship between individuals or groups that is characterized by mutual cooperation and responsibility, as for the achievement of a specified goal.* To partner with parents is to form a relationship based on cooperation and shared responsibility. Partnerships move beyond a superficial relationship to one in which the educator and the family are intimately and mutually involved in the process.

Genuine partnerships begin when teachers make a deliberate effort to form relationships with parents and to involve them in the decision-making process.

59

Conversations with parents are viewed as opportunities for learning about the child and his/her family: their areas of expertise, how they might contribute to the curriculum, and ideas on how their children learn best. Rather than serving merely as "helpers," parents are seen as being integral to the instructional process.

Parent Involvement

To better understand the difference between parent involvement and partnership, consider the ways that "involvement" has traditionally been understood. According to Epstein et al. (1997), there are basically six types of parent/family involvement. The first is the basic obligation families have to the child in providing a home in which the child is safe and healthy, and education is supported. The second is the basic obligation schools have to the family. Schools are obligated to communicate through multiple means so as to ensure that the parents are completely aware of what occurs at school. School-to-home communication happens when the student excels and when he has problems. The third type of parent/family involvement occurs inside the school building and includes opportunities for parents to serve in a multitude of volunteer capacities, e.g., social events, field trip chaperones, playground monitors, and other school-defined duties (Ladky & Peterson, 2008). It also includes additional opportunities such as tutoring students and assisting school administration. The fourth type of involvement occurs in the home. These are activities that support learning in school, such as enrichment activities, having the child read aloud to a parent or older sibling and of course, homework (De Gaetano, 2007; Scribner, Young, & Pedroza, 1999).

The fifth type of involvement for parents/families is serving on advisory panels or governance (decision-making) committees and the PTA/PTO. These are prime opportunities for parents to participate in influencing educational policies and procedures for school improvement. The sixth type of involvement moves the parent into the community as a whole. These are volunteer opportunities to either support others in the community or to receive assistance themselves, such as community support groups, childcare centers, and cultural activities. The challenge is for schools to communicate with parents through open dialogue about which of these types of involvement is important to parents prior to implementing varying programs and opportunities for service. If all a family can do is be minimally involved, then this is to be accepted and appreciated.

Parent Partnerships

Contrast these definitions of involvement with what Sanders (1996) defines as true educator–family partnerships. She points out that there are ten facets to true partnerships. The first is that partnerships are a shared responsibility between teachers, families, administrators and community members. The second is that partnerships take time to develop, whereas involvement is immediate. Partnerships take commitment and perseverance from all involved. The third facet is that true partnerships reach out to all family members, not just the immediate parent(s). This is recognition of the importance of extended family members in the child's life.

The fourth facet is that partnerships improve incrementally. Partnership formation demands thoughtful planning, implementation, evaluation, and improvement. Fifth, a true partnership acknowledges the fact that families are vital for student success across all of the grades, not just in elementary school. The sixth feature of teacher-parent partnerships acknowledges the role of students, for without them, educator and family partnerships would not be necessary. The seventh facet points to the community as vital towards developing strong partnerships. It is through such community connections that many different forms of improvements can come to a school. Eighth, partnerships must include the hard-to-reach family. Some families are dealing with extreme stressors, but even these families can partner with educators when the right strategies are in place (Sanders, 1996). The ninth facet stresses the need for a link with student learning and curriculum. This is a real recognition of the "funds of knowledge" families possess and the value they can bring to the classroom for all students (González, Moll, & Amanti, 2005). Finally, the tenth facet holds that true partnerships include the six types of involvement. It is through such activities that educators can take the first steps in creating strong connections with families that will hopefully develop into a partnership.

Benefits of Educator–Parent Partnerships

We must remember our purpose for becoming educators—to assist children academically and socially in becoming the best they can be. We must also remember that the concept of "partnership" acknowledges that neither educators nor parents alone can educate and socialize children for productive citizenship (Hidalgo, Bright, Epstein, Siu, & Swap, 1995). Thus, if we are to achieve our purpose, we must appreciate that a child's parent is their primary educator, and as such, they play a critical role in the child's academic success

61

(Edwards and Turner, 2008; Levine and Lezotte, 1995). When we collaborate with families, there are many positive benefits for all involved.

Research is clear on the importance of parent/school collaboration. Fifty years of studies reveal that the family influences student success regardless of family structure, socioeconomic status, race, and level of parent education, size of the family or the age of the child. Evidence also points to the fact that when schools and educators develop relationships and form partnerships, families acquire a greater appreciation for the opportunity to be involved in their child's learning, and subsequently increase their involvement. This increased parental participation leads to improvement in student achievement, attitudes, and behaviors (Hidalgo et al., 1995).

Research by Matuszny, Banda, and Coleman (2007) supports these findings. They found that partnerships increased student achievement, increased student educational aspirations, increased length of time spent attending school overall, created a drive for personal independence, increased parental efficacy in regards to parenting ability, increased parental aspirations to improve their own educational standing, and increased ratings/opinions of schools (in general).

Similarly, Levine and Lezotte (1995) found that in schools where educators and families partnered, students had higher academic achievement rates than students in other schools, even when compared to those students of similar socioeconomic status. These researchers also found evidence of parents who were willing to work within the community to obtain resources for the school, and who were instrumental in improvement efforts within the school. Parents helped to maintain orderly environments in various locations in the building, observed in classrooms to ensure positive teacher performance and student interaction, informed administration of when homework was no longer productive but had become busy work, and actively participated in building-level governance activities.

Harry (2008) discusses the many benefits of partnerships. These include positive, understandable, respectful communication, a greater sense of commitment to the child, a relationship based on equal power, a shared sense of competence in setting and achieving academic goals for children and, most importantly, a development of mutual trust and respect (see also Hughes & Kwok, 2007). Her research demonstrates that when such a shared model (partnership) was not in place, families and educators worked from states of confusion, misunderstanding, and isolation. Grantham, Frasier, Roberts and Bridges (2005) concur with these findings and add that such partnerships increase the likelihood for consistency of academic and social expectations between the home and the classroom. They found that when the family and the educator share and reinforce the same values, students were more likely to project achievement-oriented attitudes and work ethics.

Finally, Robinson and Fine (1994) share significant findings from research conducted by Christenson and Cleary (1990) on the benefits of partnerships. These researchers found direct benefit to all four of the participants in the process: the student, the educator, the family and the school. For the student, it was noted that generally grades and test scores improved, homework was completed more regularly, and students were more engaged in their learning in the classroom. Educators developed a greater sense of job satisfaction and received many more positive evaluations from their principals (see also, Cassity & Harris, 2000). Families increased in their understanding of how the system functions and improved in home to school communication. There was also an increase in their willingness to support student learning at home through additional activities. Finally, the school benefited overall due to such partnerships and were found to be more effective and successful in the mission of educating all children.

With all of this supporting data, why haven't schools, parents, and communities united in creating an educational atmosphere which leads all children towards academic success? One very basic answer may be found in the general understanding of and attitude toward the family unit.

A New Understanding of Family

The socially accepted definition of family has undergone many changes. The dominant norm that defined the "average" family in the 1950s was that of a working father, stay-at-home mother, and their children (Sanacore, 2004). Current statistics regarding family structure reveal that 27% are single parent family households, with more than 2 million fathers in the role of primary caregiver. One out of every 25 children does not live with either parent, and 2.4 million grandparents are primary caregivers. Approximately 2 million children are being raised by lesbian or gay parents and unmarried partner households raising children has increased significantly (US Department of Education, 2000, Census data).

Families also face greater challenges than ever before. The statistics continue to demonstrate that of all American families with children, 1.35 million are homeless and 13.2% are projected to live in poverty (US Department of Education, 2000, Census data). This becomes a more complicated issue when you also consider the diversity America has and the challenges those families face. Government statistics demonstrate that 2.8 million children are born into families of mixed races or ethnicities. Two-thirds of all 5–24-year-olds whose native language is not English were born in the United States. Nearly 3.4 million children do not speak English at all or have limited proficiency, and of those

3.4 million, 2.7 live in "linguistically isolated" home situations where no one over the age of 14 speaks English well (Herrera & Murray, 2005).

Although there has been a dramatic shift away from the 1950s' "ideal family," it still has a powerful influence over what is considered the "better" family unit by current society (Turner-Vorbeck & Marsh, 2008). When one form is accepted as being better than another, it is what sociologists call "hegemonic construction." These are the constructions which meet with the greatest amount of "spontaneous" approval. A hegemonic notion of the "ideal" family has cultural power. This image of the ideal family has been viewed through history as a symbol for safety, success, and happiness. In essence, the hegemonic family ideal need not be the most common form, but it remains the most valued.

Families that depart from this accepted hegemonic form are faced with increasing challenges of being stereotyped and encountering prejudice. As a profession, education must take the necessary steps towards accepting the diversity of families. For the classroom teacher, the goal is to be able to function comfortably with families who live in ways that differ from their own (Turner-Vorbeck & Marsh, 2008). These are the modern families educators must come to appreciate, value, and partner with. Understanding the family unit in which a child lives provides insight and opportunity to develop effective ways in which families can become involved and partnerships can be developed (Rockwell, Andre, & Hawley, 2010).

Challenges to Creating Partnerships

Building collaborative relationships with parents and families of our students is not an easy task. This task becomes even more daunting when those parents and families speak languages or come from cultures that differ from our own. Yet as educators, it is important to recognize the important benefits of developing productive relationships with the families we serve. In this section, we explore some of the barriers that exist in forming such relationships.

Our first challenge as educators is to acknowledge that we view the world through a dominant lens. Establishing partnerships with families requires that we respect the families and children that we serve. It also requires that we recognize the many resources that families bring to learning. For instance, speaking a language other than English can be regarded as a strength that can be used in the classroom. Knowledge of agriculture, cooking, homemaking, auto mechanics, carpentry, etc. can all be infused into the literacy curriculum if teachers are committed to making important home–school connections. Using families' "funds of knowledge" empowers parents and families as they come to see themselves as active and equal participants in their children's education (González et al., 2005).

Yet because most teachers are members of the dominant culture, there is often a tendency to view many families—particularly those from under-represented groups—from a deficit perspective (Harry, 2008). We all operate from our own cultural framework, and we subsequently make decisions about what is correct and "normal" through this framework. When the language and behaviors of children and their families vary from mainstream norms, it is tempting to regard these families as inferior and as having nothing of value to contribute to the educational enterprise. Thus, the challenge for us as educators is to overcome our own "deficit thinking" and to learn from the families we serve.

When we are not knowledgeable about the lives, backgrounds, and expectations of families, prejudices are reinforced and we are more likely to view them as "problems" (Rockwell et al., 2010; Tomlinson, 1993). Hence, establishing personal relationships with families becomes essential. To do so, it is important that we as teachers "step outside of our comfort zones" and make a concerted effort to learn about the lives and cultures of our students and their families.

It is also important that we recognize that we may harbor biases that stem from our own socialization. In their book, *White Teachers/Diverse Classrooms* (2006), Landsman and Lewis write: "taking a look at the parts of ourselves that we don't wish to face may be uncomfortable. However, when you are responsible for children's lives, this kind of honesty is vital" (p. 120). Many in our society harbor biases against alternative family structures, divorced families, families living in poverty, and the specific cultural beliefs and behaviors of many of the families we serve, and educators are no exception (Gray & Cosgrove, 1985; Hong & Hong, 1991; Kalyanpur & Harry, 1997; Rockwell et al., 2010; Trask & Hamon, 2007). Yet as educators, it is important that we recognize that the strongest and most consistent indicator for any parent–teacher partnership is the educator who encourages, supports, and guides all parents towards finding their niche (Dauber & Epstein, 1993).

Indeed, it can be argued that the culture of schooling has established particular norms for "appropriate" parent involvement; that is, schools have created an official set of rules that all parents are expected to follow (Tett, 2001). We believe that parents should support classroom rules and structures; they should participate whenever we need them; they should ensure the child's full compliance with all academic requests; and they should attend parent–teacher conferences. When families do what we request, they are typically labeled as "good parents." These are often the traditional, middle-/upper-class, mainstream families who know the rules of the school game and who have the necessary resources (such as time and transportation) to follow them. In essence, they are familiar with the dominant cultural norms that define schooling and teacher–parent interaction. It is important to recognize, however, that in some cultures, parents believe that the educator is solely responsible for providing the child with academic behavior, while their role is to educate the child in proper social behaviors (Chamberlain, 2005; Ladky & Peterson, 2008). Hence, parents and teachers can have very different expectations as to the roles that each should assume. There can also be differences in behavioral expectations: what is considered punctual, how one is to communicate with those in positions of authority or of a differing gender (male to female), or appropriate norms for non-verbal communication such as personal space (Gudykunst & Kim, 1997).

Further, when educator–parent communication does occur, it is far too frequently on the "educational professional's" terms (Bastiani, 1989). All too often, our communication with families is conducted using educational jargon, which can build barriers between educators and parents. The resulting relationship therefore becomes one that is distant, and places the parent in a subordinate role (Bastiani, 1989; Tett, 2001). Thus, the conversation becomes one in which the teacher "expert" tells the parents(s) how best to help their child, rather than a genuine opportunity for teachers and parents to learn from one another. Most parents want to be supportive, encouraging and positive of their children's educational process, but this is difficult to achieve if they perceive that they are constantly being ignored and left out (Tett, 2001).

It is also important to examine the reasons why parents are sometimes reluctant to initiate partnerships with educators. Facing the bureaucracy called education in this country can cause many families to feel intimidated, confused, or just plain lost (Johnson, Pugach, & Hawkins, 2004). For many immigrants, the educational process as it is conducted in the United States may be quite different from their country of origin. Language barriers can further contribute to their sense of alienation (Chamberlain, 2005; De Gaetano, 2007; Herrera & Murray, 2005). Similarly, for parents who may find themselves under-educated or who live in poverty, the system can be quite daunting to traverse.

Additionally, families sometimes sense that they are discouraged from participating in the educational process (De Gaetano, 2007; Street, 2005; Voltz, 1994). Hence, families begin to feel unsure of themselves and question if they have anything of value to offer (Hensley, 2005; Raffaele & Knoff, 1999). This sense of diminished control and inferiority can cause families to feel vulnerable (Johnson, Pugach, & Hawkins, 2004; Robinson & Fine, 1994); therefore, it behooves teachers to examine the manner in which they conduct business and strive to discover the issues which may be preventing families from becoming partners in the educational process. Schools must create an environment and structure through which families become empowered (Hensley, 2005; Johnson, Pugach, & Hawkins, 2004; Scribner et al., 1999). In culturally responsive classrooms, all families are made to feel welcome from the very first interaction and are included in the dialogue on effective educational practices for their child

(Cassity & Harris, 2000; Hughes & Kwok, 2007; Raffaele & Knoff, 1999). It is this very type of proactive approach which will assist in developing partnerships and communication based on mutual respect and trust.

Finally, some parents are reluctant to develop educational partnerships because of a history of mistreatment when they attended school (Cassity & Harris, 2000; Dodd & Konzal, 2000; Levine, 2009; Robinson & Fine, 1994; Scribner et al., 1999; Voltz, 1994). If a parent was made to feel inferior as a child in school, they most likely harbor resentment towards the system as an adult (Raffaele & Knoff, 1999). For instance, Williams and Baber (2007) suggest that African American parents who endured a faulty educational system may not believe there has been a clear demonstration of equity in the educational system towards their children. Examine the comments of an African American parent:

> I look at what I have seen in my lifetime and what I have seen specifically since I have been challenging this school system, and it is the most frightening thing I have ever seen. But when you are talking about miseducating and "dumbing down" generation after generation, after awhile you can keep diluting something until it is just as weak, to where you almost have to start all over again.
>
> (Williams & Baber, 2007. p. 7)

Research has demonstrated repeatedly that parents of color want their children to succeed in school. They place a high value on education and attempt to contribute substantially to the cognitive and intellectual development of their children (Hidalgo et al., 1995). Yet when they believe that the system does not equally value them, the parents find themselves in a difficult position. Trust, or the lack of it, is a powerful thing. If one has been mistreated, trust is forever damaged.

Ultimately the lack of trust can undermine the development of productive parent–teacher partnerships. All too often, cultural differences result in deficit thinking, whereby educators place blame on the parents and the child for not reaching academic goals (Chamberlain, 2005; Kalyanpur & Harry, 1997). Genuine partnerships with families necessitate mutual trust, whereby teachers and parents learn from one another for the benefit of the child. Voltz (1994) points out that education as a system has forgotten that it is the family (parent) who is the primary educator for any child and that when educators fail to listen to and work cooperatively with families, the effectiveness of the system is compromised. Thus, education as a system must work diligently to convey the message to families that their input is valued and desired.

PRACTICAL APPLICATIONS

Establishing relationships with parents and families that can lead to productive partnerships requires a different set of strategies than many of us have used in the past. These strategies are based on two pivotal concepts: establishing a welcoming environment and developing positive communication skills.

Establishing a Welcoming Environment

The physical environment of the culturally responsive and welcoming school is one that conveys respect for all cultural groups. The building is in good repair and clean, and the walls are brightly colored, with pictures that convey an appreciation for diversity. The entrance area is warm and inviting and says to all who enter, "This is a place where learning occurs." Student work floods the hallways. If a school has linguistic diversity, it is acknowledged with signage in multiple languages.

The culturally responsive school is a loving community where everyone is welcome, including parents. Parents are constantly sought to assist in any way they feel comfortable and the building envelops them in the sense that something wonderful happens in this place for their child.

To show that parents are valuable assets, schools can set aside space for parent centers—a designated room, perhaps, in the school building where parents perform certain volunteer tasks, hold meetings, and network and interact with other parents (Rockwell et al., 2010; Scribner et al., 1999). Ideally, schools serving underrepresented populations might even provide access to health services, social services, and adult education classes, thus reinforcing the idea of school as community (Cassity & Harris, 2000).

Open Communication

Harry (2008) offers six characteristics that need to be in place to create effective partnerships with families. First, all communication needs to be open, positive, understandable, and respectful. Some suggested easy communication tools include notes and letters, activity calendars, conferences/meetings, email, home visits, notebooks or journals, surveys and questionnaires, web pages, classroom and school newsletters, telephone calls, handbooks, learning compacts, orientations, open houses, portfolios, and progress reports (report cards). Local radio stations can be asked to broadcast school events, keeping in mind also to utilize radio stations that broadcast in the home language when

68

possible. Another suggestion is to place school information in community areas such as the local market, child care facility, library, and even the local church.

In communicating with families, culturally responsive teachers are not condescending but use vocabulary that families can understand. For instance, they avoid using "educationese" in both written and oral communication (Baruth & Manning, 1992; Flett & Conderman, 2001). Additionally, using titles such as Mr., Mrs., and Ms. demonstrates respect. Remember that in some cultures, addressing another adult by using their first name is seen as forward and disrespectful (Baruth & Manning, 1992). It is important to use a polite, respectful tone of voice which sets a positive tone for the conversation (Baruth & Manning, 1992). Culturally responsive teachers also make an effort to ensure that written communication is as clear and concise as possible, and if necessary, have it translated into the home language. Important materials, such as school policies, can be made available in audiotape and/or videotape form for those families unable to read in either their home language or American English (Linan-Thompson & Jean, 1997).

When conversing with parents, it is important to listen actively (Olion, 1988). Repeat what they say to ensure that what they were trying to communicate is what was understood. Ensure that the parent feels valued by giving them full attention when they are speaking. Further, never allow a conversation with a parent to go without some form of response, and never avoid a difficult situation. Many people dislike confrontation, yet parents who feel you and they are a team in the difficult times as well as the good are likely to maintain their partnerships.

It is vital to get to know families and their communication expectations and to treat them all uniquely. Different cultures have different norms for interaction, and teachers are wise to learn about these differences. Clearly, providing interpreters for parents who speak a language other than English is crucial; however, it is essential to keep in mind that confidentiality can be an issue. Thus, interpreters need to be carefully selected and trained, and district guidelines followed.

While formal conferences with parents can be useful, it is also important to recognize that not all parents feel comfortable coming to the school. Thus, culturally responsive teachers consider less formal events for getting to know parents, such as picnics at a local park, or social gatherings at a local community center. Hosting fun activities with families off the school grounds communicates that teachers want to establish a genuine relationship with them.

In order to ensure that parents participate actively in the educational process, some educators ask parents to sign a compact with the school (Crosby, 2006). Unlike a handbook, these compacts serve as a written agreement between the school, educators, families, and students intending to improve academic and home behaviors. One of the most popular is the compact for reading. Typically such compacts include such things as extra reading practice at home or working on various reading activities. Unique to such compacts is also a section which addresses alternatives to television and video game time, such as looking at magazines or local newspapers together as a family.

Culturally responsive educators encourage the development of workshops and parent groups for the differing families represented in the building (Cassity & Harris, 2000; De Gaetano, 2007; Flett & Conderman, 2001; Levine, 2009; Scribner et al., 1999). Language support groups, homework help sessions, how-to workshops, and district opportunities for parents who want more information on how to assist their child with specific academic tasks are opportunities to explore different interests of parents. Traditionally, parents have been given little information as to how best to contribute to their children's learning (Epstein and Jansorn, 2004; Hidalgo et al., 1995), but it is a priority of the culturally responsive school's administration to generate programs within the building to enable these families to become effective partners.

Mavis Sanders (1996) shares how program development has changed the face of three different schools in the Baltimore, Maryland, area. Two of the most unique programs these schools put into place were called "Pops on Patrol" and the "100% Club." Pops on Patrol is comprised of teams of six grandfathers and six grandmothers, who spend the day patrolling the halls. Their purpose is simple—to provide a message of the importance of school by being an example, to provide a safe environment, and to assist students with being punctual. The teams are rotated so multiple grandparents can participate. The 100% Club was developed in response to a need to improve communication between school and home. So for every newsletter, school calendar, cafeteria menu, message from the principal, or other school-to-home communication, parents are asked to sign an attached piece of paper. Every time a class successfully brings 100% of the slips back signed, the class wins an award. This program has seen an increase in communication between school and home.

Development of programs like these creates a true sense of commitment by the educator and the family. Through such programs, parents find the self-confidence necessary to move beyond their perceptions of inadequacy or inability to help their child be successful in school. It's important to note, however, that such programs are generally more successful when parents are involved in the planning phase and are thereby invested in the program (Schmidt, 1999). Inviting parents to collaborate in program planning moves beyond mere "parent involvement" to genuine partnership, which can only be established when educators are committed to learning from the families that they serve. It is to this topic that we now turn.

TEACHERS' VOICES

Welcoming Family Collaboration

Debbie Carter

First grade teacher, Western Elementary, Georgetown, KY

Approachable, open, and *welcoming* are words I hope will define my teaching when it comes to working with the families of my students. Despite my best attempts to welcome and embrace the diverse cultures of these families, I realized how challenging this really is when I once asked a student why his mother didn't attend a special program in which the children would sing songs in both English and Spanish. My heart sank when he replied to me, "She's embarrassed she doesn't speak English."

Embarrassed sounded like a bad word to me—vulgar and unacceptable. *Embarrassed* was a word I wanted to replace with *valued.* I wanted this parent to know and understand her value to her child and what an honor her presence in his classroom would be. I believe that every parent is a child's first teacher. Once a child enters a classroom, a partnership is forged. The strength of that partnership depends on the teacher.

Alisa

Alisa (pseudonym) was a quiet girl, shy and unsure. She was an English Language Learner (ELL) student in my multi-aged primary classroom. I was fortunate to have her as a student for two consecutive years. Her parents arrived together for the first parent–teacher conference. Her father walked ahead, and her mother, equally as shy as Alisa, was practically hiding behind him. I understood her apprehension. It was caused by the language barrier and her feelings of inferiority to me, the teacher. She thought I knew everything, and she thought she knew little.

I began by praising them for their support of Alisa. I told them how happy I was that she was in my classroom. I spoke about my interest in understanding second language acquisition. I told them their language was important. I invited them to visit the classroom to share their funds of knowledge. I apologized that I couldn't speak Spanish. That day was the beginning of a fruitful partnership. Over the next two years we would work together to make a difference for Alisa, who began to blossom.

She made steady progress in reading, despite the challenge of learning English. Over the summer, I met with her at the public library once a week to borrow books

71

on her reading level. She and I discovered bilingual books in English and Spanish. She beamed at the prospect each week of carrying a new armload of books home.

A year later, during another meeting in the conference room, I marveled over the bond her parents and I had forged and the rapport we had developed. I noted the difference in Alisa's mother who seemed much more comfortable, and began to greet me with a smile each time we met. A few moments after I was back in my classroom, a knock sounded at the door. It was Alisa's parents. They had one more question. They had noticed that on the bottom of Alisa's math homework, the sheets were labeled: Grade One.

I had been told that year to ability group my students with my team teachers. I had fought this directive because it is against best practice and I had lost. Alisa had scored low on the placement test and she was assigned to grade one level math again. But here at my classroom door stood my salvation—Alisa's salvation—her parents. They had been empowered. They were asking why, and I told them. In addition to the placement test, another teacher said that Alisa worked very slowly, that she wasn't able to keep up. I explained that I would see to it that she was moved to a grade two math group. I asked them to provide extra help at home on homework if needed. In the end, Alisa came through. She completed the assigned math in class, learned to work a little faster and performed well on assessments. Our expectation—her parents' and mine—was that she could succeed, and she did.

Later in her second year, Alisa's reading progress slowed. Finally, she stopped progressing at all and her reading level did not climb for three months. What she read, she seemed to comprehend; however, her pronunciation was difficult to decode. I was discouraged. I couldn't seem to pinpoint the cause or work towards a solution. Finally during a home visit, I asked an essential question. "Did Alisa have any trouble with her speech in her native language?" I asked. Yes. Her parents shared that she could not pronounce her r's in Spanish and they were able to understand her three-year-old sister better than her. I suspected that this was the reason for her plateau! I referred Alisa to the speech pathologist.

How many times does information such as this go undiscovered by teachers? It took me two years of working closely with Alisa's family to learn this essential fact. How often do we give up on our students and instead accept a deficit perspective? Without regard for the expertise of families and the importance of collaboration with them, educators often make assumptions. We sometimes believe that our students are in some way lacking. We believe that our students' families have no regard for education. We might even believe that students are lazy.

We must embrace partnerships with the families of our students. Herein lies our hope.

Establishing Collaborative Partnerships

While many schools have implemented opportunities for family involvement such as those noted above (e.g., regular communication through workshops, newsletters, conferences), very few have moved to Endrizzi's (2008) notion of "mutualism," whereby the teacher becomes a co-learner with the parent(s) and child. Endrizzi writes:

> When family–school partnerships are perceived as opportunities for families and teachers to learn together deliberately, they transform parent–teacher interactions . . . [teachers] intentionally set out to build bridges and work to unite community, home, and school learning experiences . . . teachers value the funds of knowledge that each child brings from family, peer, and community life, and they use these resources in the learning process.
>
> (p. 18)

The primary difference between teacher–family involvement and teacher–family partnerships is this: *in a partnership, teachers become the learners and parents become the experts.* Parents teach the educator what they know—about how their child learns, about their areas of expertise, about their cultural ways of interacting and "being in the world." Teachers, in turn, use this information to create a culturally responsive learning environment, to plan ways for connecting new information to what the child already knows, and to showcase parents' funds of knowledge in the formal curriculum.

Collaborative partnerships require that we develop genuine relationships with parents. Yet consider what is involved in establishing such relationships. Essentially, both parties need to be willing to "be human"—to share their thoughts, ideas, and personal experiences. Schmidt (1999) has developed a procedure that she has termed the "ABCs of Cross-Cultural Communication," whereby teachers intentionally learn about families and then engage in cultural comparison. She suggests that teachers begin by writing down the significant events of their own lives, recording all of the details that they can recall. Then, teachers conduct unstructured interviews with parents, asking them to tell about early school and home experiences. Families are encouraged to share their stories in detail. Next, teachers compare the similarities and differences between their personal stories, and analyze those differences. Experiences such as this encourage teachers to recognize the norms of their own culture and to determine what cultural differences make them the most uncomfortable. Schmidt documents one successful experience in K-6 classrooms:

> [Teachers] modeled autobiography by telling personal and family stories, sharing written accounts, and showing personal artifacts . . . This stimulated classroom interest and students began to share stories, written and oral, about their families. Students invited their family members to show pictures, explain family objects, and tell family stories. Several families created albums or stories of their lives with photos, illustrations, and written narratives.
>
> (p. 336)

Schmidt reports that such activities helped teachers to make positive connections to students and families early in the school year.

Ada, Campoy, and Zubizarreta (2001) share a project in which parents and teachers engage in book discussions, and parents are invited to relate the stories they read to their own life experiences. Parents are then provided with blank books to take home and are encouraged to create their own books. The authors report that parents have written books such as *Celebrations of My Childhood, Our Grandparents, Our Dreams for Our Children and How We Can Help Them Come True*. Not only do projects such as this one provide educators with windows into families' histories and visions for the future, but they also provide important information on how best to shape the educational experiences for their students. Ada et al. (2001) conclude:

> Teachers participating in the program reported a greater understanding of the children in their classroom and of the challenges faced by those children on a daily basis . . . Teachers also reported that children who had the opportunity to see their parents recognized as authors by the school gained a greater sense of self-esteem and a new-found appreciation for the wisdom of their parents' words and their parents' life experiences.
>
> (p. 180)

Another important way for teachers to get to know families is to attend events in their students' communities. By attending social activities in the community, educators can learn a great deal about the families they serve (Voltz, 1994). Many communities have cultural celebrations, picnics, or block parties. Attending such events provides the opportunity for educators to develop positive relationships with parents and families. Schools might even organize such events, thereby demonstrating a sense of respect for the families and their home communities (Cassity & Harris, 2000).

Another effective means for building partnerships and a bond of trust is the home visit (Hensley, 2005; Rockwell et al., 2010). While some educators are apprehensive to venture into unknown parts of the community, home visits are nevertheless an integral part of the process of establishing parent–teacher partnerships, for they provide educators with an opportunity to learn from parents and families. When teachers are reluctant to go on home visits, they can arrange to visit in pairs. Visiting with a family on neutral ground, such as the local park, library, or a local restaurant, can be viable alternatives as well.

During quality home visits, the teacher allows the family to do the majority of the sharing and questioning. Teachers listen very attentively to what parents have to say (Hensley, 2005). A home visit will backfire if it is perceived by the family as an away from school parent conference. Too many times educators have gone to students' homes to discuss progress, report inappropriate behaviors, and to "teach" families what they feel the "family needs to know" (Street, 2005). Teachers can expect some feedback about school-related issues, but the focus of the visit remains solidly on getting to know the parents (McIntyre, Kyle, Moore, Sweazy, & Greer, 2001). In this way, home visits are an opportunity to step into the child's world.

For instance, home visits allow the teacher to gain valuable understanding as to how the child interacts in his/her home environment and how the family members share their knowledge with one another (Street, 2005). By listening to the family's stories and gaining an understanding of what the family "knows"—i.e., their "funds of knowledge" (González, Moll, & Amanti, 2005)—teachers can gain vital information that can be used in educating the child. The educator can then take this information and use it to provide a more effective and sensitive educational experience for the child by creating these meaningful connections between school and home (Hensley, 2005; Rockwell et al., 2009; Street, 2005). Research has demonstrated repeatedly that education is much more meaningful when it connects the child's home knowledge with school curriculum (McIntyre et al., 2001). Hensley (2005) states: "Classroom learning can be greatly enhanced when teachers learn more not just about their students' lives in an abstract sense but about their particular students and their households" (p. 146). When educators take advantage of this information and utilize it, the education of the child becomes a family affair, and parents become much more willing participants in the educational process for their child.

Research shows that there are many positive benefits to conducting home visits (Rockwell et al., 2010). Families tend to change their attitudes towards the educational process, their ability to work successfully with their child improves, and they begin to utilize outside resources more often. Children demonstrate positive behavior changes and their self-esteem improves. Most importantly, the gap between home and school is bridged. Families begin to feel empowered and a real sense of partnership develops. Friendships are formed and mutual trust and respect can be found. We believe that the many positive outcomes from home visits are worth the challenges they present to teachers.

Building on Families' "Funds of Knowledge"

Literacy learning begins at home, not in the school (Compton-Lilly, 2003; Edwards & Turner, 2008). While some families may not have ready access to a home library, this does not mean the home is devoid of literacy. All homes are rich in print, and all families engage in some form of literate activity every day. From writing notes, using recipes, making a simple grocery list, or reading closed television captions, to reading from the family Bible or Qur-an, literacy abounds in the home (Edwards & Turner, 2008). This is also very true in homes where English is not the primary language. It must be stressed that literacy is present, just not perhaps in forms that educators readily identify (Kenner, 2005). Barton (1994) puts it best when he states, "The family is an ecological niche in which literacy survives, is sustained, and flourishes" (p. 149).

As noted previously, social events with families, such as picnics, potlucks, and home visits, afford the educator with the opportunity to learn about the family's many interests, their "ways of knowing," their social routines (McIntyre et al., 2001). Educators can explore the families' "funds of knowledge" and based on such information, can build instruction on what the child knows and has experienced. Through such experiences, educators explore meaningful ways to build connections with the child and family and as a result, begin to create those partnerships that are so important to academic success. In fact, I would argue that it is impossible to create literacy experiences that are truly culturally responsive without an integral knowledge of the cultural experiences of the children and families that we serve. Thus, establishing positive and productive relationships with parents is vital.

In their book, *Funds of Knowledge: Theorizing Practices in Households, Communities, and Classrooms*, González, Moll and Amanti (2005) provide numerous examples of how the knowledge of families and communities can be used to enhance instruction. Teachers who participate in the "funds of knowledge project" are trained to become ethnographers, stepping into the worlds of their students in order to document their home lives. Teachers then engage in a process of "contextualization," in which the knowledge of students and families is utilized as a basis for further learning. The teachers attend to every detail of the neighborhood: family yard sales, building projects, gardening, restored automobiles, ornaments, and other artifacts. They then interview families on their family and labor histories. The authors write: "The narratives that [emerge] from these household histories are incredibly powerful and often are testimonies to the resiliency and resources of people whose lives are often lived at the economic margins" (p. 11).

Due to time constraints, teachers typically conduct complete interviews with only three students and their families, with visits spaced over a period of several months. Teachers then engage in study groups in which they discuss related professional literature, revise interview procedures, review findings from their visits, and discuss practical implications for instruction. Amanti writes that the study groups "create the conditions where teachers can become risk-takers, willing to experiment and try out new strategies and practices in their classrooms" (González, Moll, & Amanti, 2005, p. 20).

In learning about families' histories and funds of knowledge, teachers begin to acknowledge the strengths and resources of families that can be leveraged for instruction. For instance, Amanti (2005) discovered that many of her students and their families had experiences with horses. She subsequently developed an inquiry module whereby her students researched the various questions they had about horses. She was able to connect this study to several social studies topics, such as the role of Spanish explorers in bringing horses to the Americas, and the early history of the domestication of horses. Students read stories about horses and engaged in research in order to find answers to their questions. Science and math topics included cells and multi-celled living organisms, graphing the heights of different horse breeds, horse anatomy, and a live demonstration of horse shoeing.

In her ethnographic work with families from Mexico, Browning-Aiken (2005) found a common historical theme of mining and the importance of the copper mining industry. She used this discovery to enhance the middle school science and language arts curriculum. Utilizing local resources, students studied geology, ecology, and mining processes and operations. They read folktales about mining towns and settlers and wrote family anecdotes, journals, and descriptive essays. Messing (2005) reports the discovery of an uncle's coin collection led to a study of money. The children learned about the barter system, how an economy works, and how money is made. Soon many of the children were bringing in their own collections and sharing them with the class.

Messing (2005) also writes about a young girl who was a "discipline problem" in the classroom. Her teacher noticed that the student liked to play singing and clapping games, so she invited the young girl to write the games on a chart and teach them to the other students. The children subsequently performed the games for the parents and principal. This project emerged from visiting the student's home and developing critical observation skills that were used to discover the child's area of expertise. By tapping into the child's natural leadership abilities, the teacher was able to develop a positive relationship that led to improved student engagement.

Compton-Lilly (2004) writes about various projects that she completed with her first grade students: writing down their jump rope rhymes and using them as early reading experiences; investigating the levels of lead in students' homes and reading and writing about the effects of lead poisoning; asking parents to take cameras to work and using the pictures to create personalized books; investigating the many uses of literacy in her students' households and communities. Like the aforementioned literacy activities, these "funds of knowledge" projects connect to and address the required state and national language arts standards; however, the medium through which the standards are taught varies based upon the cultural experiences of students and families.

It is also important to note that in all of these cases, teachers did not depend on a standardized literacy program for teaching reading. Rather, literacy in all of its forms—reading, writing, speaking, and listening—was taught in authentic ways using the knowledge and resources of the students and their families. Creative teachers can teach literacy skills and strategies using authentic texts created by students and their families, such as:

- simple picture books using pictures from the students' neighborhood and/or school;
- family experience stories written on charts or in books;
- family artifacts or student collections that are labeled;
- common songs and chants;
- written publications (reports, brochures, presentations) based upon students' inquiries.

Because literacy is embedded in our life experiences, opportunities for making home-school connections abound. Parents can be invited to write books about their experiences to place in the classroom library. Parents who speak a language other than English can contribute books in their native language (DeGaetano, 2007). Books of children's poetry, folk stories, folk sayings, songs and even books of recipes in varying languages written by family members would make a wonderful addition to any school library. Classroom walls can be filled with pictures and charts of students' experiences that can be used to teach concepts about print, sight words, phonics skills, and to develop reading fluency.

Parents can be asked to cook with the students, which can lead to a written sequence map and perhaps a class recipe book. They can be asked to assist with a construction project, which can result in a "how to" book. Family and community members can be interviewed on specific topics and students can compile their findings in articles, reports, and PowerPoint presentations. Indeed, the possibilities are endless. Of course, parents can also be encouraged to read to their children and to participate in various literacy experiences at home. Even parents who have extended conversations with and read to their child in their primary language are helping their children learn language; literacy activities do not have to be in English to be valuable (Ladky & Peterson, 2008).

Another literacy activity in which parents could be very supportive is the use of performing arts. Dramatic activities include the use of puppets, pantomime, and singing, dancing, and acting out small portions of favorite books, using improvisation or Reader's Theater (Sanacore, 2004). Imagine how books about Native American dance such as *Star Boy* (Goble, 1990) would come to life for students if a parent came and demonstrated Native American dance in full costume. Similarly, imagine how books like *How Sweet the Sound* (Hudson & Hudson, 1995) or *I See the Rhythm* (Igus, 1998) would engage students if shared by parents who could either sing or play the music for the class, or how heartfelt a book such as *Reaching Out* (Jimenez, 2008) would be if read to the class by a parent who had endured a similar past. Customs, historical events, ethnic pride, and cultural understanding can be brought to life for all of the children through the simple reading of a book.

CONCLUSION

Families provide children with things like love, togetherness, consideration, respect, communication, and commitment (Raffaele & Knoff, 1999). Although different families may show more or less of any of these characteristics, generally they are a child's greatest support system. They are the child's source of strength. They are the child's primary educator. A bridge built from school to home allows families the opportunity to play a meaningful role in the educational process of their child. Yet this bridge must be traveled from both directions.

Administrators, educators, and parents must begin to accept that the roles they play are not independent from each other. Education can be represented by the image of a puzzle; if just one piece of the puzzle is missing, the overall image is incomplete. By the same token, if one important member of the team does not participate, the child's academic success can suffer. This form of partnership develops a sense of shared responsibility between the school and the parents (Christenson, 1995). A child's education is only partly completed at school; the remainder of learning is done at home. If parents and educators are going to build partnerships, it must be based on both forms of education—the kind that happens at school and the kind that happens at home. This shared sense of responsibility for the child's success will become part of the foundation for partnership. Family–educator partnership is only one piece to the answer to improving the current system, but it is a vital piece.

We have explored the many benefits to families, educators, administrators and most importantly, the student, when partnerships are formed. We have explored how content can be wonderfully enriched for all children in the classroom when partnerships are formed. The impact of partnership is a

79

life-altering event for all. Let us remember why we became teachers—to enhance the development of the child. May we never forget.

"Whose child is this?" I asked once more,
Just as the little one entered the door.
"Ours," said the parent and the teacher as they smiled.
And each took the hand of the little child.
"Ours to love and train together.
Ours this blessed task forever."

(Author unknown)

Table 4.1 Summary of CRIOP Component: Parent Collaboration

Element	What you would expect to see in a classroom where CRI practices are occurring	What you would expect to see in a classroom where CRI practices are not occurring
The teacher establishes genuine partnerships (equitable relationships) with parents/caregivers.	Parents'/caregivers' ideas are solicited in how best to instruct the child; there is evidence that the teacher has made the effort to get to know the "whole child" (his/her background, family culture, out-of-school activities) by getting to know his/her parents/caregivers, and families.	No effort has been made to establish relationships with caregivers; there's evidence of a "deficit perspective" in which families and caregivers are viewed as inferior and/or as having limited resources that can be leveraged for the education of the child.
The teacher uses parent expertise to support student learning and welcomes parents/caregivers in the classroom.	Parents'/caregivers' "funds of knowledge" are utilized in the instructional program; parents/caregivers are invited into the classroom to share experiences and areas of expertise.	Parents/caregivers are never involved in the instructional program; their "funds of knowledge" are never utilized.
The teacher reaches out to meet parents in positive, non-traditional ways.	Teacher conducts home visits, meets parents in the parking lot or other "neutral" locations outside of the school, and makes an effort to develop a relationship with parents through planning various social activities outside of school.	Teacher makes phone calls and sends personal notes to parents for negative reports only (e.g., discipline); when communication occurs, it is through newsletters or similar correspondence, where parents are asked to respond passively (e.g.,

Table 4.1 Continued

Element	What you would expect to see in a classroom where CRI practices are occurring	What you would expect to see in a classroom where CRI practices are not occurring
		signing the newsletter, versus becoming actively involved in their child's learning); the only interaction with parents is through formal parent–teacher conferences that are conducted on the school grounds.

REFLECTIVE ACTIVITIES

1 Take a moment to reflect on how you as the classroom educator interact with the parents/caregivers of the children in your classroom and jot down these interactions in two lists: *Parents as Partners* and *Parents as Teacher Assistants*. Which is longer? If parents primarily serve as assistants in your classroom, what action could you take in the near future to add items to the *Parents as Partners* list?

2 Take a look at the demographics of your classroom. Record, for example, the gender, neighborhood, family birth order, parent configuration, and income of the families represented. What challenges do you recognize to creating partnerships?

3 As a teacher, in what ways do you communicate in "educationese" with parents? How can you begin to change these words and phrases to make your information more accessible to more parents?

4 Use one of the examples in the chapter (or create your own activity) to explore and record the ways your students' families use literacy at home. In what ways do children engage with these family-focused activities?

5 In what ways could you use families' "funds of knowledge" to teach current state standards? In what ways can the parents and families be "experts" in your classroom?

REFERENCES

Ada, A. F., Campoy, F. I., & Zubizarreta, R. (2001). Assessing our work with parents on behalf of children's literacy. In S. R. Hurley, & J. V. Tinajero (Eds.), *Literacy assessment of second language learners* (pp. 167–186). Boston: Allyn & Bacon.

Amanti, C. (2005). Beyond a beads and feathers approach. In N. González, L. C. Moll, & C. Amanti (Eds.), *Funds of knowledge: theorizing practices in households, communities, and classrooms* (pp. 131–141). Mahwah, NJ: Lawrence Erlbaum.

Barton, D. (1994). *Literacy: An introduction to the ecology of written language.* Oxford: Blackwell.

Baruth, L. G., & Manning, M. L. (1992). *Multicultural education of children and adolescents.* Boston: Allyn & Bacon.

Bastiani, J. (1989). Professional ideology versus lay experience. In G. Allen, J. Bastiani, I. Martin, & K. Richards (Eds.), *Community education: An agenda for educational reform.* Milton Keynes: Open University Press.

Browning-Aiken, A. (2005). Border crossings: Funds of knowledge within an immigrant household. In N. González, L. C. Moll, & C. Amanti (Eds.), *Funds of knowledge: Theorizing practices in households, communities, and classrooms* (pp. 167–181). Mahwah, NJ: Lawrence Erlbaum.

Cassity, J., & Harris, S. (2000). Parents of ESL students: A study of parental involvement. *NASSP Bulletin, 84,* 55–62.

Chamberlain, S. (2005). Recognizing and responding to cultural differences in the education of culturally and linguistically diverse learners. *Intervention in School and Clinic, 40,* 195–211.

Christenson, S. L. (1995). Families and schools: what is the role of the school psychologist? *School Psychology Quarterly, 10,* 118–132.

Christenson, S. L., & Cleary, M. (1990). Consultation and the parent–education partnership: A perspective. *Journal of Educational and Psychological Consultation, 1,* 219–241.

Compton-Lilly, C. (2003). *Reading families: The literate lives of urban children.* New York: Teachers College Press.

Compton-Lilly, C. (2004). *Confronting racism, poverty, and power: Classroom strategies to change the world.* Portsmouth, NH: Heinemann.

Crosby, B. (2006). *Smart kids, bad schools.* New York: St. Martin's Press.

Dauber, S. L., & Epstein, J. L. (1993). Parents' attitudes and practices of involvement in inner city elementary and middle schools. In N.F. Chavkin (Ed.), *Families and schools in a pluralistic society* (pp. 53–71). Albany, NY: SUNY Press.

De Gaetano, Y. (2007). The role of culture in engaging Latino parents' involvement in school. *Urban Education, 42,* 145–162.

Dodd, A. W., & Konzal, J. L. (2000). Parents and educators as real partners. *Education Digest, 65,* 18–22.

Edwards, P. A., & Turner, J. D. (2008). Family literacy and reading comprehension. In S. E. Israel, & G. G. Duffy (Eds.), *Handbook of research in reading comprehension* (pp. 622–639). Mahwah, NJ: Lawrence Erlbaum.

Endrizzi, C. K. (2008). *Becoming teammates: Teachers and families as literacy partners.* Urbana, IL: NCTE.

Epstein, J. L., Coates, L., Salinas, K. C., Sanders, M. G., & Simon, B. S. (1997). *School, family, and community partnerships: Your handbook for action.* Thousand Oaks, CA: Corwin Press.

Epstein, J. L., & Jansorn, N. R. (2004). School, family, and community partnerships link the plan. *Education Digest, 69,* 19–23.

Flett, A., & Conderman, G. (2001). Enhance the involvement of parents from culturally and linguistically diverse backgrounds. *Intervention in School and Clinic, 37,* 53–55.

Goble, P. (1990). *Star boy.* New York: Aladdin Paperbacks.

González, N., Moll, L. C., & Amanti, C (Eds.), *Funds of knowledge: Theorizing practices in households, communities, and classrooms.* Mahwah, NJ: Lawrence Erlbaum.

González, N., Moll, L., Tenery, M. F., Rivera, A., Rendón, P., Gonzales, R., & Amanti, C. (2005). Funds of knowledge for teaching in Latino households. In N. González, L. C. Moll, & C. Amanti (Eds.), *Funds of knowledge: Theorizing practices in households, communities, and classrooms* (pp. 89–117). Mahwah, NJ: Lawrence Erlbaum.

Grantham, T. C., Frasier, M. M., Roberts, A. C., & Bridges, E. M. (2005). Parent advocacy for culturally diverse gifted students. *Theory into Practice, 44,* 138–147.

Gray, E., & Cosgrove, J. (1985). Ethnocentric perception of childrearing practices in protective services. *Child Abuse and Neglect, 9,* 389–396.

Gudykunst, W. B., & Kim, Y. Y. (1997). *Communicating with strangers: An approach to intercultural communication.* Boston, MA: McGraw-Hill.

Harry, B. (2008) Collaboration with culturally and linguistically diverse families: Ideal versus reality. *Exceptional Children, 74,* 372–388.

Hensley, M. (2005). Empowering parents of multicultural backgrounds. In N. Gonzalez, L.C. Moll, & C. Amanti (Eds.), *Funds of knowledge: Theorizing practices in households, communities, and classrooms* (pp. 143–151). Mahwah, NJ: Lawrence Erlbaum.

Herrera, S. G., & Murray, K. G. (2005). *Mastering ESL and bilingual methods: Differential instruction for culturally and linguistically diverse students.* Boston, MA: Pearson.

Hidalgo, N. M., Bright, J. A., Epstein, J. L., Siu, S., & Swap, S. M. (1995). Research on families, schools, and communities: A multicultural perspective. In J. Banks, & C. Banks (Eds.), *Handbook of research on multicultural education* (pp. 498–524). New York, Macmillan.

Hong, G. K., & Hong, L. K. (1991). Comparative perspectives on child abuse and neglect: Chinese versus Hispanics and Whites. *Child Welfare, 70,* 463–475.

Hudson, W., & Hudson, C. (1995). *How sweet the sound.* New York: Scholastic.

Hughes, J., & Kwok, O. (2007). Influence of student–teacher and parent–teacher relationships on lower achieving readers' engagement and achievement in primary grades. *Journal of Educational Psychology, 99,* 39–51.

Igus, T. (1998). *I see rhythm.* San Francisco, CA: Children's Book Press.

Jiménez, F. (2008). *Reaching out.* Boston, MA: Houghton Mifflin.

Johnson, L. J., Pugach, M. C., & Hawkins, A. (2004). School–family collaboration: A partnership. *Focus on Exceptional Children, 36,* 1–12.

Kalyanpur, M., & Harry, B. (1997). A posture of reciprocity: A practical approach to collaboration between professionals and parents of culturally diverse backgrounds. *Journal of Child and Family Studies, 6,* 487–509.

Kenner, C. (2005). Bilingual families as literacy eco-systems. *Early Years, 25,* 283–298.

Ladky, M., & Peterson, S. S. (2008). Successful practices for immigrant parent involvement: An Ontario perspective. *Multicultural Perspectives, 10,* 82–89.

Landsman, J., & Lewis, C. W. (2006). *White teachers/diverse classrooms.* Sterling, VA: Stylus Publishing.

Levine, D. (2009). Tellin' stories: Finding common ground. *Rethinking Schools, 23,* 38–45.

Levine, D. U., & Lezotte, L. W. (1995). Effective schools research. In J. Banks, & C. Banks (Eds.), *Handbook of research on multicultural education* (pp. 498–524). New York: Macmillan.

Linan-Thompson, S., & Jean, R. E. (1997). Completing the parent participation puzzle: Accepting diversity. *Teaching Exceptional Children, 52,* 46–50.

Matuszny, R. M., Banda, D. R., & Coleman, T. J. (2007). A progressive plan for building collaborative relationships with parents from diverse backgrounds. *Teaching Exceptional Children, 39,* 24–31.

McIntyre, E., Kyle, D., Moore, G., Sweazy, R. A., & Greer, S. (2001). Linking home and school through family visits. *Language Arts, 78,* 264–272.

Messing, J. (2005). Social reconstructions of schooling: Teacher evaluations of what they learned from participation in the funds of knowledge project. In N. González, L. C. Moll, & C. Amanti (Eds.), *Funds of knowledge: Theorizing practices in households, communities, and classrooms* (pp. 183–194). Mahwah, NJ: Lawrence Erlbaum.

Olion, L. (1988). Enhancing the involvement of Black parents of adolescents with handicaps. In A. A. Ortiz, & B. A. Ramirez (Eds.), *Schools and the culturally diverse exceptional student: Promising practices and future directions* (pp. 96–103). Reston, VA: Council for Exceptional Children.

Raffaele, L. M. & Knoff, H. M. (1999). Improving home–school collaboration with disadvantaged families: Organizational principles, perspectives, and approaches. *School Psychology Review, 28,* 448–466.

Robinson, E. L., & Fine, M. J. (1994). Developing collaborative home–school relationships. *Preventing School Failure, 39,* 9–15.

Rockwell, R. E., Andre, L. C., & Hawley, M. K. (2009). *Families and educators as partners.* Belmont, CA: Wadsworth.

Sanacore, J. (2004). Genuine caring and literacy learning for African American children. *The Reading Teacher, 57,* 744–753.

Sanders, M. (1996). Building family partnerships that last. *Educational Leadership, 54,* 61–66.

Schmidt, P. R. (1999). Know thyself and understand others. *Language Arts, 76,* 332–340.

Scribner, J. D., Young, M. D., & Pedroza, A. (1999). Building collaborative relationships with parents. In P. Reyes, J. D. Scribner, & A.P. Scribner, (Eds.), *Lessons from high performing Hispanic schools: Creating learning communities* (pp. 36–60). New York: Teachers College Press.

Street, C. (2005). Funds of knowledge at work in the writing classroom. *Multicultural Education, 13,* 22–25.

Tett, L. (2001). Parents as problems or parents as people? Parental involvement programmes, schools and adult educators. *Journal of Lifelong Education, 20,* 188–198.

Tomlinson, S. (1993). Ethnic minorities: Involved parents or problem parents? In P. Munn (Ed.), *Parents and schools: Customers, managers, or partners.* London: Routledge.

Trask, B. S., & Hamon, R. R. (2007). *Cultural diversity and families: Expanding perspectives.* Thousand Oaks, CA: Sage Publications.

Turner-Vorbeck, T., & Marsh, M. M. (2008). *Other kinds of families: Embracing diversity in school.* New York: Teachers College Press.

Voltz, D. (1994). Developing collaborative parent–teacher relationships with culturally diverse parents. *Intervention in School and Clinic, 29,* 288–291.

Williams, E. R., & Baber, C. R. (2007). Building trust through culturally reciprocal home–school–community collaboration from the perspective of African American parents. *Multicultural Perspectives, 9,* 3–9.

Part II

Core Instructional Practices

Chapter 5

Culturally Responsive Assessment: Creating a Culture of Learning

Rebecca Powell

[T]he United States has currently reached the highest volume of testing and the highest stakes testing in its history. We are reminded of a definition of fanaticism as the act of redoubling one's efforts while having forgotten what one is fighting for.

(Johnston & Costello, 2005, p. 265)

Has our nation, as this quote suggests, become obsessed with standardized testing? It would seem so. Standardized tests have become the primary gauge for determining individual success; students who consistently do not perform well on "the test" are deemed to be inferior academically, doomed to a life of mediocrity. Yet at the same time, we hear cries for developing future citizens who are innovative, creative, thoughtful—precisely those practices that are *not* assessed by standardized tests. Add to this list the desirability of other abilities such as multilingualism and working collaboratively with others, and the limitations of large-scale testing become clear.

Standardized tests originally were developed to make education more efficient by categorizing and grouping students for instruction. E. L. Thorndike, a prominent educational psychologist during the progressive period, advocated for widespread use of standardized testing, stating that: "Reading tests . . . will mean . . . an ultimate differentiation in training for the different types of children, with which teachers now have to deal." (1918, pp. 280–281, cited in Shannon, 1998, p. 82). Such tests were based upon the premise that standardized evaluation can be objective, and that one's potential for learning is largely biologically predetermined.

Given that the original purpose of standardized testing was to sort students, consider that such tests were designed to *promote* an achievement gap. It is important to recognize that our current testing practices are derived from this legacy. As Shannon (1998) notes, the scientific management of schooling has become ingrained in the American mind, and tests have been used to standardize the educational enterprise. Such tests encode cultural biases found within the larger society and tend to divide children along cultural and socioeconomic lines. Indeed, standardized tests were designed to do just that, so as to promote the efficiency required for the scientific management of schools.

In recent years, in an effort to hold schools and teachers accountable for student success, standardized testing has become pervasive in our nation's schools. Schools can be characterized by a "culture of evaluation"—a culture whereby the test and its contents define both the skills and the content that are taught and how they are presented. While the expressed purpose for standardized testing has shifted from social efficiency to accountability, the results are nevertheless the same: some students are determined to be "less capable" than their peers, and these students tend to be those from marginalized populations.

In this chapter, I argue that the classroom environment needs to be transformed from a "culture of evaluation" to a "culture of learning." That is, the educational paradigm needs to shift from assessing students to determine what they know and can do—their strengths and weaknesses—to assessing students to determine what they are *able* to do—their learning potential. The first approach views the student as someone who is in need of "remediation," and our task as teachers is to determine what needs to be "fixed." The second approach, however, views the student as a learner who is capable of academic success, given the appropriate learning environment and instructional support. The role of assessment, then, is to *learn from the students and families we serve* so that we can appropriately scaffold their learning.

MOVING TOWARD A CULTURE OF LEARNING

Effective assessment informs instruction. This statement is almost becoming a cliché in educational circles. Quality assessment helps to assure that all students master the concepts we are teaching. Quality assessment also focuses on what students can do—their strengths, competencies, and resources that they bring to learning—versus their deficits. Effective assessment is motivating; it encourages students to set goals and to work to achieve those goals. Stiggins, Arter, Chappuis, and Chappuis (2006) write: "[U]sed with skill, assessment can motivate the unmotivated, restore the desire to learn, and encourage students to keep learning, and it can actually create—not simply measure—increased achievement" (p. 3). Yet more often than not, our current assessment practices allow too many students to become demoralized and to "fall through the cracks," thus actually contributing to student failure.

Consider these scenarios. All of the third grade teachers at this particular elementary school are teaching about the water cycle, yet their assessment practices are very different. In one class, after the teacher introduces the concepts, the teacher asks various children to tell what they know by asking probing questions. A typical classroom interaction might go something like this:

T: Who can describe the water cycle? [a few hands are raised] Dillon?
Dillon: Well, the water e- e-
T: Evaporates.
Dillon: The water e-va-por-ates and makes a cloud. Then it comes down when it rains.
T: Very good Dillon. Can anyone else add to that?

This is the typical Initiation–Response–Evaluation (IRE) pattern found in most classrooms (Cazden, 2001). The IRE pattern has become so embedded in the "way that we do school" that teachers seem to perform this ritual without examining its limitations.

Now consider another classroom. After introducing the water cycle, the teacher directs her students to take out a sheet of paper and demonstrate their learning in any way that makes sense to them. She then circulates around the room as they complete their work and publicly affirms the various ways that students are representing their knowledge. She makes comments such as "Brianna is making a list and putting the parts of the water cycle in order. That's a good way to show the sequence." "I see that Marcos is drawing a picture of the water cycle. He's labeling it with some of the words that we talked about. Good job, Marcos." When the students are finished, they turn to one another and share their work with a peer. The teacher then collects their papers and examines each one carefully to determine student learning.

Both of these teachers are using formative assessment. Yet in the first classroom, with the exception of the few students who responded to her initial prompt, the teacher really has no way of knowing which students in the class have grasped the concepts, and which have not. Perhaps just as damaging, those students who are not able to arrive at the specific response that the teacher is seeking may come to perceive themselves as less capable than their peers. Further, there is evidence to suggest that after teachers call on a particular student, other students feel that they are "off the hook" and remain passive (Clarke, 2005; Walsh & Sattes, 2004). Thus, such assessment practices do little

91

to determine students' knowledge, and may even be counterproductive in that they undermine students' motivation to learn.

In contrast, the assessment practices used by the teacher in the second classroom will encourage students to achieve. In this classroom, every student is asked to provide evidence of learning, and even those with limited English proficiency can complete the task. By requiring every student to respond and by allowing students to share their responses with one another, the teacher sends the message that she believes every student can learn, and that they are also capable of enhancing the knowledge of their peers. In this classroom, students cannot "get by"; every student is required to demonstrate their learning. In this way, the teacher gains specific information on each child's level of understanding. At the same time, they are allowed to show their learning in multiple ways, e.g., through diagrams with simple labels, through a written list, or through more extended discourse, depending upon their level of literacy or language proficiency. The emphasis is not on getting "the one correct answer," but rather on exhibiting what you know. Through her assessment practices, this teacher is creating a culture of learning versus a culture of evaluation in her classroom.

Quality formative assessment is at the heart of good instruction. Indeed, formative assessment is essential to assure the success of every student. Yet I suggest that while quality assessment is important for every student, it is particularly important for those students who historically have experienced failure in our educational institutions. These are the students who may be overlooked in our classrooms, who may feel that they don't have the verbal competence or the facility in English to respond, or who simply have become so disengaged with schooling that they no longer make the effort to learn. As I will discuss throughout this chapter, quality literacy assessment considers the *social dimension* of literacy and learning and the critical importance of student–teacher relationships in acquiring valid data on students' understanding.

With our current emphasis on accountability, however, summative assessments—in the form of standardized tests—have assumed prominence. While such tests may provide some useful information to teachers, they nevertheless have a number of limitations, particularly for English language learners. Further, rather than viewing literacy as a social process, formal tests tend to promote a very narrow conceptualization of literacy, which can have a profound effect on instructional practice. We turn now to the research base on standardized testing and on quality assessment for learners from diverse populations.

SUPPORTING RESEARCH

One of the more prominent themes in the research literature on assessment practices in our nation's diverse schools is that there are a number of concerns with standardized testing. Thus, we begin this discussion with an examination of the problems with standardized tests and the challenges for diverse student populations.

Concerns with Standardized Testing

As Murphy (1998) aptly points out, reading tests reflect and reinforce particular conceptualizations of literacy. In sampling popular standardized reading tests, Murphy found that most used short reading passages instead of the connected discourse that is typical of authentic reading. In summarizing her findings for group tests, Murphy concludes that "[t]he tests reviewed did not contain a lot of reading material. None of the standardized tests surveyed contained half their items at the discourse level" (p. 54). She found similar findings in her evaluation of individualized reading tests. She writes that, while one would expect individualized tests to require more reading of extended text, in fact, the opposite is the case: "by and large most items for all tests emphasize the word, subword, or nonword level" (p. 71). Thus, reading tests tend to reflect a reductionist perspective of literacy, where literacy is reduced to its parts, versus a language process that is developed in authentic sociocultural contexts (Johnston & Costello, 2005).

A real concern with such reductionist measurements is that tests tend to drive instruction. In discussing the "consequential validity" of standardized testing, Johnston (1998) examines the many ways that the use of standardized literacy tests can have a negative impact on students' academic success, and most particularly on the success of historically marginalized student populations. First, a reductionist perspective results in a narrow literacy curriculum that focuses on teaching the parts of literacy versus its varied uses in authentic social contexts (Harlan & Crick, 2003; McNeil, 2000; Morrison & Joan, 2002; Smith, 1991). Research shows that more complex literacy tasks which require purposeful, extended uses of oral and written texts tend to be eliminated because they "aren't on the test." Indeed, skills that we ought to be encouraging, such as bilingualism, collaborative inquiry, and creative thinking, can become handicaps on standardized tests. Consider that a narrow focus on the subskills of literacy can actually hinder students' linguistic development, in that students rarely have the opportunity to engage in activities that require extended uses of oral and written language (Darling-Hammond, 1994).

Reductionist → teach to the test

Beyond this, however, the reductionist perspective associated with standard-ized testing ignores the importance of peer collaboration and social activity that has been found to be important to learning, particularly for students of color (Ladson-Billings, 1994; Vaughan, 2002). In fact, some research suggests that a focus on test scores leads to a "dumbing down" of the curriculum, resulting in peer resentment of students who require extra preparation for the test (Moon, Brighton, Jarvis, & Hall, 2007). Johnston notes that, "The competitive individ-ualism fostered by testing . . . systematically devalues cooperative literate activity and ensures the perpetuation of a narrow and privileging form of literacy" (p. 97). He further suggests:

> The format that requires simple right or wrong answers may foster a view of knowledge as the accumulation of right answers from authorities such as teachers and texts. Such a concrete, dualistic view of knowledge is non-dialectic and is unlikely to foster inquiry approaches to instruction.
>
> (p. 101)

Because of the accountability pressures on schools that serve economically disadvantaged students and students of color, there tends to be even more time devoted to "teaching to the test" in these schools (Cunningham & Sanzo, 2002; Herman & Golan, 1990; Moon, Brighton, Jarvis, & Hall, 2007). Further, research shows that in schools serving lower socioeconomic students, there is a greater dependence on test scores and less time spent in consulting with parents and teachers in developing case studies for instructional intervention (Milofsky, 1989). Hence, the child's performance in the classroom and at home—i.e., in social contexts where literacy is actually practiced—is devalued as a source of data for making important instructional decisions about the child.

Perhaps one of the most harmful effects of standardized testing, however, is the negative impact that it can have on students' perceptions of themselves as learners. Studies show that students who do poorly on standardized tests come to see themselves as failures, and thereby tend to give up more easily and invest less energy in learning (Firmin, Chi-en, Copella, & Clark, 2004; Moon, Brighton, Jarvis, & Hall, 2007). The notions of "learned helplessness" and "low self-efficacy" resulting from continued failure are well documented in the research literature (Burhans & Dweck, 1995; Diener & Dweck, 1978; Schunk, 2003). Research has also documented the anxiety associated with standardized testing, especially among underachieving students (Moon, Brighton, Jarvis, & Hall, 2007; Smith, 1991).

Research even suggests that standardized tests can have deleterious effects on high-achieving students, who may perceive that inadequate performance on the test can reinforce negative stereotypes associated with their group. Such perceptions can lead to anxiety that one's actions will confirm a negative stereotype, thereby affecting performance. This phenomenon has been called "stereotype threat," and it applies to all social settings in which a negative stereotype about one's group would limit how an individual might be viewed. Steele and his colleagues (Aronson et al., 1999; Steele, 2003) have studied the effects of stereotype threat on the test performance of a variety of student populations (e.g., Black students, female students who excel in mathematics, White males). Invariably, when a negative stereotype is elicited prior to the testing event, students' performance suffers. For instance, in one study, a group of White males was told that Asians tend to score higher on a test they were about to take; a similar group of White males, however, did not receive this comment. The lower performance of the first group of males supports the idea that stereotype threat can negatively affect even those students who are members of the dominant group, and are therefore unlikely to sense any inferior perceptions about their group. Research shows that the anxiety produced by stereotype threat causes students to "try too hard," making them "inefficient on a test that, like most standardized tests, is set up so that thinking long often means thinking wrong" (Steele, 2003, p. 121).

Standardized Testing and Second Language Learners

As we have seen, our emphasis on standardized testing is problematic for a number of reasons; however, it can be particularly problematic for students whose native language is not English. García, McKoon, and August (2008) provide a comprehensive summary of the research on assessment practices with language minority students. In summarizing the findings of the National Literacy Panel on Language-Minority Children and Youth, they suggest that standardized tests typically do not reveal students' true competence. Often, second-language learners (SLLs) are able to comprehend more than they are able to demonstrate on the test when asked to respond in a second language. Time limitations may also be a factor, as SLLs may need more time to process the language prior to responding. SLLs may know different vocabulary in each language, and therefore it is difficult to assess their knowledge when the test is in only one language. The authors write:

> They may have well-developed cognitive skills that underlie comprehension, such as integrating background knowledge with textual knowledge or drawing inferences across propositions, but may not be able to apply these skills to English text because their limited English proficiency interferes with their accessing enough of the text's meaning to apply the skills.
>
> (p. 253)

95

Finally, the tests themselves may be culturally biased, in that few English language learners were included in the norming samples. Hence, the validity of the test scores for language-minority students can be seriously compromised. Citing the Standards for Educational and Psychological Testing (American Education Research Association, American Psychological Association, & National Council on Measurement in Education, 1999, p. 118), when a test is

> administered in the same language to all examinees in a linguistically diverse population, the test user should investigate the validity of the score interpretations for test takers believed to have limited proficiency in the language of the test [because] the achievement, abilities, and traits of examinees who do not speak the language of the test as their primary language may be seriously mismeasured by the test.
>
> (cited in García, McKoon, & August, 2008, p. 254)

The authors note that test validity may be a concern even with tests given in the students' native language, as the test developers may have used populations for norming that are different from the population being tested.

Similarly, tests of language proficiency have their own set of problems. The authors note that such tests do not assess students' ability to use language in real-life settings or for academic purposes. Some popular tests, such as the Language Assessment Scales (LAS), have been shown to have little predictive value in that they do not predict how well students will perform on a standardized reading test or content assessment in English (De Avila & Duncan, 1990; Duncan & De Avila, 1988). Research also shows that the assessment practices of school psychologists and speech and language pathologists tend to present a limited view of students' language development (Ochoa, Galarza, & González, 1996). Teachers, too, can over-identify students as having learning disabilities based upon their assessment of students' oral language proficiency in English (Limbos & Geva, 2001; Miramontes, 1987).

In suggesting alternatives for testing language-minority students, García, McKoon, and August (2008) identify a few promising practices from the research literature. Testing accommodations, such as increased time, providing a bilingual dictionary or glossary, and oral test administration, have resulted in improved performance for ELLs (Abedi, Lord, Boscardin, & Miyoshi, 2001; García, 1991). Side-by-side assessments, in which students receive parallel versions of a test in both English and their primary language, have been tried with some success (Durán, Brown, & McCall, 2002). At the same time, many researchers have noted the difficulty of developing equivalent tests in two languages (American Educational Research Association, American Psychological

Association, & National Council on Measurement in Education, 1999; August & Hakuta, 1997; García & Pearson, 1994).

Effective Classroom Assessment Practices

The basic premise underlying much of the research on effective assessment practices for culturally and linguistically diverse students suggests that assessment must reflect a definition of literacy as a social process. All forms of literacy—reading, writing, speaking, listening, viewing—require active involvement in which participants are engaged in acts of communication and interpretation. Thus, for assessment to be a valid indicator of proficiency, it must occur while students are participating in authentic literacy tasks. Ongoing assessment that occurs while students are using oral and written language in authentic contexts is particularly important with SLLs in order to determine their level of language proficiency (Hurley & Blake, 2001; Lenski, Ehlers-Zavala, Daniel, & Sun-Irminger, 2006). That is, to be valid, students' linguistic competence must be evaluated over time, while they are actually using language in purposeful ways.

Further, culturally responsive assessment views every student as a capable learner, and evaluates students' competence versus their deficits. Culturally responsive assessment practices *measure students' potential*, and not merely what they know. This is a major paradigm shift from traditional evaluation practices. In her edited volume *Vygotsky in the Classroom*, Dixon-Krauss (1996) argues for the use of "dynamic assessment" that reflects the social nature of learning. Dynamic assessment not only measures students' past learning, but also their potential for future learning within a supportive environment. Even an informal reading inventory (IRI), which assesses students' reading ability through actual reading, "ignores the social context of instruction because it is a static test of the student's individual reading performance . . . The IRI does not actually measure the students' potential to benefit from assistance" (p. 128). In contrast, dynamic assessment provides the teacher with information on the amount and types of support that students will require to complete a task successfully.

Stanley (1996, p. 139) writes that the basic assumptions that underlie Vygotsky's (1978) theory of social interaction are these:

1 A true measure of a learner's potential must involve measuring both unassisted and assisted performance.
2 Traditional or static tests that measure only independent performance underestimate the learner's potential.
3 Emerging learning processes are observed when the learner is engaged in highly difficult learning tasks under adult guidance or with capable peers.

4 Instruction leads development and should be aimed at the "ripening" or maturing, not the "ripe" or mature, mental functions of the student.

Thus, beyond using assessment practices that use authentic texts in assessing students' oral and written language proficiency, effective assessment provides opportunities for students to be evaluated within the context of instruction, i.e., while they are being provided with various support structures. Research shows that dynamic assessment shows promise for identifying students from under-represented populations who may be eligible for gifted programs. Stanley (1996) writes that Hispanic students' test scores in receptive vocabulary dramatically increased when they were provided with "minimal instruction upon approaching the vocabulary task" (p. 141).

In their research investigation with an English-language learner, Brock and Raphael (2005) note the importance of considering interaction structures in assessing students with limited English proficiency. The researchers videotaped literacy lessons that occurred in a fifth grade classroom in which Deng, a second language learner from Laos, was a student. They later played back the video excerpts and, with the assistance of Deng and an interpreter, were able to determine when confusion had occurred during instruction. Importantly, Deng's comprehension tended to break down the most during whole-group instruction. Yet the teacher's assessment practices during this time, which consisted primarily of questioning, were not effective in determining Deng's misunderstanding. In fact, their data on whole-group literature discussions show that only a small number of students participated, and Deng "never once spoke voluntarily in the whole group" (p. 40). Thus, the teacher had no way of know-ing that communication was breaking down and that he was failing to learn, as she had no information on which to base her assessment of his learning. Interestingly, Deng's participation in small group activities was relatively high, and his peers were able to clarify confusing points. Brock and Raphael write that in the small group setting,

> Knowledge of the text and U.S. culture were not prerequisites to successful interactions within the group. In fact, in the small group it was acceptable to reveal confusions about the story and U.S. culture. Further, the nature of the interpersonal interactions amongst the boys influenced the understandings constructed as they worked through the assigned tasks.
>
> (p. 66)

Consistent with a Vygotskian perspective discussed previously, Brock and Raphael suggest that "there is much to be learned from really listening to students that can inform the ways that teachers design and implement literacy learning opportunities in their classrooms" (p. 28). They also suggest that, as a regular part of whole-group instruction, teachers need to build in opportunities for students to communicate with their peers and to voice their learning so that their thinking is "made public."

PRACTICAL APPLICATIONS

As discussed previously, I argue that an emphasis upon standardized and summative testing has resulted in a "culture of evaluation" in our schools and classrooms. Within this environment, there has emerged a cycle of instruction that is driven by the testing schedule and by a narrow conceptualization of what constitutes "literate behavior." In contrast, I suggest that our assessment practices ought to create a "culture of learning," whereby assessment is used to illuminate students' capacity for learning and every student feels validated as a learner. A primary goal of assessment ought to be to discover as much as we can about every student in our care—their background knowledge, their areas of expertise, their learning strengths, their linguistic competence, their potential for learning—so that we can appropriately scaffold our instruction. Another primary goal of assessment is to send the message to students that they are capable learners. In this section, I provide a discussion of assessment practices that can create a "culture of learning" in the classroom.

Discovering Students' Strengths and Literacy Competence

The fundamental underlying principle of culturally responsive literacy assessment is that literacy is a social process. Assessment practices that are culturally responsive examine students' literacy proficiency while they are actively engaged in authentic, purposeful literacy acts. Reading, writing, speaking, listening, viewing—all are social events that are embedded within particular social and cultural contexts. Thus, I suggest that ignoring the social dimension of literacy and the context within which it occurs will always result in invalid results. Indeed, a primary theme in the literature on culturally responsive assessment practices is that assessment must be conducted while students are actually using literacy (García & Pearson, 1991; Lenski, Ehlers-Zavala, Daniel, & Sun-Irminger, 2006; Philpott, 2007; Tinajero & Hurley, 2001). Literacy assessments that occur as students are reading, such as running records (Clay, 2000) and miscue analysis (Goodman, Watson, & Burke, 2005), provide windows through which we can observe the strategies that students use while they are engaged in the act of reading. They also provide important information on students' language growth. Such assessments should be an integral part of instruction.

In writing instruction, holistic scoring guides can provide important information on students' writing ability. In our state, for example, teachers are provided with "marker papers" that include samples of students' writing at various developmental levels and in various genres. These writing samples have been annotated to point out skills that the writer is using, and possible "next steps" in teaching. Teachers use these marker papers to examine their own students' writing against these prototypes, to determine the students' developmental level, and to plan for instruction. When coupled with authentic writing tasks in which students are writing for real audiences and for genuine purposes, such assessment practices can provide useful and valid information on students' writing proficiency.

Running records, miscue analysis, writing portfolios—all are practices that can inform our instruction in important ways. At the same time, these assessments generally occur outside the context of instruction. As research shows, it is important to recognize that assessment also needs to occur throughout instruction (Hansen, 1998; Brock and Raphael, 2005). That is, *assessment ought to be an integral part of instruction*; as culturally responsive teachers, we need continuous information—during the flow of instruction—on which students are grasping the skills and concepts we are teaching, and which are not. Fisher and Frey (2007) call this type of assessment "checking for understanding," and suggest that it should occur at least every 15 minutes during instruction, and ideally more frequently.

In her book, *Formative Assessment in Action*, Clarke (2005) outlines an assessment framework that includes the use of accountable talk throughout the instructional event. Through the use of "talking partners" and teacher questioning/prompting, students construct meaning together throughout the lesson. Further, every student is held accountable for their own learning and for the learning of their partner. The use of "talking partners" is part of a comprehensive instruction/formative assessment process, which includes several elements:

1 Develop "success criteria" based upon the learning objectives. For instance, in a kindergarten class, the learning objective might be to be able to make a simple list, and the context for learning would be to list the food and drink for a class party. The success criteria could then be: put each thing on a new line; include food and drinks; include things to hold the food and drinks. At a higher level, the success criteria would be related to a particular writing genre.
2 Provide an authentic example and ask students to tell you what features they see, "thus generating the success criteria for themselves" (p. 9).

3   Use "talking partners" in which students discuss a question in pairs prior to giving a response.
4   Ask worthwhile questions. It is particularly helpful to ask questions that provide a range of responses, in order to deepen students' understanding.

In discussing the benefits of "talking partners," Clarke writes:

> Having talking partners as a regular feature of lessons allows all children to think, to articulate and therefore to extend their learning. Shy, less confident children have a voice, and over-confident children have to learn to listen to others, so the benefits extend to a more respectful, cooperative ethos and culture: fundamental to the success of assessment for learning.
>
> (p. 55)

The use of talking partners not only provides important information to teachers on the learning of every student, but it also equalizes their participation during instruction.

Observing Students' Potential for Learning

Viewing assessment as an integral part of instruction has the added benefit of being able to determine students' *potential* for learning, e.g., what students are capable of with support, as well as what type of scaffolding is most helpful. As indicated in the literature, effective assessment practices allow teachers to ascertain students' competence and potential for learning, versus their deficits and current level of proficiency. Dynamic assessment, in which students perform under varying conditions of teacher support, provides important information on students' capabilities for learning literacy given the appropriate learning conditions. In discussing ways to implement dynamic assessment in classrooms, Stanley (1996) suggests that teachers use "trial lessons" in which students' literacy ability is determined while they are engaged in literate activity with teacher guidance. Trial teaching can provide teachers with important information on the level at which students can perform with instructional guidance (which is typically a higher reading level than standardized tests or informal inventories would indicate). At the same time, careful observation during trial instruction can provide important insights on how best to scaffold student learning.

Indeed, "kidwatching" is an essential skill for teachers (Owaki & Goodman, 2002). Teachers must become careful observers of their students and be able to document students' literacy practices and conceptual understanding *while they are engaged in the learning process.* Johnston and Costello (2005) write:

> The essence of formative assessment is noticing details of literate behavior, imagining what they mean from the child's perspective, knowing what the child knows and can do, and knowing how to arrange for that knowledge and competence to be displayed, engaged, and extended.
>
> (p. 262)

This statement points to the importance of closely examining students' literate behavior in order to celebrate their competence and scaffold further learning. Clearly, "kidwatching" is most effective in classroom environments that promote authentic uses of literacy. Literacy events that require students to use literacy within the context of social interaction, such as children's play and small group discussions, provide especially rich opportunities for assessing students' literacy development (Genishi & Dyson, 2009; Hall, 1998; Powell & Davidson, 2005).

TEACHERS' VOICES

Kindergarten Voices

Laura Hampton

KINDERGARTEN TEACHER, BOURBON CENTRAL ELEMENTARY, PARIS, KY

In my kindergarten classroom of 24 children, there are many different voices. These voices come from children from very different backgrounds, experiences, and families. Within each planned writing lesson, I strive to allow my students the opportunity to create pieces that meet curriculum standards and also allow their precious voices to be heard.

When introducing writing in the kindergarten classroom, I often meet with children who confess, "I can't spell that word," or "I don't know what to write about," or "I am too little to write." I meet these excuses armed with quality picture books, modeling, and good classroom conversation. Before any student takes pencil (or crayon) to paper, they are given the opportunity to hear stories, see stories, and discuss stories.

During our personal narrative unit we wrote many stories about ourselves. We wrote stories about what life is like at age five, nightmares we have had, and stories about our families. It is always a lot of fun to hear what the world looks like from the perspective of a 5-year-old! We began the family pieces by reading the story *In My Family/En Mi Familia* by Carmen Lomas Garza. This is a book that shows similarities and differences between various family routines and customs. There were two English Language Learners (ELLs) in my class, so I tried to use many stories that include Hispanic families along with other culture groups that are represented in my classroom. This book was read aloud and discussed at length. I frequently stopped and asked the students to discuss with a partner how each family was alike or different from their families. Many responses that I heard from the students included, "My family eats dinner like that!" and "My grandmother lives at our house too!" When my students share with partners, I usually hear more quality responses to questions than I do when I ask only one student to respond.

After reading the story, I modeled writing on chart paper. I placed a snapshot of my brothers, my sister, and me on the top of the chart paper and looked at it for a while. I wanted the students to see me thinking for a moment before I began writing. I started to write a story about a family hiking trip. I thought aloud as I wrote and asked the students to help me with the writing process (using capital letters, spelling sight words, using punctuation). After I completed my writing I told the students to go home and find a photograph of their families that would help them write their own stories. Of course, I wrote a note home to parents explaining why we were asking for pictures.

The following day many students brought in family pictures or drawings of their families. I asked the students to form groups of four to share their pictures, discussing who was in the pictures, who was not, and different things about their families.

Next, the students went to their writing spots and began writing. I allow my students to sit wherever they want during writing time as long as they are writing. Many students wrote about who was in their families, what their families like to do for fun, and what their families like to eat. I walked around and noted areas in which students excelled, areas that could be future mini-lessons, and skills that needed improvement.

The piece included here is about Nicole's family. She is an ELL student from Mexico. She wrote about her family members and how much they like to swim together. She included a very detailed drawing of her family swimming. This is a student who is typically very apprehensive about writing. I have learned that when she has a visual or can make a connection to something, her writing is much stronger. Nicole's favorite thing to write about is her family (Figures 5.1 and 5.2).

The last step in the writing process for our family pieces was "show off" time. Due to time constraints, we do not use the traditional "Author's Chair" to share writing in my classroom. We use the "Line Dance." The students sit in two lines facing each other and share their writing with the person that is sitting across from them. Both students share, ask questions, and give compliments. Then one row scoots to the right (the last person in the row gets up and walks to the far end of the line and sits down across from a new partner) and they share again. This is repeated one more time. This enables the students an opportunity to share with three people,

Figure 5.1 Photo of Nicole's Family

Figure 5.2
Photo of Nicole's
Writing

to practice speaking, and to listen. It also gives me the chance to listen to their use of language and academic vocabulary.

The students were proud of their writing and could not wait to take them home to share with their families. However, before letting them go, I displayed them on our Family Wall and saw many students reading them throughout the day with delight on their faces. By going through this entire process using a quality picture book, modeling, good student conversation, and strong family connections (photographs), I was able to hear the many kindergarten voices that may otherwise not have been heard.

REFERENCE

Garza, C. L. (1996). *In my family/En mi familia.* San Francisco: Children's Book Press.

Assessing students' literacy while they are engaged in literate activity is particularly important in determining the developing linguistic competence of second-language learners. In writing about effective assessment for SLLs, Lapp, Fisher, Flood, and Cabello (2001) suggest that assessment practices should be used that provide information to teachers on students' development of biliteracy. They write that "[a]ssessment and instruction should be viewed as interactive processes" (p. 11), involving the use of performance evaluations that are completed while students are actually engaged in literacy. The authors provide several recommendations for appropriate assessments for SLLs, including: (1) story retelling inventories that can be used to determine students' comprehension, knowledge of sentence structure, and vocabulary development as they retell a story; (2) speaking checklists that include criteria for evaluating students' public speaking abilities; (3) writing portfolios, in which both the teacher and the student are involved in evaluating the student's writing progress; and (4) reciprocal questioning, whereby readers take turns posing questions to one another on the ideas in a text.

Tinajero and Hurley (2001) suggest that in addition to checklists, teachers can use instruments such as fluency rubrics to record SLLs' use of particular language patterns and structures. For instance, a fluency rubric might include a classification system that allows the teacher to document whether a student uses mostly drawings with some isolated words to communicate her thoughts, short phrases and simple spellings, complete sentences with some grammatical inaccuracies, or connected text with conventional English spelling. (For an example of a fluency rubric, see Hurley & Tinajero, 2001, p. 30.) Similarly, teachers can use anecdotal records to document students' communication skills while they are using sustained and connected discourse, such as while they participate in a story dramatization, present a report, or share their journal entries with a peer.

Similar to reciprocal questioning, Ruiz, Vargas, and Beltrán (2002) found that the use of interactive journals was highly effective in determining the linguistic competence of a second-language learner, "Diego," who had been labeled as linguistically incompetent. Because he appeared to be essentially non-verbal in both English and his native language, Spanish, Diego had been referred for special education testing. He subsequently received services through the Optimal Learning Environment (OLE) Project, which implements the following principles in instructing English language learners: (1) connect literacy lessons to students' background knowledge; (2) use the students' primary language in literacy lessons; (3) have students apply literacy in authentic contexts; and (4) foster increased levels of interaction. Through dialoguing with his teachers in an interactive journal, Diego was able to use his talent in drawing to communicate with them, and the teachers in turn were able to build upon this talent to promote the development of writing conventions. The authors write, "After communicating in the interactive journals with drawings, Diego soon attempted to spell words, which later resulted in letter strings" (p. 301). His teachers praised his efforts and continued to write back to him, modeling conventional spelling and writing mechanics. After one academic year in the OLE Project, Diego wrote extended discourse in his journal and all of his words were either spelled conventionally or phonetically. Through the use of interactive journals, the teachers were able to provide appropriate support for Diego's language development and were also able to see his *potential* for learning. Ruiz, Vargas, and Beltrán share that they later learned about Diego's educational history:

[Diego] had not attended school in Guatemala, and all of his schooling had been in Los Angeles. His kindergarten teacher was an English-only teacher, whom Diego did not understand. His first-grade teacher, though of Hispanic descent, did not speak Spanish to him, and his second-grade teacher was under the impression that he spoke "some Indian language." Diego also shared that he had never understood what was going on in these classrooms because no one had ever tried to demonstrate what was being said. At his previous school, people rarely talked to him.

(pp. 304–305)

The story of Diego illustrates the critical importance of viewing assessment holistically. Students are members of various social, cultural, and linguistic groups and come with a history of language and literacy use. To create a "culture of learning," it is important that our assessment practices include ascertaining the resources that students and families possess that can be used to scaffold students' learning, and discovering students' language and literacy backgrounds (Lenski, Ehlers-Zavala, Daniel, & Sun-Irminger, 2006). That is, the focus of our assessment ought to be to get to know our students "in the round." Yet because their assessment practices did not allow his former teachers to assess Diego's strengths and capacity for learning, he was labeled as learning disabled and as having limited oral language proficiency in both English and Spanish. In contrast, his OLE teachers focused on his strengths as displayed through his writing. By embedding assessment within the context of instruction, they began to uncover Diego's linguistic competence. Fortunately for Diego, this discovery spared him from what promised to be a reductionist instructional program that taught and assessed the "pieces" of literacy—a program that would have done little to promote his language and literacy development.

Considering the Social Context in Assessment

Culturally responsive assessment practices go beyond using "best practices" in assessment. Assessment does not occur in a vacuum; rather, assessment takes place within a social context, and social contexts always involve relationships of power. Every social context, including classrooms, is a social space where participants negotiate for voice. In discussions about assessment, however, typically teacher–student relationships are ignored. Yet the relationship between a teacher and her students can have a profound effect upon students' test performance. For instance, Labov (1985) found that Black children became essentially non-verbal when faced with an investigator in a testing situation. These same children were found to have great verbal ability when their linguistic competence was evaluated in their natural surroundings—on city streets, while communicating with their peers. Labov notes that "The social situation is the most powerful determinant of verbal behavior . . . an adult must enter into the right social relation with a child if he wants to find out what a child can do; this is just what many teachers cannot do" (1985, p. 191; cited in Powell, 2001, p. 178). Consider, too, the ramifications of Labov's research on our obsession with standardized testing, where the test itself exerts authority over the social event, thereby establishing an environment of intimidation and control.

Research on stereotype threat reinforces the importance of considering the social context in assessment. In a study designed to determine if Black college students react differently from White students to teachers' feedback, researchers found that race relationships can have a significant impact on students' ability to accept that feedback (Cohen, Steele, & Ross, 1999). Steele writes that neither straight feedback nor feedback preceded by the "niceness" of a cushioning statement ("There were many good things about your essay") was trusted by Black students. They saw these criticisms as probably biased, and they were less motivated than White students to improve their essays (2003, p. 126).

Consider the significance of this finding. As teachers, we are often told to provide "direct feedback" to students on their performance. Yet without first establishing relationships of trust with our students, they may ignore our advice. Steele goes on to state that this same experiment revealed ways to counteract stereotype threat when providing feedback:

> [T]ell the students that you are using high standards (this signals that the criticism reflects standards rather than race), and that your reading of their essays leads you to believe that they can meet those standards (this signals that you do not view them stereotypically). This shouldn't be faked. High standards . . . should be an inherent part of teaching, and critical feedback should be given in the belief that the recipient can reach those standards.
>
> (p. 126)

Steele suggests that for students who are affected by stereotype threat, it is important to reinforce our belief in them as learners. That is, teachers must *make explicit* their belief in the student's capability to realize high standards. In this particular study, students who received the dual message that high standards were being used to evaluate their work and that they were capable of meeting the challenge subsequently viewed the feedback as unbiased "and were motivated to take their essays home and work on them even though this was not a class for credit." In fact, Steele reports that the Black students were actually more motivated than other groups in the study, and responded "as if this combination of high standards and assurance was like water on parched land, a much-needed but seldom-received balm" (p. 126).

I suggest that involving students in self-assessment can enhance the assessment process in that it equalizes relationships of power within the classroom. When students become integrally involved in analyzing their work and setting learning goals, they essentially become partners in the teaching/learning process. Teachers, too, send the message to their students that they have confidence in their ability to make important decisions in their own learning; that is, students are *validated as learners*. Stiggins states that "[t]he key is to understand the relationship between assessment and student motivation . . . When students are involved in the assessment process, they can come to see themselves as competent learners" (in Sparks, 1999, p. 2).

One of the most useful forms of reading self-assessment is retrospective miscue analysis, in which students listen to recordings of their own reading with the teacher and discuss their reading miscues. Teachers find this tool to be

108

extremely useful in providing additional information on students' thinking during the act of reading and their reasons for applying particular reading strategies (Goodman, Watson, & Burke, 2005). A similar approach is to include space on written assessments for students to write why they selected particular answers. Deuel, Nelson, Slavit, and Kennedy (2009) have found that teachers who use this approach tend to focus more on student thinking rather than simply on which students "got it" and which did not, which helps them to create lessons to correct students' misconceptions.

Jones, Clarke, and Enriquez (2010) provide a useful tool for implementing student self-assessment in literacy instruction. In their book *The Reading Turn-Around*, the authors argue that the label "struggling reader" presents a negative identity that does nothing to inform our instruction. They state that "our language is robust in naming potential things wrong with students but not in thinking and talking about *who students are, what they do well*, and *how they can teach us to teach them better*" (p. 2; italics in original). Consistent with the notion of dynamic assessment, the authors share several examples in which careful "kidwatching" resulted in Powerful Reading Plans (PRPs) for students. For instance, Cassidy needed to work on reading fluency. Her plan included the goal to read more smoothly and with more speed. She listed several action plans, and the teacher also listed ways that she planned to help Cassidy reach her goals: "Not interrupting you or correcting you when you read aloud," and "giving you plenty of fun opportunities to read aloud in class" (p. 50). Gary, who had become disruptive during vocabulary instruction, required a very different plan. His PRP involved learning more vocabulary, and his teacher's plan included "helping you grow in your word knowledge through prefixes and suffixes" and "using more engaging strategies in my own teaching beyond vocabulary lists" (p. 74). These engaging strategies included helping the student keep a vocabulary journal and starting a "sesquipedalian chart" for the class to add long, unusual, and interesting words.

Consider how the use of individualized instructional plans in which both teachers and students commit to certain goals and actions can impact the social dynamics in the classroom. In creating the PRP together, the student becomes an active participant in her literacy growth and is empowered to reach her goals. In assisting the student in setting standards and ways for achieving those standards, the teacher conveys the message that she believes that the student can achieve her goals. Further, when the teacher contributes to students' plans by committing to assist them in reaching their goals, a relationship of trust is established. The teacher has presented concrete evidence that she will provide the necessary guidance to assure their success.

One of the most powerful forms of self-assessment that I have witnessed is the student–parent conference, in which the student directs the conversation with her parents/caregivers and they subsequently develop together a plan for her continued academic growth. Stiggins (in Sparks, 1999, p. 2) has suggested that the student-led conference "is perhaps one of the biggest breakthroughs in communicating about student achievement in the last century." In student-led conferences, the student shares her work with the parent/caregiver and discusses her strengths and learning goals. The discussion generally centers around a portfolio or collection of work that includes the student's best products along with those that demonstrate the learning process. I have also witnessed effective student–parent conferences where students share a lengthy letter that they have written outlining what they do well, their goals for learning, and the support that they need to reach those goals. Consistent with research on stereotype threat, such practices allow students to internalize the high standards that are being used to evaluate their work, and can reinforce our expectations that they are capable of reaching those standards. In effect, students take on a role of teacher as they are responsible for gathering evidence of their learning and reflecting on their work. For readers who are interested in student–parent conferences, I recommend the book, *Implementing Student-Led Conferences* by Jane Bailey and Thomas Guskey (2001). In their book, Bailey and Guskey provide a comprehensive plan for scaffolding the reflective processes and procedures necessary for successful student-led conferences.

As indicated previously, the use of "talking partners" as a regular formative assessment practice can change the social context of the classroom. Throughout this book, we emphasize that an important element of culturally responsive instruction is building on the learning preferences of students. As shown by the research on culturally relevant instruction (Ladson-Billings, 1994; Reyes, Scribner, & Scribner, 1999), many students prefer collaborative learning environments over the more individualistic, competitive environments that dominate most classrooms. In addition to providing the teacher with important information on student understanding during instruction, the use of "talking partners" contributes to a community of learners, whereby students are able to assist one another in their learning. Clarke (2005) shares this important observation:

> We have tended to over-focus on individual children when they have responded to a question, so that the child's name is often repeated and maybe public congratulations given, thus reinforcing the comparison effect for those children who have not responded. With talking partners, the pair is asked to respond, which changes the emphasis from the *child* to the *response*.
>
> (p. 55)

As Clarke notes, the social dynamics of the classroom shift when we move from a whole-class IRE competitive form of discourse, to a more collaborative

 110

form of discourse through the use of "talking partners" and/or small groups. Asking pairs or small groups of students to respond versus calling on individuals emphasizes collective achievement over the achievement of the individual, and encourages students to work together to assure the academic success of their peers.

CONCLUSION

In this chapter, I have argued that literacy is a social process, and thus our assessment practices ought to occur during literacy-in-action. Standardized tests tend to conceptualize literacy as a narrow range of codified "skills" that can be measured outside of their use in actual social settings. Dependence on such instruments for accountability and instructional decision-making can be exceedingly detrimental to students, and particularly for those students who tend to underachieve in our schools. Such tests do not assess students' true linguistic competence, nor do they determine students' potential for learning.

Culturally responsive assessment necessitates evaluating students while they are engaged in authentic literacy tasks. To assure that every child is acquiring the skills and concepts being taught, teachers need to provide opportunities for students to demonstrate their understanding in multiple ways and at frequent intervals during instruction. Further, it is important for teachers to become skilled observers of students' literate behaviors. Formative assessments such as checklists, running records, miscue analyses, dialogue journals, and purposeful written products provide information to teachers that can be used to scaffold students' literacy development.

Every social setting involves relationships of power that can undermine students' performance, including their performance on assessment tasks. Hence, when considering effective assessment practices, it is critical to consider the social environment of the classroom and the relationships between teachers and students. Valid assessment can only occur within social environments where students are viewed as capable learners and they trust that the teacher believes in their ability to learn. Engaging students in self-assessment and helping them to set individual goals can enhance their motivation for learning.

I end this chapter with an example that I believe illustrates the ways in which our assessment practices can, and must, change in order to be truly culturally responsive. The Nunavut province of Canada serves a large indigenous population, whose culture embraces a holistic perspective and emphasizes the group over the individual. The Nunavut assessment system views assessment as a process that begins on the day that the students enter the classroom and we, as teachers, begin to learn who they are, what they know, and what they want to know . . . it is linked closely to goal setting and learning outcomes.

(Department of Education, Curriculum & School Services, 2005, p. 3; cited in Philpott, 2007, p. 26)

Consider that this perspective on assessment validates students, their families, and the cultural knowledge that they bring to learning; an integral part of student assessment involves uncovering the resources of the students and families we serve (González, Moll, & Amanti, 2005).

Importantly, assessment practices in Nunavut reflect the idea that assessment is a collaborative process, and the school and home community are partners in gathering the information necessary for meeting students' educational needs (Philpott, 2007). Teachers in Nunavut come to know students "in the round" so that they can design appropriate instructional strategies that link new concepts to students' cultural knowledge. Effective assessment involves carefully observing students while they are engaged in actually practicing what they have learned in authentic social contexts. Nunavut assessment practices connect to the authentic learning that occurs in the community whereby the elders exercise their role of "guiding students to find their strengths and to use those strengths to help the community":

Just as becoming expert at using the *sabgut* or *naukkuti* involves a hands-on application and accumulated experience over time, our students' learning has to be grounded in real life experiences. Students need to participate actively in connecting the learning outcomes from the curriculum to their personal realities. Effective assessment must be real as well as developmentally and culturally appropriate

(Department of Education, Curriculum & School Services, 2006, p. 3; cited in Philpott, 2007, p. 27)

Among its seven key principles of culturally appropriate assessment, Nunavut's model "emphasizes the interdependence, growth, and success of the group." In Nunavut, as in other communities that are culturally and linguistically diverse, culturally responsive assessment practices are those that promote group over individual achievement.

In Nunavut, literacy is seen as social practice, and examining real-world literacy use within the larger community is considered to be an essential component of assessment. The primary purpose of assessment is to discover who students are and what they know, so that instruction can build on students' strengths. Such assessment practices honor students, their families, and their cultures, and place learning—and not testing—at the center of instruction.

Table 5.1 *Summary of CRIOP Component: Assessment*

Element	What you would expect to see in a classroom where CRI practices are occurring	What you would expect to see in a classroom where CRI practices are not occurring
Formative assessment practices are used that provide information throughout the lesson on student understanding.	Teacher frequently assesses students' understanding throughout instruction; students may have "talking partners" for reviewing information; students are able to voice their learning throughout the lesson.	Assessment occurs at the end of the lesson.
Students are able to demonstrate their learning in a variety of ways.	Students with limited English proficiency and/or limited literacy can show their conceptual learning through visual or other forms of representation.	Most or all tests are written and require reading/writing proficiency in English.
Formative assessment practices are used that provide information on the learning of every student.	Teacher uses formative assessments that determine individual learning.	The primary formative assessment is whole class review where teacher calls on individual students (Initiate-Respond-Evaluate pattern).
Authentic assessments are used as the primary means for assessing literacy development.	Students' literacy is assessed while actively engaged in reading, writing, speaking extended discourse; students' linguistic competence is evaluated while they are actually using language in purposeful ways.	Assessments measure discrete, isolated skills and/or use short, disconnected passages.
Students are evaluated within the context of scaffolded instruction to determine their potential for learning.	Teacher assesses students' ability to learn with appropriate support; teacher may implement "trial lessons" that use texts at a higher level than students' performance; teacher uses frequent "kidwatching" to determine students' capabilities.	Assessment is solely used to determine what students already know or can do.
Teacher sets high standards and students understand the criteria by which they are being assessed.	Teacher bases feedback on established high standards; students are provided with a sense that they can meet those standards.	Teacher feedback is subjective; students do not know the criteria upon which they are being assessed; and/or standards are not rigorous.

Table 5.1 Continued

Element	What you would expect to see in a classroom where CRI practices are occurring	What you would expect to see in a classroom where CRI practices are not occurring
Students have opportunities for self-assessment.	Students are involved in analyzing their work and in setting their own goals for learning.	Assessment is always teacher-controlled.
Assessment practices promote the achievement of the group, and not just individuals.	Teacher encourages students to work together to learn difficult concepts, and assesses the work of the group.	Teacher emphasizes individual achievement; working together is viewed as "cheating."

REFLECTIVE ACTIVITIES

1 Examine the standardized tests that you are required to give to your students. How do these tests seem to define "literacy"? How often are students required to read connected text?

2 List your formative assessment practices and then analyze those practices. Do you assess students while they are engaged in authentic literacy tasks? Are you able to tell if every student is developing the skills and concepts that you are teaching? Do you provide students with multiple ways to demonstrate competence? Are you able to determine students' potential for learning through the assessments that you use?

3 Modify a lesson that you plan to teach to include formative assessments throughout the lesson. Make sure that you check for understanding at least every 15 minutes, and that you are able to determine the learning of every child.

4 Prepare a "trial lesson" that utilizes the principles of "dynamic assessment." Using a text (or task) that is above students' instructional level, consider how you might scaffold their learning to assure success. For instance, if you choose to have them read a more difficult text, you might read the text orally prior to asking them to read it, and pre-teach important vocabulary and concepts. Include the formative assessments you will use to determine whether students are able to be successful with the support that you provided.

5 Consider the notion of "stereotype threat" and how it might be affecting your students' performance. Develop an action plan for

counteracting stereotype threat that includes appropriate feedback on student work.

6 Consider how you involve students in assessing their performance and setting their learning goals. Try your hand at implementing some suggestions included in this chapter, such as developing a Powerful Reading Plan with individual students or helping students to prepare for student-led conferences.

REFERENCES

Abedi, J., Lord, C., Boscardin, C. K., & Miyoshi, J. (2001). *The effects of accommodations on the assessment of limited English proficient (LEP) students in the National Assessment of Educational Progress (NAEP)* (Technical Report No. 537). Los Angeles: University of California, Center for the Study of Evaluation/National Center for Research on Evaluation, Standards, and Student Learning.

American Education Research Association, American Psychological Association, & National Council on Measurement in Education (1999). *Standards for educational and psychological testing 1999*. Washington, DC: American Educational Research Association Publications.

Aronson, J., Lustina, C., Good, C., Keough, K., Steele, C., & Brown, J. (1999). When White men can't do math: Necessary and sufficient factors in stereotype threat. *Journal of Experimental Social Psychology, 35*(1), 29–46.

August, D. L., & Hakuta, K. (Eds.). (1997). *Improving schooling for language-minority learners*. Washington, DC: National Academy Press.

Bailey, J. M., & Guskey, T. R. (2001). *Implementing student-led conferences*. Thousand Oaks, CA: Corwin Press.

Barrs, M., Ellis, S., Hester, H., & Thomas, A. (1989). *The primary language record: Handbook for teachers*. London: Inner London Education Authority/Centre for Language in Primary Education.

Brock, C. H., & Raphael, T. E. (2005). *Windows to language, literacy, and culture: Insights from an English-language learner*. Newark, DE: International Reading Association.

Burhans, K. K., & Dweck, C. S. (1995). Helplessness in early childhood: The role of contingent worth. *Child Development, 66,* 1719–1738.

Cazden, C. B. (2001). *Classroom discourse: The language of teaching and learning*. Portsmouth, NH: Heinemann.

Clarke, S. (2005). *Formative assessment in action: Weaving the elements together*. London: Hodder Murray.

Clay, M. M. (2000). *Running records for classroom teachers*. Portsmouth, NH: Heinemann.

Cohen, G. L., Steele, C. M., & Ross, L. D. (1999). The mentors' dilemma: Providing critical feedback across the racial time. *Personality and Social Psychology Bulletin, 25,* 1302–1318.

Cunningham, W. G., & Sanzo, T. D. (2002). Is high-states testing harming lower socioeconomic status schools? *NASSP Bulletin 86*(631), 62–75.

Darling-Hammond, L. (1994). Performance-based assessment and educational equity. *Harvard Educational Review, 64*(1), 5–30.

De Avila, E., & Duncan, S. (1990). *Language assessment scales: Oral*. Monterey, CA: CTB McGraw-Hill.

Department of Education, Curriculum & School Services (2005). *School enrollment report for 2005/06*. Iqaluit, NU: Government of Nunavut.

Department of Education, Curriculum & School Services (2006). *Inclusive education in Nunavut schools: Student support handbook*. Iqaluit, NU: Government of Nunavut.

Deuel, A., Nelson, T. H., Slavit, D., & Kennedy, A. (2009). Looking at student work. *Educational Leadership 67*(3), 69–72.

Diener, C. & Dweck, C. (1978). An analysis of learned helplessness: Continuous changes in performance, strategy, and achievement cognitions following failure. *Journal of Personality and Social Psychology, 39*, 940–952.

Dixon-Krauss, L. (1996). *Vygotsky in the classroom: Mediated literacy instruction and assessment*. White Plains, NY: Longman.

Duncan, S., & De Avila, E. (1988). *Language assessment scales: Reading and writing*. Monterey, CA: CTB McGraw-Hill.

Durán, R. P., Brown, C., & McCall, M. (2002). Assessment of English-language learners in the Oregon statewide assessment system: National and state perspectives. In G. Tindal, & T. M. Haladyna (Eds.), *Large-scale assessment programs for all students*. St. Paul, MN: Assessment Systems Corporation.

Firmin, M., Chi-en, H., Copella, M., & Clark, S. (2004). Learned helplessness: The effect of failure on test taking. *Education, 124*(4), 688–693.

Fisher, D., & Frey, N. (2007). *Checking for understanding: Formative assessment techniques for your classroom*. Alexandria, VA: ASCD.

García, G. E. (1991). Factors influencing the English reading test performance of Spanish-speaking Hispanic children. *Reading Research Quarterly, 26*(4), 371–392.

García, G. E., McKoon, G., & August, D. (2008). Language and literacy assessment. In D. August, & T. Shanahan (Eds.), *Developing reading and writing in second-language learners* (pp. 251–274). New York: Routledge.

García, G. E., & Pearson, P. D. (1991). *Literacy assessment in a diverse society* (Technical Report No. 525). Champaign, IL: University of Illinois at Urbana-Champaign, Center for the Study of Reading.

García, G. E., & Pearson, P. D. (1994). Assessment and diversity. In L. Darling-Hammond (Ed.), *Review of research in education* (vol. 20, pp. 337–392). Washington, DC: American Educational Research Association.

Genishi, C., & Dyson, A. H. (2009). *Children, language, and literacy: Diverse learners in diverse times*. New York: Teachers College.

González, N., Moll, L. C., & Amanti, C. (2005). *Funds of knowledge: Theorizing practices in households, communities, and classrooms*. Mahwah, NJ: Lawrence Erlbaum.

Goodman, Y. M., Watson, D. J., & Burke, C. L. (2005). *Reading miscue inventory: From evaluation to instruction* (2nd ed.). Katonah, NY: Richard C. Owen.

Hall, N. (1998). Real literacy in a school setting: Five-year-olds take on the world. *The Reading Teacher, 52*, 8–17.

Hansen, J. (1998). "Evaluation is all day, noticing what is happening": Multifaceted evaluation of readers. In S. Murphy, *Fragile evidence: A critique of reading assessment* (pp. 105–123). Mahwah, NJ: Lawrence Erlbaum.

Harlan, W., & Crick, R. D. (2003). Testing and motivation for learning. *Assessment in Education 10*(2), 169–207.

Herman, J., & Golan, S. (1990). *Effects of standardized testing on teachers and learning: Another look:* CSE Technical Report #334. Los Angeles: Center for the Study of Evaluation, Standards, and Student Testing.

Hurley, S. R., & Blake, S. (2001). Assessment in the content areas for students acquiring English. In S. R. Hurley, & J. V. Tinajero (Eds.), *Literacy assessment of second language learners* (pp. 84–103). Boston: Allyn & Bacon.

Hurley, S. R., & Tinajero, J. V. (Eds.). (2001). *Literacy assessment of second language learners.* Boston: Allyn & Bacon.

Johnston, P. (1998). The consequences of the use of standardized tests. In S. Murphy, *Fragile evidence: A critique of reading assessment* (pp. 89–101). Mahwah, NJ: Lawrence Erlbaum.

Johnston, P., & Costello, P. (2005). Principles for literacy assessment. *Reading Research Quarterly, 40*(2), 256–267.

Jones, S., Clarke, L. W., & Enriquez, G. (2010). *The reading turn-around: A five-part framework for differentiated instruction.* New York: Teacher's College.

Labov, W. (1985). The logic of nonstandard English. In P. Giglioli (Ed.), *Language and social context* (pp. 179–215). New York: Viking Penguin.

Ladson-Billings, G. (1994). *The dreamkeepers: Successful teachers of African American children.* San Francisco: Jossey-Bass.

Lapp, D., Fisher, D., Flood, J., & Cabello, A. (2001). An integrated approach to the teaching and assessment of language arts. In S. R. Hurley, & J. V. Tinajero (Eds.), *Literacy assessment of second language learners* (pp. 1–26). Boston: Allyn & Bacon.

Lenski, S. D., Ehlers-Zavala, F., Daniel, M. C., & Sun-Irminger, X. (2006). Assessing English-language learners in mainstream classrooms. *The Reading Teacher, 60*(1), 24–34.

Limbos, M., & Geva, E. (2001). Accuracy of teacher assessments of second-language students at risk for reading disability. *Journal of Learning Disabilities, 34*(2), 136–151.

McNeil, L. M. (2000). *Contradictions of school reform: Education costs of standardized testing.* New York: Routledge.

Milofsky, C. (1989). *Testers and testing: The sociology of school psychology.* New Brunswick, NJ: Rutgers University Press.

Miramontes, O. B. (1987). Oral reading miscues of Hispanic students: Implications for assessment of learning disabilities. *Journal of Learning Disabilities, 20*(10), 627–632.

Moon, T. R., Brighton, C. M., Jarvis, J. M., & Hall, C. J. (2007). *State standardized testing programs: Their effects on teachers and students.* Storrs, CT: National Research Center on the Gifted and Talented.

Morrison, K., & Joan, T. F. H. (2002). Testing to destruction: A problem in a small state. *Assessment in Education, 9,* 289–317.

Murphy, S. (1998). *Fragile evidence: A critique of reading assessment.* Mahwah, NJ: Lawrence Erlbaum.

Ochoa, S. H., Galarza, A., & González, D. (1996). An investigation of school psychologists' assessment practices of language proficiency with bilingual and limited-English-proficient students. *Diagnostique, 21*(4), 17–36.

Owaki, G., & Goodman, Y. M. (2002). *Kidwatching: Documenting children's literacy development.* Portsmouth, NH: Heinemann.

Philpott, D. F. (2007). *Assessing without labels: Inclusive education in the Canadian context.* Thunder Bay, Ontario: Lakehead University, Centre of Excellence for Children and Adolescents with Special Needs.

Powell, R. (2001). *Straight talk: Growing as multicultural educators.* New York: Peter Lang.

Powell, R., & Davidson, N. (2005). The donut house: Real world literacy in an urban kindergarten classroom. *Language Arts, 82*(5), 248–256.

Restrepo, M. A. (1998). Identifiers of predominantly Spanish-speaking children with language impairment. *Journal of Speech, Language, and Hearing Research, 41*(6), 1398–1411.

Reyes, P., Scribner, J. D., & Scribner, A. P. (Eds.). (1999). *Lessons from high-performing Hispanic schools: Creating learning communities.* New York: Teachers College.

Rolheiser, C. & Ross. J. A. (n.d.). Student self-evaluation: What research says and what practice shows. Retrieved Jan. 9, 2010 from http://www.cdl.org/resource-library/articles/self_eval.php.

Ruiz, N. T., Vargas, E., & Beltrán, A. (*2002*). Becoming a reader and writer in a bilingual special education classroom. *Language Arts, 79,* 297–309.

Schunk, D. H. (2003). Self-efficacy for reading and writing: Influence of modeling, goal setting, and self-evaluation. *Reading and Writing Quarterly, 19,* 159–172.

Shannon, P. (1998). A selective social history of the uses of reading tests. In S. Murphy, *Fragile evidence: A critique of reading assessment* (pp. 75–87). Mahwah, NJ: Lawrence Erlbaum.

Smith, M. L. (1991). Put to the test: The effects of external testing on teachers. *Educational Researcher, 20*(5), 8–11.

Sparks, D. (1999). Assessment without victims: An interview with Rick Stiggins. *Journal of Staff Development, 20*(2). Retrieved on Jan. 9, 2010 from: http://www.nsdc.org/news/jsd/stiggins202.cfm.

Stanley, N. V. (1996). Vygotsky and multicultural assessment and instruction. In L. Dixon-Krauss (Ed.), *Vygotsky in the classroom: Mediated literacy instruction and assessment* (pp. 133–148). White Plains, NY: Longman.

Steele, C. (2003). Stereotype threat and African-American student achievement. In T. Perry, C. Steele, & A. Hilliard III (Eds.), *Young, gifted, and Black: Promoting high achievement among African-American students* (pp. 109–130). Boston: Beacon Press.

Stiggins, R., Arter, J., Chappuis, J., & Chappuis, S. (2006). *Classroom assessment for student learning: Doing it right – using it well.* Portland, OR: Educational Testing Service.

Thorndike, E. L. (1918). Fundamental theories of judging men. *Teachers College Record, 19,* 278–288.

Tinajero, J. V., & Hurley, S. R. (2001). Assessing progress in second-language acquisition. In S. R. Hurley, & J. V. Tinajero (Eds.), *Literacy assessment of second language learners* (pp. 27–42). Boston: Allyn & Bacon.

Vaughan, W. (2002). Effects of cooperative learning on achievement and attitude among students of color. *Journal of Educational Research 95*(6), 359–364.

Vygotsky, L. (1978). *Mind in society.* Cambridge, MA: Harvard University Press.

Walsh, J. A., & Sattes, B. D. (2004). *Quality questioning: Research-based practice to engage every learner.* Thousand Oaks, CA: Corwin.

Chapter 6

Curriculum and Planned Experiences: Bridging the Classroom with Students' Worlds

Angela Cox

> Every curriculum decision also says something about the values, expectations, hopes and dreams that a teacher has for his or her students.
>
> (Nieto & Bode, 2008, p. 28)

At the first meeting of one of my foundational graduate classes, the professor began by posing the question, "What is the purpose of public education in the United States?" She asked us to respond individually in writing and then share our responses with the entire group. Responses varied widely. Some opinions emphasized "the basics": reading, writing, arithmetic. Others expressed the goal of producing independent adults who could navigate society. A few asserted that school should serve to supplement the home as a secondary learning environment. The professor facilitated discussion by asking questions designed to flesh out the perspectives. First, she asked us to consider the idea of teaching the basics as the primary purpose of public schooling. The faces in the room seemed to indicate agreement. Then, the professor asked, "So what are the basics? How do you define the basics? What should we expect students to know when they complete high school?"

A few spoke up and shared skills and competencies they felt high school graduates should be able to demonstrate. The professor then said, "Okay, so will the student then be prepared to be an independent adult who can navigate society?" There was an awkward pause. The skills listed on the board were broad and somewhat general: read fluently, communicate in writing, perform computations and equations. A few students commented that the basic skills mentioned would not necessarily produce active citizens. Soon a chasm developed, as one student stated that he did not feel that it was the role of schooling to prepare students for active citizenship.

A fervent discussion followed regarding power and privilege in American society. Some in the room advocated for schools to serve to equalize the power disequilibrium in society, while a few argued for maintaining the status quo. As I pondered the discussion, I was struck with the realization that some do not acknowledge the unequal playing field pervasively present in American schools and, furthermore, some will actively oppose efforts to equalize educational opportunities for disenfranchised students. I also was left with a feeling that although this was a small group of people who had quite a lot in common as graduate students in education, we could not come to consensus regarding the knowledge and skills American students should be able to demonstrate upon completing public schooling.

As multicultural educators, we assert that the role of American public schools is to prepare students for active citizenship in a democracy. Indeed, we would suggest that this is its primary role. Kelly (1994) argues that: "Schools in a democracy should intentionally cultivate in students, *regardless* of students' political ideology, the understandings, dispositions and capacities to act effectively as citizens" (p. 65, emphasis in original). Thus, the school curriculum ultimately must empower students and provide them with the tools to share in the process of collective governance. Giroux writes: "When wedded to its most emancipatory possibilities, democracy encourages all citizens to actively construct and share power over those institutions that govern their lives" (1993, p. 13). Literacy instruction plays a major role in preparing students for participating in a democratic state. Such instruction should encourage critique and provide students with a voice, so that they can understand the power of literacy for agency and social transformation.

The installment of No Child Left Behind (NCLB) and a return to a traditional, transmissive literacy approach threaten to exacerbate educational dysfunction in the United States. The focus on prescribed curricula and content chosen to meet explicit standards, with the primary goal of raising scores on standardized assessments, is scanty instruction for a democratic electorate. Democratic ideals cannot be measured by standardized test scores. In fact, we would argue that our national obsession with testing undermines the realization of a literacy that would preserve our democratic way of life. Absent is the opportunity for critique, for creative thought and analysis, for considering diverse perspectives. Such skills are vital in a democratic state, yet these are the very skills that are discounted on tests that require a single correct response.

It is important to recognize that school curricula are not neutral or objective. The material we teach and the way we teach it communicate our stance on the purpose of public education. Edelsky (1991) argues that the form of literacy promoted in school positions students as "objects" versus "subjects" in that they have little control over literacy events. She writes that the literacy curricula that students typically experience consist of "exercises" rather than authentic opportunities for communication. Hence, students generally perceive that the role of literacy is solely for instruction or evaluation, rather than as a means for actively constructing meaning. Such curricula can have a particularly detrimental effect on historically marginalized groups who, rather than seeing literacy as a means for empowerment and social transformation, may come to view literacy as having little (or negative) significance for their lives.

Researchers have documented the fact that teachers teach what they know and often in the way they themselves were taught (Irvine, 2003; Oakes & Lipton, 2003). Au (1993) emphasizes that "Teachers need to be aware that when students from diverse backgrounds participate in school literacy activities, they are in essence being socialized into the literacy practices of a different culture, the culture of the school" (p. 29). We suggest that teachers need to recognize that the culture of school often promotes a literacy that encourages conformity rather than critique and positions students as "objects" versus "subjects" who are capable of innovative thought and agency.

Despite the increasing diversity of American schools, traditional literacy curricula persist. As Gollnick and Chinn (1998) describe it, multicultural education is the broad-based educational strategy in which students' cultural backgrounds help develop effective classroom instruction and school environments. We would add that effective instruction needs to include a consideration of curricula and materials that reflect our diverse human experience, and that promote the "habits of mind" that are important for active participation in a democratic state. Unfortunately, under NCLB, the focus has shifted to teaching to the test through prescribed curricula and methods that have been designed without much regard to the diversity of the student population being served.

In this chapter, we present an alternative perspective on curricula that promotes the academic achievement and empowerment of students from historically underrepresented groups. The curriculum in culturally responsive classrooms is designed to do the following: (1) to make explicit links to students' cultural knowledge; (2) to affirm students' identities; (3) to prepare students to understand multiple perspectives; and (4) to involve students with real-world, relevant issues in order to empower them to transform their communities. Regardless of the demographics of the particular classroom in the United States, all students benefit from a culturally responsive perspective. The aim of this chapter is to provide information to guide educators in developing and adjusting curricula to meet the needs of students who are living in a pluralistic society.

SUPPORTING RESEARCH

As Oakes and Lipton (2007) observe, "For teachers today, multiculturalism cannot be a lesson, a curriculum, a teaching style or even a philosophy . . . Multiculturalism is simply a fact – a condition of culture" (p. 3). But the reality of multiculturalism in the US population has yet to become a reality in our schools. Nieto and Bode (2008) define the goals of multicultural education as:

1. Tackling inequality and promoting access to an equal education.
2. Raising the achievement of all students and providing them with an equitable and high quality education.
3. Giving students an apprenticeship opportunity to become critical and productive members of a democratic society.

Certainly, the goals of multicultural education are laudable. Yet a growing number of researchers note that the dominant school curricula reinforce the notion of the superiority of privileged populations and fail to validate the cultures of students outside the mainstream (Bennett, 1995; Grant & Sleeter, 1986; Irvine, 1990). Researchers provide approaches that enable teachers both to examine and to extend their understanding of multicultural practices and then to integrate ethnic content into their curricula.

Sociocultural Theory and the Literacy Curriculum

Several theoretically-based assumptions support this chapter's discussion of literacy curricula. Most basic to the foundation of this research is a sociocultural learning view. As Lipson and Wixson (1997) explain, "Social theories of learning and language suggest that meaning is not an individual construction, but a social negotiation that depends on supportive interaction and shared use of language" (p. 8). In relation to literacy, specific assumptions underlie social perspectives. Reading and writing, as well as other forms of literacy, are social and cultural phenomena; knowledge is constructed through an individual's interaction within the sociocultural environment; and cognitive processes related to literacy activities are acquired through contextualized activity and assisted learning (Englert & Palincsar, 1991; McCarthey & Raphael, 1992). Oakes & Lipton (2003) suggest that given new understandings of learning, community-like images of classroom life should replace the mass schooling factory-like settings of the past. They explain that by following Dewey, Piaget, and Vygotsky (and their current counterparts), teachers focus on developing classroom learning relationships that allow students to use knowledge in ways that transform their thinking, promote their development and over time help them to participate and benefit from societies' multiple cultures (p. 212).

Yet our obsession with higher test scores and our contemporary emphasis on a scientific rationality tends to discourage schools from implementing socio-cultural principles in literacy instruction. As noted previously, the curriculum is not neutral. Educational institutions choose to invest in particular programs, texts, and literacy instructional materials. Embedded in these texts is a particular ideological perspective on what is important to know, and how that information is best transmitted. Powell (1999) writes:

> Often these materials promote an "input/output" ideology, whereby students are required to master "basic skills" and "comprehension" of text through successful completion of various exercises versus meaningful and authentic uses of print. Hence, literacy instruction is viewed as "objective" in that the ideological perspective of the texts themselves—as well as the underlying assumptions of such "scientifically" managed programs—are ignored. One of the primary aims of such instructional programs is to teach students how to conform to the materials so that their responses will be "accurate," rather than to teach them the relevance of literacy for their lives.
>
> (p. 8)

A number of educational theorists have noted the ways in which schooling in general, and literacy instruction in particular, promote student apathy and passivity (Edelsky, 1991; Freire & Macedo, 1987; Greene, 1978). Rather than using the students' own words and worlds as texts, pre-packaged programs control both what is taught and how it is taught. Thus, students have little ownership of their literacy learning. Further, pre-packaged instructional programs tend to emphasize singular, "correct" responses that discourage divergent and creative thought. Literacy is reduced to a technical model that consists of a narrow set of skills that can be transmitted to learners ("input") and then regurgitated on a test ("output"), versus a dynamic, interactive, and purposeful process that positions the student as agent.

Within this ideological context, literacy is regarded as a neutral "tool" or "skill" that can be removed from its sociopolitical context. "What is important to know" is determined by outside "experts" who have little knowledge of the experiences of our students. Such literacy materials not only control students by promoting passivity and requiring that they conform to a narrow conceptualization of literacy, but they also subject teachers to increased technical control. Teachers are reduced to the role of "managers" of the instructional program, which inhibits their ability to make curriculum decisions that best meet their students' needs. Over two decades ago, Gerald Duffy expressed his concerns about the deskilling of teachers in his 1990 Presidential Address to the National Reading Conference:

> We are participating in a system which encourages teachers to compliantly follow rather than to take charge . . . when we take control away from [teachers] by directing them to follow materials or codified approaches or tested procedures, we make them into technicians who follow directions. In doing so, we rob them of their professional dignity.
>
> (1991, pp. 3–5)

A shift to a sociocultural perspective focuses on the classroom as a community of learners. From a sociocultural perspective, activities that are authentic—that is, worthwhile, significant, and meaningful in the real world—provide the basis for the curriculum and for classroom learning. While traditional transmission models view the prepackaged literacy program or textbook as the source of knowledge and the teacher as the transmitter of that knowledge, the sociocultural perspective views literacy as a dynamic process whereby students actively construct meaning in the acts of reading, writing, speaking, and listening. Literacy is used for authentic communicative purposes. Au (1993, p. 48) summarizes the differences between constructivist and transmission models of literacy that are shown in Table 6.1.

Multicultural educational theories, culturally responsive pedagogy and culturally responsive literacy curriculum and instruction flow from a sociocultural perspective. Sociocultural theory is supported by brain-based research, which confirms that learning is social. That is, optimal learning occurs when students' need for social interaction is honored. (See the work of Caine, Caine, McClintic, & Klimek [2005] and Caine [2008], who provide a framework that integrates research from neuroscience, psychology, biology, and other disciplines.) Further, this research confirms that variations in students' experiences affect learning, and that learning is enhanced when students' individual talents, abilities, and capacities are engaged in the learning event.

The Theory of Structural Inequality and the "Official Knowledge" of the School

Curriculum decisions are also affected by notions about what is most important to know. The structural inequality theory posits that schools reflect the social stratification that operates in society and that this stratification defines what and whose knowledge is of most worth (Gibson, 1988). These cultural mismatches can have a profound effect on student achievement. As McIntyre, Roseberry, and

Table 6.1 *Comparison of Constructivist and Transmission Models of Literacy*

Constructivist models	Transmission models
Learners actively construct their own understandings	Skills and knowledge can be transmitted or passively absorbed
Teaching proceeds from whole to part	Teaching proceeds from the part to the whole
Literacy is embedded is social contexts	Literacy is taught through skills in the abstract, without regard for social context
Students are encouraged to explore the functions of literacy	Little or no emphasis is placed on the functions of literacy or the relationship of skills to these functions
Instruction is student-centered; individual differences are taken into account	Instruction is skill-driven; little emphasis is given to individual or group differences
Instruction emphasizes the process of thinking; recognizes the place of students' life experiences and cultural background	Instruction focuses on product; little recognition given to students' life experiences and cultural background
Instruction allows for cultural diversity	Instruction may reflect the values of the mainstream, to the exclusion of other cultures

González (2001) explain, "Children from middle class homes, where funds of knowledge correspond nicely to those of school, experience much less discontinuity" (p. 3). Most educational institutions are designed to maintain the status quo (Gollnick & Chinn, 1998) by perpetuating what Apple (1993, 2003) calls the "official knowledge" of the school. Apple suggests that cultural inclusion in school texts typically involves "mentioning," whereby information that would benefit marginalized populations is given cursory exposure, but not developed in depth. Powell writes, "By merely adding such information but minimizing its significance, the knowledge of dominant groups maintains its legitimacy and the cultural, regenerative knowledge of subordinate groups is subsumed within the official knowledge of the school" (1999, p. 44). Thus, in evaluating classroom curricula, we must look not only at what is present, but also at what is absent.

Geneva Gay (2000) advises educators to examine the adopted curricula and related materials with a critical eye. We ought to examine materials with the following in mind: Are ethnic minorities invisible? Marginalized? Portrayed erroneously? Assimilated? Teachers should evaluate the quality of content to avoid the typecasting of colorful characters. A combination of resources is necessary to teach about ethnic and cultural diversity. In addition, we can extend

125

the examination of curriculum outside the information taught in schools to consider students' perspectives. Thus, we must think of the curriculum as dynamic rather than fixed.

Culturally Responsive Pedagogy

Culturally responsive pedagogy emerged from the work of scholars who were concerned about the serious academic achievement problems among low-income students and students of color (Au, 1993, 2008; Boykin, 1982; Delpit, 1995; Gay, 2000; Irvine, 1990; Ladson-Billings, 1994; Nieto, 2003; Tharp & Gallimore, 1988). Their work documents the prevalence of a pattern of "blaming the victim," also called a "deficit model" for addressing the persistent achievement gap. They have also revealed the fact that some of the academic achievement disparity is due to racism or cultural hegemony.

The theory of culturally responsive pedagogy (also known as culturally sensitive pedagogy and culturally relevant instruction/pedagogy) gives hope and guidance to educators striving to improve the academic achievement of historically disenfranchised students. As Banks (1991) explains, the theory postulates that discontinuities between the school and the language and cultural experiences of historically marginalized groups largely account for their low academic achievement. The theory also asserts that the academic achievement of these students will increase if curricula and instructional practices reflect and draw on their cultural and linguistic strengths. Culturally responsive pedagogy demands using multicultural/multiethnic frames of reference with classroom curricula and instruction. Culturally responsive pedagogy assumes cultural diversity to be a strength. A number of researchers (Allen & Butler, 1996; Au, 2008; Lee, 2007; Tharp & Gallimore, 1988) have provided pervasive evidence that when students' learning and cultural backgrounds enter into the classroom experience and their cultural and linguistic resources are used to solve academic problems, task engagement and performance increase. Culturally responsive pedagogy rejects the use of checklists or prescribed instructional or curriculum models because no ethnic group is ethnically or intellectually monolithic.

Consistent with educating students for a democracy, culturally responsive pedagogy focuses on civic engagement and asserts that students must be taught to relate to people of different racial, ethnic, cultural, language and gender backgrounds. Gay (2000) calls these "relational competencies" and explains that they must encompass "knowing, valuing, doing, caring and sharing power, resources and responsibilities" (p. 20). Therefore, developing social and civic skills for effective action is an important goal.

126

As defined in the literature, culturally responsive pedagogy is comprehensive, multidimensional, empowering, transformative and emancipatory (Au, 1993; Gay, 2000; Ladson-Billings, 1994). According to Ladson-Billings (1994), culturally responsive teachers tend to be comprehensive because they seek to develop intellectual, social, emotional, and political learning by using "cultural referents to impart knowledge, skills, and attitudes" (p. 382). Gay (2000) explains that culturally responsive teaching is multidimensional because it "encompasses curriculum content, learning context, classroom climate, student–teacher relationships, instructional techniques, and performance assessments" (p. 31).

Banks (1991) contends that culturally responsive pedagogy is transformative, and explains that being transformative involves helping students "to develop the knowledge, skills, and values needed to become social critics who can make reflective decisions and implement their decisions in effective personal, social and political action" (p. 31). A number of researchers have noted the liberating effects of culturally responsive teaching including Asante (1991/1992), Au (1993), Foster (1995), Hollins (1996), and Ladson-Billings (1992, 1994). In a synthesis of the scholarship on culturally responsive pedagogy, Gay (2000) observes that "Culturally responsive pedagogy lifts the veil of presumed absolute authority from conceptions of scholarly truth typically taught in schools. It helps students realize that no single version of 'truth' is total and permanent" (p. 35).

The ideas of a culturally responsive curriculum are consistent with those of John Dewey, a strong advocate of educating students for democratic life. Over 100 years ago, Dewey (1902) asserted that curriculum content should be seen as a tool to help students develop their capabilities, attitudes, and experiences. Therefore, the curriculum should have the malleability to adapt to the cultural identities of students. Curriculum content should be chosen with the dual purpose of validating students' personal experiences and cultural heritages, and teaching content entirely new to students in ways that make it comprehensible. Curriculum content should also be chosen that will provide students with opportunities to question the text and that will expose them to diverse perspectives. When these democratic goals are articulated, the importance of using authentic, real-world texts in literacy instruction becomes clear.

Cultural Data Sets

As has been noted throughout this book, students whose language, ethnicity and race are not represented in the school's dominant culture experience varying degrees of success in school, resulting in persistent gaps in reading achievement. Fortunately, some researchers have begun to reverse this trend with culturally responsive instruction that "capitalizes on the knowledge and literacy strategies students learn in their homes and communities, the ways students reason about and make sense of the world, and the language and communicative patterns of students" (Risko & Walker-Dalhouse, 2007, p. 1).

As educators prepare to work with an increasingly ethnically- and linguistically-diverse student population and attempt to navigate mandated curricula and standards, a framework developed by Carol Lee (2007) can offer a practical structure. This model was developed for use with African American students in need of educational support. Cultural modeling (Lee, 2007) is a way of designing culturally responsive curricula and instruction as it is focused on making explicit connections between content and literacy goals and the knowledge and experiences students share with family, community, and peers. In cultural modeling, units of instruction are organized around interpretive problems. Cultural data sets (Lee, 2007) are a collection of artifacts from students' everyday experience that pose a problem of interpretation similar to those posed by required canonical texts. Teachers can intentionally use cultural data sets to bridge academic expectations with students' backgrounds. Using students' cultural data sets to bridge the knowledge and experiences students bring to school with the information we are required to teach represents one aspect of cultural modeling. The use of data sets provides a rich example of adapting curriculum to highlight student knowledge and experience. The "texts" included in these data sets go beyond traditional written texts to include R&B and rap song lyrics, videos, film clips, television programs, and oral stories and sayings. Beyond the opportunity for rich discussion that expands students' perspectives, the use of thoughtfully constructed materials that are intentionally chosen can meet multiple language arts goals. Lee (2007) explains that cultural data sets "represent practices and knowledge that schools not only devalue, but which schools have historically viewed as detrimental to academic progress" (p. 58).

In order to identify data sets that students bring to the classroom, teachers provide multiple opportunities for students to share how they reason about interpretive problems. The teacher then intentionally uses the perspectives and experiences of students to make connections between what students know and what they are expected to do with canonical school-based texts. For example, the teacher may ask the students to share how they would respond to the idea of forbidden love before embarking on a study of *Romeo and Juliet*. Through these studies, teachers provide opportunities to elicit specific memories of family activities and dialogues and invite students' connections, feelings, and interpretations. "This work can be the beginning of an intellectual journey for both teachers and students" (Lee, 2007, p. 3, as cited in Risko & Walker-Dalhouse, 2007, personal communication).

Integrating Families' "Funds of Knowledge" in the Curriculum

In 1988, González and Moll began the Funds of Knowledge research project with a study funded by the Office of Bilingual Education and Minority Language Affairs of the U.S. Department of Education. Over the past two decades, González, Moll, and Amanti (2005) have focused on the significance of the values and life skills of adults in a community. The concept of "funds of knowledge" is based on the simple premise that every person has knowledge and competence, and knowledge is the culmination of life experience. Thus, by intentionally researching and learning about the knowledge of families and adults in the community, teachers can capitalize on the many skills and experiences available in developing curriculum. It is important to distinguish this process from home visits designed to teach parents how to "do school." Within a culturally responsive framework, the primary purpose of home visits is to foster a relationship of trust so there can be an exchange of ideas, information, and stories. Teachers can then use this information to examine the school curriculum in terms of what is taught and why it is taught.

As a first step in preparing to use funds of knowledge in the development of curriculum and planned learning experiences, teachers became familiar with the concept of ethnographic research. That is, rather than a top-down approach to the adoption and implementation of prescribed curricula, this requires teachers' commitment to understanding what makes sense to others and then developing experiences and choosing materials and tools that will facilitate learning based on how others make sense of their lives. Teachers are encouraged to visit the homes of at least three families of their students and to make careful note of the families' areas of expertise. They conduct these visits as researchers, with the intentional goal of learning about families' areas of knowledge and expertise and then using that knowledge in designing curricular experiences. For instance, a family's favorite heirloom might lead to a classroom book about quilts, or their knowledge of agriculture might result in interviews with family members that serve as a basis for student writing. In determining how to use families' "funds of knowledge" in the curriculum, it is important to recognize that literacy—reading, writing, speaking, listening, viewing—are embedded in the everyday events of our lives. A commitment to learning about families' funds of knowledge requires that teachers acknowledge that all families have important resources that can be leveraged for literacy instruction. For many teachers, making the shift to using funds of knowledge authentically requires intentional self-reflection, practice, and study.

Effective Literacy Curriculum for English Language Learners

The literature suggests that a curriculum that fails to consider the unique needs of English Language Learners can have a detrimental effect on their literacy development. For instance, in detailing the conflict her own son experienced at an all-White private school, Gutiérrez (2004) recounts how a teacher's understanding of literacy was "complicated and constrained by a mandated school curriculum that was conceptualized and implemented independent of the knowledge and practices of its students" (p. 102). She explains that her son entered an elite private school as a confident and fluent reader and writer. Soon after his entrance she responded to an urgent call for a conference. As she waited to learn of the reason for the conference, she became concerned because she knew that the school had experienced some difficulty adjusting to the first Latino student (a Chicano/African American) to enroll there. She soon learned that the reason for the conference was that her son did not know phonics and thus had not completed a series of required phonics workbook pages. The teacher explained that although he was probably the best reader in the class, the knowledge of phonics was a part of the mandated curriculum and assessment structure. Gutiérrez was able to mediate this situation for her child, but other parents may lack the tools to do so.

Schools are mired in "English-only" debates which usually focus on eliminating languages other than English. Research reveals that many ELL students often receive highly scripted phonics-only reading curriculum (Gutiérrez, Asato, Santos, & Gotada, 2002; Wolfram, Adger, & Christian, 1999). These programs represent a "one-size fits all" approach to literacy development, and because students are assigned only "school work" and not authentic oral and written communication, they do little to facilitate students' language acquisition. In order to facilitate literacy development, it is important to understand how beliefs and assumptions about language impact the reading and writing curriculum. If we acknowledge that language is dynamic—that it changes according to the user's purpose and the social context—we must deliberately engage children in conversation and writing activities designed to assist their growing understanding of why particular forms of language are used and required in particular settings.

A study conducted by Campano (2007) illustrates the power of using ELL students' experiences as a source of knowledge. A fifth grade teacher, Campano's investigation occurred in an urban classroom with immigrant children from a variety of backgrounds. In his interactions with students during and outside of the structured instructional day, he recognized a need to blend the experiences of the students with the academic expectations of school. He found that the students were perceived as underachievers in the classroom, yet many of them worked hard to help their families survive. He also found that many of the students exceeded academic expectations but their diligent work both inside and outside of the classroom did not translate into empowerment in the school system.

Campano valued his students' experiences and was frustrated with the thought that they might see themselves as failures in school, so he became invested in helping students produce their stories. He says the stories "were about survival, unimaginable loss, separation from home and community and continued social exclusion and estrangement. They were also about possibility, social action and hope" (p. 18). The stories his students produced were epic and from the heart. They provided rich opportunities to empower students through valuing their own personal histories, as well as teaching the necessary conventions of English.

Through blending what Campano calls the "first classroom," i.e., the space of traditional classroom activity and instruction, with that of the "second classroom"—the activity that lies outside the normal boundaries of academic requirements—children's own experiences become important academic and intellectual resources. Campano likens the "second classroom" with what Gutiérrez, Baquedano-Lopez, and Tejada (1999) term "third space" (hybrid) literacy practices. The resources provided by the "second classroom" and "third space" resemble the funds of knowledge of working-class minority students which are often disregarded or overlooked in favor of a "one size fits all" approach to literacy. Campano found that the stories generated by tapping into the "second classroom" revealed "real histories and experiences that are buried by the pressure of standardization" (p. 41). This exploration of the "second classroom" through speaking, putting words on paper, dance, drama and recitation of verse became the alternative curriculum and brought the children into contact with the larger world.

The research and theoretical perspectives discussed in this section underscore that our decisions about the curriculum are political ones. If we believe that public education is merely to transmit basic skills, then we perpetuate a White, upper-class dominant ideology that promotes the language and experiences of those in power. Within this paradigm, curriculum is static or fixed and the teacher becomes the transmitter of knowledge rather than one who learns alongside her students. In this case, the teacher simply begins the school year by changing the nametags on the desks and cubbies, and dusting off the plans and texts from the previous year to implement in a "ready-made" fashion. The curriculum is predetermined without specific regard for the individual identities and experiences of the children who will live there for the school year.

On the other hand, if we believe that education is for transformation and empowerment, our curriculum and educational practices will be very different.

131

The curriculum will be inclusive, representing all voices within the national and global narrative. The curriculum will be authentic, in that it will involve the use of oral and written language for real purposes. The curriculum will be dynamic, reflecting the ever-changing knowledge and experiences of our students.

Admittedly, school practices and policies often militate against the use of culturally responsive practices, and thus implementing curricula that is culturally appropriate for the students you teach can become a challenge. Yet it is important to note here that it is virtually impossible to use a standardized, "one-size-fits-all" instructional package and teach in a way that is culturally relevant. No packaged curriculum can meet the needs of all students. Further, such curricula tend to be reductionist in that they diminish literacy to a series of discrete skills, thereby obscuring the social nature of literacy learning and the importance of the social dimension in literacy and language acquisition. As teachers, it is important that we challenge such policies. We also must commit ourselves to learning from our students and their families, so that we honor their experiences by making them an integral part of the curriculum.

PRACTICAL APPLICATIONS

How can we develop a culturally responsive curriculum in an environment of mandates? Essentially, we must know the standards for which we are accountable and know our students as individuals. This requires teachers to think broadly, personally, and authentically. As we implement state and national standards, it is essential for teachers to become thoroughly familiar with the expectations for proficiency so they may select resources and plan experiences that meet the school's curricular requirements while capitalizing on the cultural knowledge that students bring to the classroom. It is also important to acknowledge that a primary goal of literacy instruction in a democracy ought to be preparation for civic action. Thus, our curricular decisions ought to reflect this fundamental purpose of literacy.

This section outlines a framework for guiding our curricular decisions and provides examples of how this framework can be implemented in practice. This framework includes:

- Using what students know;
- Affirming students' identities;
- Presenting diverse perspectives;
- Examining real-world issues.

Using What Students Know

Culturally responsive teachers build on what students know to help them make connections to new concepts. Although such teachers remain accountable to educational standards, culturally responsive teachers work within the required curricular content to engage students in meaningful ways. For example, in her book *The Dreamkeepers: Successful Teachers of African American Children* (1994), Ladson-Billings provides an example of how a fifth grade teacher might use a culturally relevant approach in a lesson about the U.S. Constitution. The teacher might begin with a discussion of the bylaws and articles of incorporation used to organize a local church or African American civic association. Then, the teacher might ask students to examine how their own people build institutions so that they acquire the new knowledge within a familiar cultural context. Ladson-Billings explains that "this kind of moving between the two cultures lays the foundation for a skill that the students will need in order to reach academic and cultural success" (p. 18). Basically it is a matter of viewing content from many perspectives to build the bridges that help children increase their under-standing—in short, a bicultural mode of thinking, seeing, and valuing.

Several researchers (Dudley-Maring, 1997; Kruse, 2001; Lee, 1993) have acknowledged the fact that there is a lack of cross-cultural networks available to teachers and parents, and thus it is often difficult to know our students "in the round" in order to make important cultural connections. Often, teachers travel to a school outside their own neighborhood to teach. Thus, opportunities for families and school personnel to get to know each other are limited. In order for teachers to be culturally responsive, they need opportunities to know the personal lives and "funds of knowledge" their students bring to the classroom. As noted previously, it is important for teachers to conduct home visits with the intent of learning about the funds of knowledge of the families being served (González, Moll, & Amanti, 2005).

Knowing students so as to build on students' cultural knowledge also requires intentionally and consistently including opportunities for discussion and sharing. Although student discussion will be examined in other chapters, it is important to note the implication to the curriculum. In a culturally responsive classroom, authentic, purposeful reading and writing tasks (e.g. letters or other texts written for real purposes, personal narratives, literacy performances, and other "real-life" uses of literacy) are integral to the curriculum. Through these authentic literacy experiences, teachers come to know their students on a personal level.

Some researchers have developed projects that are specifically designed to promote cross-cultural relationships. For instance, Allen, Fabregas, Hankins, et al. (2002) report on a project called Photographs Of Local Knowledge

Sources (PhOLKS) whereby classroom teachers provided students with disposable cameras to take pictures of "things that were important to them in their homes and neighborhoods" (p. 313). With the permission of their parents and the support of their teachers, the students gathered pictures and then wrote or dictated stories about each picture. Family members also wrote narratives about pictures that the students had taken. Projects such as this one allow the teacher to have a glimpse into the knowledge and experiences that students bring to the classroom. These experiences can then be used to plan instruction and to determine ways that parents can be included in class discussion and projects.

As a first grade teacher, Compton-Lilly (2004) used children's jump rope rhymes and pictures of their parents at work as texts to teach literacy. Indeed, the possibilities for including the world of our students in literacy instruction are endless. For instance, teachers can take pictures in their students' communities and use them to develop big books for shared reading. Students can interview family members and write down their family stories for the class library. Students can develop a series of texts that feature their favorite poems, phrases, animals, and other interests. One kindergarten teacher we know takes pictures of her students making various faces and they use these photos to create a classroom "Feelings" book. Before long, 5-year-old students are reading words such as *frustrated*, *bored*, and *confused*.

This same teacher extends the traditional unit on community helpers to highlight the expertise and skills of the families in her classroom. For instance, this past year, one parent brought his 18-wheel commercial truck to school. The students had the opportunity to climb inside the truck and to learn about his profession. This event also became a source of literacy learning, as the students subsequently wrote about his visit and read their final texts. Including parents' funds of knowledge in the formal curriculum opens the door for parents to contribute to students' learning and also engenders pride in their areas of expertise.

In middle school, teachers can use popular texts such as video games, raps, and film to teach skills and concepts. For instance, we recently observed a sixth grade teacher who used excerpts from the film *October Sky* (Cramer & Johnston, 1999) to teach characterization. The students were required to discuss the traits of the various characters and to defend their ideas with examples from the text. The first classroom vignette included with this chapter describes how one middle school teacher uses rap to teach core language arts content for middle school, such as point of view and various literary devices. Using students' "cultural data sets" (Lee, 2007) as springboards for teaching literacy concepts is not only motivating to students, but it can help students to see the relevance of literacy for their lives.

TEACHERS' VOICES

Pop Culture

Victor Malo-juvera

EIGHTH GRADE LANGUAGE ARTS TEACHER, REDLAND MIDDLE SCHOOL, MIAMI, FL

Open up your books to page 324. Who would like to read?

Something similar to this starts lessons in language arts classes across America each school day, and with it comes a myriad of groans and sighs released by students under their breath as another lesson begins . . .

I never liked this method of teaching as a student, and as a teacher it still continues to lull me into a soporific state. When teaching language arts, there are so many ways to engage students, since all of the entertainment they consume, whether it is television, films, video games, comic books, or music, contain the same elements studied in a language arts classroom. Why not use these media as the textbook?

When introducing literary terms, I prefer to use a medium that my students are familiar with: rap music. I start with *What Can I Do?* (Jackson, 1994), a hip hop hit by Ice Cube. It is a political rap that tells the story of a high school drop out who turns to selling drugs. The lyrics describe his life through the moment he gets 25-to-life in prison for his third criminal conviction. It is a song that contains many of the literary elements examined in a secondary classroom. The song begins with a narrator's voice in third person, then switches to first person for the verses and to second person for the chorus. I often use this person-switching to reinforce knowledge of personal pronouns in addition to the literary use of point of view. In addition, the song tells a story that can be broken down for plot structure in terms of exposition, rising action, climax and dénouement. The various types of conflict can be taught as the song has man vs. man, man vs. society and man vs. himself conflicts. It uses similes, rhetorical questions, verbal irony, and situational irony. There are allusions to political events, policies and slogans in the song that can be researched and used for advanced literary analysis.

Students really get into this lesson, which usually takes two full class periods. I make sure I explain to them that Ice Cube was part of NWA,[1] who are considered, along with Public Enemy, to be the founders of the modern rap era. I do not give them the lyrics; I make them listen carefully to every line to work on their listening skills, and as the song progresses, I introduce definitions and concepts. After introducing students to analyzing songs, I let them bring in songs they choose and

135

we examine the ones that have depth of meaning and enough literary elements to warrant analysis.

Rap music is not the only element of pop culture I use to make connections with my students. When teaching the Hero's Journey, we read *The Odyssey* (Homer, eighth century BC) and I have students examine *SpongeBob: The Movie* (Hillenberg, 2004), for elements of the journey and for elements of the Odyssey. Students respond to this unit as it shows them that the entertainment they enjoy has its antecedents in classical literature. In *SpongeBob: The Movie*, SpongeBob is out to prove he is a man, much like Telemachus. He receives help from a princess Mindy, close to Minerva (the Roman name for Athena); he is given a bag of winds but the wind is let out by accident; he must visit a visual representation of a fiery hell; and he must even face a Cyclops before returning home for his final battle. All straight out of *The Odyssey*.

Tragedy can also be found in the films youth watch and I use *Star Wars: Revenge of the Sith* (Lucas, 2005), to connect to *Julius Caesar* by Shakespeare (c. 1599). In *Revenge*, Cassius and Brutus are represented by Chancellor Palpatine and Anakin Skywalker, Portia is Padme, Mark Antony and Octavius Caesar are Yoda and Obi Wan, and Julius Caesar is represented by all the Jedi who are assassinated when Anakin turns to the dark side. Both Shakespeare's and Lucas's works revolve around dreams and the interpretations of them; in *Caesar* it is Calpurnia's dream of Caesar's statue spouting blood, and in *Revenge of the Sith* it is Anakin's dream of Padme dying in childbirth. Love plays a central role in both as Brutus's love for Rome is his tragic flaw, while Anakin's love for Padme is his. Even the dual light-saber battles at the end of *Revenge of the Sith* mirror the battles between Octavius and Mark Anthony's armies against those of Brutus and Cassius.

I like to ask my students if they can see how the creators of *SpongeBob* and *Revenge of the Sith* must have obviously read the classic texts in their education. They unanimously respond YES! Students become much more excited to read classics when they can see for themselves how the traditional canon forms the foundation for much of the entertainment they consume. I have had students do projects comparing the television series *Lost* (Abrams, Lindelof, Bender, & Williams, 2004–2010) and William Golding's *Lord of the Flies* (1954), identifying the elements of the Byronic Hero in *Pirates of the Caribbean* (Bruckheimer & Verbinski, 2003) and *Twilight* (Meyer, 2005), and analyzing video games such as *Halo* (Bungie, 2001) for the Hero's Journey. Video games are an especially fertile ground for teaching, as most of the new video games have entire story lines that go with them that can be used to teach all the core elements of a language arts class. Imagine how excited a student is who gets to do his homework on a video game!

I also use pop culture to let students do tragic analyses of pop icons. Students will take the fall of icons such as Michael Vick, Britney Spears, or John Edwards, and chart them out according to the elements of tragedy such as the incentive moment, hamartia, peripetia, and anagnorisis. Television and the internet seem to be dominated by stories of heroes that have fallen, and students jump at the chance to turn Tiger Woods' affair or David Hassellhoff's viral video into a class project.

Modern pop culture and entertainment are rife with all of the elements we teach in language arts/English classes, so to me, it is only logical that I try to use as much of what students are familiar with to get them excited about learning the material in my class. The best part is that once your students get the hang of being critical consumers of their own entertainment, they will become the teachers and you will learn lessons from them that you can use in the future. Isn't that what teaching is all about?

NOTE

Editor's Note: According to the Urban Dictionary online, NWA is an acronym for "Niggaz With Attitudes: American rap music group from California (considered one of the first "gangsta rap" groups)." See http://www.urbandictionary.com/define.php?term=nwa.

REFERENCES

Abrams, J. J. & Lindelof, D. [Producers] & Bender, J., & Williams, S. [Directors]. (2004–2010). *Lost*. United States: Bad Robot.

Bruckheimer, J. [Producer] & Verbinski, G. [Director]. (2003). *Pirates of the Caribbean: The curse of the black pearl*. United States: Walt Disney Productions.

Bungie [Developer]. (2001). *Halo: Combat evolved*. United States: Microsoft Game Studios.

Golding, W. (1954). *Lord of the Flies*. New York, NY: Perigree.

Hillenberg, S. [Producer & Director]. (2004). *SpongeBob: The movie* [Motion Picture]. United States: Paramount Pictures.

Jackson, O. (1994). What can I do? [I. Cube]. On *Bootlegs and b-sides* [CD]. Los Angeles, CA: Priority Records.

Lucas, G. [Producer & Director]. (2005). *Star wars: Revenge of the Sith* [Motion Picture]. United States: LucasFilm.

Meyer, S. (2005). *Twilight*. New York, NY: Little Brown.

When we consider the endless possibilities for connecting literacy to students' lives, the limitations of pre-packaged standardized curricula become clear. Culturally responsive teachers create meaningful curricula with students, and they use those curricula to teach knowledge of language and literacy (phonemic awareness, letter–sound relationships, vocabulary, comprehension, written language conventions, and other literacy standards). Skills and strategies are taught within the context of students' own words and worlds.

Affirming Students' Identities

One of the most basic ways to begin to reflect a diverse perspective in classroom curriculum is through the use of multicultural literature; the use of multicultural/multiethnic texts is an effective way for teachers to move toward a more inclusive, empowering classroom. However, this powerful literature is not, of itself, effective in acquiring the knowledge necessary for transforming the curricula. We must remain aware that firsthand experience of visiting students' homes, attending cultural events, and interacting with colleagues and students from diverse cultural groups is the best way to learn more about cultures that differ from our own (Ford, Howard, Harris, & Tyson, 2000).

It is essential in choosing these texts to avoid the perpetuation of stereotypes or misconceptions and to facilitate meaningful discussion and activity. Louie (2006) has developed several principles for classroom use of multicultural literature which are worth noting here.

1 Check the text's authenticity.
2 Help learners understand the characters' world.
3 Encourage children to see the world through the characters' perspectives.
4 Identify values underlying the characters' conflict resolution strategies.
5 Relate self to the text and critique the portrayal of characters in the text and in popular media.
6 Use variants of the same story or collection of stories to help students build schema.
7 Encourage students to talk, write, and respond throughout reading the multicultural texts.

It is important to recognize that although our country is becoming increasingly diverse, many educators and students live in monocultural communities. Banks and Banks (1993) use the term "ethnic encapsulation" to refer to the phenomena of schools and communities with little ethnic diversity. For instance, Kruse (2001) notes that children in rural areas may not have the same opportunity to develop bicultural awareness as those who live in areas that provide a sustained multicultural experience. Ethnic encapsulation can result in cultural deprivation because the images provided by the media alone cannot provide an accurate portrayal of any cultural group (Macphee, 1997). Again, using multicultural literature can provide valuable opportunities for students to vicariously experience and reflect upon the differences students are bound to encounter in their lives. Quality multicultural/multiethnic literature can also enable students from diverse backgrounds to identify with the protagonists in the texts that they read, thereby affirming their racial and cultural identities. However, when using multicultural/multiethnic literature, it is essential for educators to be cautious of the threat of "essentializing people's identities" (Dudley-Maring [1997], as cited in Kruse, 2001). That is, we must help students resist the urge to generalize information to a particular race or ethnic group. Kruse (2001) reminds, "Just as no single piece of literature can speak for all peoples of European descent, even the most well-written multicultural literature cannot convey the experiences of all the members of a group" (p. 4).

Beyond using multicultural texts, however, students need to be able to "see themselves" in the formal curriculum. Providing opportunities for students to learn about the experiences of their particular cultural groups and the positive contributions they have made affirms their cultural/ethnic identities. At the same time, it is important that teachers provide opportunities for students to deconstruct negative portrayals of marginalized groups by explicitly addressing biases. For instance, teachers can use popular artifacts such as cartoons, advertisements, commercials, and other media to uncover cultural assumptions about particular groups and to reinforce a positive sense of self. By actively confronting negative assumptions that are based upon race, class, gender, and other attributes, teachers can help students to recognize that such biases are social constructions that are designed to perpetuate a system of privilege, rather than genuine portrayals of particular groups. These ideas are presented in greater depth in Chapter 9.

TEACHERS' VOICES

Using Native Dance to Teach Writing

Sally Samson

KINDERGARTEN TEACHER, AYAPRUN ELITNAURVIK IMMERSION SCHOOL, BETHEL, ALASKA

Alingevkenak Inareskina
(unknown author)
Alingevkenak inareskina (Do not be afraid to go to bed)
Alingevkenak inareskina (Do not be afraid to go to bed)

Alingevkenak qavangcaumakina (Do not be afraid and put yourself to sleep)
A ya nga, a ya nga, a ya, a ya nga.
Teguluku, mayurrluku, qillerrluku, nuqluku! (Take it, bring it up, tie it,
  pull it in!)

The song above is one of the Eskimo dances that students in kindergarten learn to perform. I heard it about 11 years ago when I taught kindergarten at Ayaprun Elitnaurvik Immersion School in Bethel, Alaska. According to Loddie Jones, kindergarten teacher and one of the founders of the immersion school, it is a lullaby song.

By the middle of the school year, students understand that when I start drumming, it is time to get into position—time to prepare for dancing. Tass'aq, a 7-year old boy, eagerly waits for my instructions and begins dancing when the song begins. During the dance, Tass'aq is vibrant, eager to learn, and eager to please. He knows that movement in dancing begins from the right, moving to the left. Like the rest of the students, Tass'aq is able to keep up with time: the beat of the drum and the rhythm of singing. When he drums, it is as if he's performed for years and years.

As I put the drum away, the students rush to the meeting area and sit on the floor. For this particular lesson, I have the chart paper and two different colored markers ready. It is the first time students will see how the song is written on paper. As I say the first word of the song, *Alingevkenak*, I hear some students say A. As I look around, I see some gesturing the letter *A* by touching both pointer fingers and both thumbs as if to make a triangle. Tass'aq and another student gesture drawing a circle and saying *akerta* (sun). As I write the rest of the words to the song, children continue to gesture, make letter–sound connections, and show their enjoyment as the lyrics fill the chart paper.

When we are finished writing, I select volunteers to point to certain letters in the song. As one student is standing in front of the chart, looking for the letter *t*, Tass'aq gives her a clue by forming the letter T with his arms. When the student doesn't understand, he says *tengssun* (airplane). The student responds and points to the letter *t* in *teguluku*.

The next day, after dancing, reading the song, and looking for known and unknown letters, I ask the students to look at the computer screen for the next part of today's lesson. As I click on the mouse, the PowerPoint pops up on the screen. The title says *Alingevkenak Inareskina* (Don't be afraid to go to bed). Each of the following slides shows a word in the song—*afraid, bed, sleep*—and a picture to go with the word. As we go through each page, Tass'aq demonstrates each word to the song by performing its companion dance movement. He listens as I once again explain the story behind the song. Each day I also ask questions such as: *Who was afraid to go to bed in the song? What did the child do in the song?* I am amazed to hear how much English vocabulary the students have acquired.

To build even more vocabulary, I use the song's popularity with the students to introduce some feeling words: *I am happy, sad, afraid, angry, sleepy, aching,* and *not afraid.* After reviewing each word and adding motions or gestures, I ask students to tell a story of when they were afraid. A few volunteer and tell their tale in Yugtun, some in English, many of them mixing the two languages. Some, like Tass'aq, add gestures as they tell their story. When the students are finished sharing their narratives, I ask them to write and/or draw their story in their journals.

Today as I look back through their journals, I am able to see the growth in their writing. When he first entered kindergarten, Tass'aq didn't know how to draw or form letters. At the end of the year he was able to draw his story with detail and he was just at the verge of discovering that letter sounds put together made a word. Tass'aq's journey into writing was his own. He responded to my instruction in his own particular way, for him a unique, developmental way. Table 6.2 shows the sequential development of this kindergartner's writing.

I discovered through this teacher action research that children go through developmental stages in writing, and by fostering them through these stages, children will discover the joy of writing. Most importantly, I learned that learners make meaning in their own way, their own style. Through *Yuraq,* the students were able to make use of their own style of learning while acquiring the written and spoken forms of both Yugtun and Standard English.

ACKNOWLEDGMENTS

This excerpt is based on my thesis titled *Yuraq: An Introduction to Writing.* This research was made possible by the Second Language Acquisition and Teacher Education Project at the University of Alaska Fairbanks, funded by the U.S. Department of Education's Alaska Native Education Program. I am grateful to the following professors who provided support throughout the project: Dr. Joan Parker

Table 6.2 Tass'aq's Journey into Literacy

Writing instruction	How Tass'aq showed knowledge
Yuraq (Eskimo Dance)	Full participation
Vocabulary build-up	Connected word and picture to gestures in Yuraq
Writing songs on chart	Verbal participation in spelling, word choice
Reading the chart/ instruction	Read while gesturing, helped others read
Activities	On task, followed directions
Journal writing	Growth in writing development

Webster, Dr. Sabine Siekmann, Dr. Theresa John, Dr. Patrick Marlow, and Dr. Marilee Coles.

Presenting Diverse Perspectives

One of the major reasons it is essential for teachers to know the curriculum and standards they are required to teach is so they can analyze the perspectives presented and provide additional resources. Available texts can be evaluated to ensure that protagonists from diverse cultural, linguistic, and/or socioeconomic backgrounds are consistently present and are presented in non-stereotypical ways. Bringing in diverse perspectives through including alternate texts serves to counteract the "official knowledge" of the school, which typically marginalizes the experiences and contributions of underrepresented groups (Apple, 1993, 2003).

It is important that teachers explicitly teach students to view texts, web-based materials and other non-print resources with a critical eye. This requires modeling and guiding students to question materials for accuracy and point of view. To prepare students for democratic engagement, students must be encouraged to question and challenge the ideas presented in print and non-print materials, and also to question what is missing from these materials (the "hidden" and "null" curricula).

For instance, Peterson (2009) provides an interesting example of a project that enabled his fifth grade students to develop their analytical skills. The teacher discovered that the school had recently received a set of CD-ROM encyclopedias, and he planned to use them to help his students to research historical figures. Knowing his student population, the teacher refined the traditional project guidelines to include the requirement that students research an American who fought for justice. Moreover, because of the ethnic background of many of his students, he extended the definition of an American to include people from Mexico and Puerto Rico. The students were excited to begin the research. Soon after beginning, a pair came to the teacher upset about the difference in the amount of information available on two people they considered investigating. It seems that the quantity of information available for Thomas Edison was much more extensive than for Harriett Tubman. The students wanted an explanation for the disparity.

Rather than squelching the discussion or trying to provide an explanation, the teacher and librarian allowed the students to present the query to the class and then guided them as they discussed possible reasons for the inequality. The students discussed several possibilities. Perhaps an inventor was more important

142

than an abolitionist. The fifth graders extended the discussion to a consideration of gender and race. The teachers guided the students to develop a set of criteria for including people in an encyclopedia and deciding how much information should be provided. The teachers ended the conversation by asking the students to consider how they might investigate accusations of racism or sexism. As the students presented the information they had gathered about the famous people they researched, they recorded the amount of information available and the sex, race, and contributions of the person. Although this project only lasted a few weeks, it provides a thoughtful example of how teachers can guide students to consider diverse perspectives.

Teachers can also provide students with specific structures that require them to view an issue from different perspectives. For instance, using authentic literary texts, teachers can ask students to take various stances as they read a text (e.g., to read from the perspective of various characters). Teachers can also use resources such as the Discussion Web (Alvermann, 1991), which requires students to look at an issue from several perspectives by providing both "yes" and "no" responses to an open-ended question, and then reaching consensus in their small groups. For many students, dramatizing a text can be useful for helping students to imagine the perspective of various protagonists. Teachers have found strategies such as the "read around" to be beneficial for encouraging students to express their ideas about a topic and to challenge the ideas of others. With the "read around," students sit in a circle and read or share their thoughts, and students are asked to respond to and expand the ideas of their peers (Christensen, 2000). With this strategy, the students' journal entries become an important part of the curriculum.

Examining Real-World Issues

If we wish to develop students who will be productive citizens in a democratic society, our classrooms must function as microcosms of the larger society. This goes beyond the usual activity of writing a persuasive letter to the principal about extending recess time. Intentional changes to the routine activities of the classroom can encourage students to take interest in the functions of their classroom, school, and immediate community.

Morning meeting is a regular occurrence in many elementary classrooms. This time can provide an effective vehicle for building classroom community and an opportunity to address important personal as well as political issues. This requires changing the routine from a primarily teacher-led conversation, with contrived participation from the students (e.g., *What day is it? What day was yesterday? What is the weather today? Who can count the days?*), and transforming it into a time to share information that is of value and concern to all present. In these meetings, teachers can present problems and ideas for discussion. The issues and concerns that are important to the children thus become the "curriculum."

In one instance (Heffernan, 2003), the teacher shared concern over behavior in the lunchroom. It seemed some children were throwing food, and as a result, the principal had asked the teachers to assign seats for lunch. The students were distressed at the idea of assigned seats, but they understood that sitting with friends was also problematic, as some students saved seats and squabbled over who sat where. As a result, the teacher introduced the idea of co-researching the interactions of the lunchroom during morning meeting. They cooperatively developed research questions, split into research teams, collected data, discussed results and proposed solutions to the lunchroom problem. In this way, the students were invested in the problem and the development of possible solutions. They owned both the process and the possible solutions so they were engaged in improving the conditions in the lunchroom. The reading and writing curriculum became their own authentic investigations and presentations.

I was fortunate enough to be collecting data for my dissertation during the 2004 presidential campaign. Rather than avoid the controversy that potentially accompanies political campaigns, one of the primary teachers I observed jumped into the campaign with both feet. She began a whole group discussion by reminding the students of the tenets of American democracy. She reviewed the election process and explained that American citizens have the right to vote and to choose who they vote for. She then talked briefly of the upcoming election and asked the students to write in their journals and then share their perceptions of the candidates. Having been a fourth grade teacher during a previous presidential election, I felt prepared for the opinions I would hear from the students. The students began sharing perceptions that revealed strong opinions of the candidates. If so and so is elected, we will not be able to be Christians anymore. If so and so is elected, we will pay higher taxes. If so and so is elected, our country won't be free anymore because he will end the war. The teacher calmly listened to and recorded the opinions shared by the students and then explained that they would be researching the opinions to try to determine the facts. Over the next month, the students worked in groups and individually read and analyzed various publications. They listened to speeches and attempted to use the words of the candidates to clarify their opinions. The second and third grade students worked diligently and respectfully to learn about the individual candidates and, along the way, they learned the importance of examining real-world issues with a critical eye. The questions and perceptions of the students drove the investigation and discussion.

Teachers often voice concern at the idea of discussing controversial or sensitive issues with their students. However, in a culturally responsive classroom, critical examination of real-world issues is essential. Consistent with a constructivist versus a transmission model of instruction, students' questions help to drive the curriculum; therefore, the teacher does not stifle students' questions, nor does she stand as the authority on all subjects. Instead, she is the guide, helping students examine issues through various perspectives and providing opportunities for students to take action to improve their communities and confront bias and inequity.

As I have talked with teachers about implementing a more critical literacy, those who teach in the primary grades are hesitant, expressing concern as to the ability of young children to relate to real-world issues. Lewison, Leland, and Harste (2008) tell the story of a first grade teacher who made the shift to use critical picture books. This shift required her to challenge the view that literacy is only a question of decoding and literal meaning-making. Although this teacher was accountable to teach phonics and comprehension, she also started asking questions that encouraged critical thinking. She asked the students to consider whose voice was heard in the story and what the author wants the reader to think. In addition, she went beyond what many teachers and parents perceive as appropriate material and subject matter for story time. She began with *The Lady in the Box* (McGovern, 1997), a story about homelessness. Although she did not think that her students would get much out of the book, she was curious to discover how her students would respond to tough social issues. The teacher found that the students made strong connections to this story and the others she included. Interestingly, she noted that the students began to treat each other with more compassion and that they became more aware of social issues. In fact, during the school's yearly canned food drive, she found that the students and their parents were much more engaged than in previous years. She was surprised and pleased to find that instead of being motivated by the class competition within the school, they were engaged because of their desire to help others. Overall, she discovered that her departure from books with happy endings and her decision to include texts that dealt with difficult issues like war, homelessness, and racism influenced her students to become more engaged in literacy activities and piqued their interest in the world beyond the classroom.

CONCLUSION

In this chapter, I have suggested that an understanding of the sociopolitical context of education is central to a genuine understanding of the significance of school curricula. The curriculum reflects who we are as a nation, what we value, and the goals that we have for our students. If a primary goal is to be able to sustain a multicultural democracy, then the history of all groups must be made visible by making their narratives a part of the curriculum (Nieto & Bode, 2008). Reconnecting with their own backgrounds and discovering the stories of their students can help teachers begin the journey of designing a curriculum that provides opportunities for students to reclaim their histories and voices.

I have also suggested that educating for democracy requires a curriculum that builds on what students know to teach new knowledge that affirms students' identities, that presents diverse perspectives, and that encourages students to examine real-world issues. Skills and concepts are taught through authentic texts: texts that emerge from analyzing a rap song, from exploring a parent's semi-truck, from examining issues in the lunchroom. In this sense, the whole world becomes the curriculum.

When we acknowledge the sociocultural dimension of literacy and literacy learning, it becomes clear that no prepackaged, standardized curriculum can be "culturally responsive." Many years ago, Sylvia Ashton-Warner (1963) wrote about her experiences in working with Maori children in New Zealand. She had no sequenced reading materials; she had no workbooks or worksheets; she had no instructional packages to help her teach literacy. What she did have, however, was the confidence that her students would learn to read using only *their* words, and the commitment to honor those words and the culture that they represented. Children's first books, she claimed,

> must be made out of the stuff of the child itself . . . And in this dynamic material, within the familiarity and security of it, the Maori finds that words have intense meaning to him, from which cannot help but arise a love of reading. For it's here, right in this first word, that the love of reading is born.
> (p. 34)

Kohn (2000) asks, "Who gets to decide what it means to be well-educated?" (p. 6). It seems, as I discovered in that graduate class, there are many perspectives. Yet how we answer this question has everything to do with the curricular decisions that we make. Will we choose to educate for conformity, asking our students to learn the same decontextualized skills that are learned by students in another geographic and social location? Will we continue to ask our students to read and write texts that are disconnected from their worlds? Or will we choose to educate for a participatory democracy, allowing students to use literacy in purposeful ways and to challenge the ideas and cultural assumptions that they find in texts? Perhaps it is only through finding answers to these challenging questions that we will find the courage and the resolve to teach in a way that makes a difference in our students' lives.

Table 6.3 *Summary of CRIOP Component: Curriculum/Planned Experiences*

Element	What you would expect to see in a classroom where CRI practices are occurring	What you would expect to see in a classroom where CRI practices are not occurring
The curriculum and planned learning experiences use the knowledge and experiences of students and their families in order to facilitate connections between students' cultural knowledge and the knowledge of the school.	Learning experiences are designed consistently to connect to and draw from the students' knowledge; the sources and products of classroom literacy experiences have authentic links to the students' lived experiences.	Classroom literacy activities are largely planned from a script or adopted program; prefabricated texts, worksheets, questions, and activities predominate.
The curriculum and planned experiences integrate and provide opportunities for the expression of diverse perspectives.	Opportunities to discuss and challenge ideas presented in texts are plentiful and encouraged; texts include protagonists from diverse backgrounds and present ideas from multiple perspectives.	The conventional point of view is predominating; few texts are available to represent diverse protagonists or multiple perspectives.
Literacy skills are taught in meaningful contexts in which students are engaged in purposeful literate activity.	The language and experiences of the students and the activity of the classroom are used to teach literacy skills and conventions; students' own writing and a variety of print materials are used to develop literacy skills.	Literacy skills are taught outside the context of meaningful literate activity; an adopted or pre-made program is used to teach skills in isolation according to a prescribed order.
The curriculum and planned learning experiences provide opportunities for the inclusion of issues important to the classroom, school and community.	Students are engaged in experiences that develop awareness and provide opportunities to contribute, inform, persuade, and have a voice in the classroom, school and beyond; literacy is used to explore real-world issues.	The curriculum and learning experiences present literacy as a "neutral skill" that ignores the sociopolitical context in which language and literacy are used; the focus of literacy instruction is to teach the skills required to "pass the test."

REFLECTIVE ACTIVITIES

1 Consider the literacy materials that you use to teach reading. Do they promote a "one-size-fits-all" perspective? Do they view literacy as a sociocultural or transmission process?

2 Review your classroom library and consider texts you use for literacy instruction. Are a variety of perspectives authentically represented?

3 Consider the literacy goals you have for your students. Are these goals consistent with the curriculum you use?

4 Consider the literacy activities and planned experiences in your classroom. How do they represent opportunities to make links to students' cultural experiences and affirm students' identities?

5 What opportunities are provided in the curriculum you use for students to investigate and take action on issues important to the classroom, school, community and beyond?

REFERENCES

Allen, B. A., & Butler, L. (1996). The effects of music and movement opportunity on the analogical reading performance of African American and White school children: A preliminary study. *Journal of Black Psychology, 22,* 316–328.

Allen, J., Fabregas, V., Hankins, K., Hull, G., Labbo, L., Lawson, H., et al. (2002). PhOLKS lore: Learning from photographs, families and children. *Language Arts, 79,* 312–322.

Alvermann, D. E. (1991). The Discussion Web: A graphic aid for learning across the curriculum. *The Reading Teacher, 45,* 92–99.

Apple, M. W. (1993). *Official knowledge: Democratic education in a conservative age.* New York: Routledge.

Apple, M. W. (2003). *The state and the politics of knowledge.* New York: RoutledgeFalmer.

Asante, M. K. (1991/1992). Afrocentric curriculum. *Educational Leadership, 49*(4), 28–31.

Ashton-Warner, S. (1963). *Teacher.* New York: Simon & Schuster.

Au, K. H. (1993). *Literacy instruction in multicultural settings.* New York: Harcourt Brace.

Au, K. H. (2008). *Multicultural issues and literacy achievement.* New York: Routledge.

Banks, J. A. (1991). A curriculum for empowerment, action and change. In C.E. Sleeter (Ed.), *Empowerment through multicultural education* (pp. 125–141). Albany, NY: State University of New York Press.

Banks, J. A., & Banks, C. M. (Eds.). (1993). *Multicultural education: Issues and perspectives* (2nd ed.). Needham Heights, MA: Simon & Schuster.

Bennett, C. I. (1995). *Comprehensive multicultural education: Theory and practice* (3rd ed.). Boston: Allyn & Bacon.

Boykin, A. W. (1982). Task variability and the performance of Black and White school children: Vervistic explorations. *Journal of Black Studies, 12*, 469–485.

Caine, R. N. (2008). How neuroscience informs our teaching of elementary students. In C. C. Block, & S. R. Parris (Eds.), *Comprehension instruction: Research-based best practices* (pp. 127–141). New York: Guilford Press.

Caine, R., Caine, G., McClintic, C., & Klimek, K. (2005). *12 brain/mind learning principles in action: The field book for making connections, teaching, and the human brain.* Thousand Oaks, CA: Corwin Press.

Campano, G. (2007). *Immigrant students and literacy: Reading, writing and remembering.* New York: Teachers College Press.

Christensen, L. (2000). *Reading, writing, and rising up: Teaching about social justice and the power of the written word.* Milwaukee, WI: Rethinking Schools.

Compton-Lilly, C. (2004). *Confronting racism, poverty, and power: Classroom strategies to change the world.* Portsmouth, NH: Heinemann.

Cramer, P. (Producer) & Johnston, J. (Director). (1999). *October Sky* [Motion picture]. Universal Pictures.

Delpit, L. (1995). *Other people's children: Cultural conflict in the classroom.* New York: The New Press.

Dewey, J. (1902). *The child and the curriculum.* Chicago, IL: University of Chicago Press.

Dudley-Maring, C. (1997). Multicultural literature and the problem of representation. *The New Advocate, 10*(2), 123–134.

Duffy, G. G. (1991). What counts in teacher education? Dilemmas in educating empowered teachers. In J. Zutell, & S. McCormick (Eds.), *Learner factors/teacher factors: Issues in literacy research and instruction* (pp. 1–8). Chicago, IL: National Reading Conference.

Edelsky, C. (1991). *With literacy and justice for all: Rethinking the social in language and education.* Bristol, PA: Falmer Press.

Englert, C. S., & Palincsar, A. S. (1991). Reconsidering instructional research in literacy from a sociocultural perspective. *Learning Disabilities Research and Practice, 6*, 225–229.

Ford, D. Y., Howard, T. C., Harris, J. J., & Tyson, C.A. (2000). Creating culturally responsive classrooms for gifted African American students. *Journal for the Education of the Gifted, 23*, 397–427.

Foster, M. (1995). African American teachers and culturally relevant pedagogy. In J. A. Banks, & C. M. Banks (Eds.), *Handbook of research on multicultural education* (pp. 570–581). New York: Macmillan.

Freire, P., & Macedo, D. (1987). *Literacy: Reading the word and the world.* South Hadley, MA: Bergin & Garvey.

Gay, G. (2000). *Culturally responsive teaching: Theory, research and practice.* New York: Teachers College Press.

Gibson, M.A. (1988). *Accommodation without assimilation: Sikh immigrants in an American high school.* Ithaca, NY: Cornell University Press.

Giroux, H. (1993). *Living dangerously: Multiculturalism and the politics of difference.* New York: Peter Lang.

Gollnick, D. M., & Chinn, P. C. (1998). *Multicultural education in a pluralistic society* (5th ed.). Upper Saddle River, NJ: Merrill/Prentice Hall.

González, N., Moll, L., & Amanti, C. (Eds.). (2005). *Funds of knowledge: Theorizing practices in households and classrooms.* Hillsdale, NJ: Lawrence Erlbaum.

Grant, C., & Sleeter, C. (1986). *After the school bell rings.* Philadelphia, PA: Falmer Press.

Greene, M. (1978). *Landscapes of learning.* New York: Teachers College Press.

Gutiérrez, K. D. (2004). Literacy as a laminated activity: Rethinking literacy for English Language Learners. In C. Fairbanks, J. Worthy et al. (Eds.), *Fifty-third yearbook of the National Reading Conference* (pp. 101–114). Oak Creek, WI: National Reading Conference.

Gutiérrez, K., Asato, J., Santos, M., & Gotanda, N. (2002). Backlash pedagogy: Language and culture and the politics of reform. *The Review of Education, Pedagogy and Cultural Studies, 24*(4), 335–351.

Gutiérrez, K., Baquedano-Lopez, P., & Tejada, C. (1999). Rethinking diversity: Hybridity and hybrid language practices in the third space. *Mind, Culture and Activity,* 6, 286–303.

Heffernan, L. (2003). Morning meeting: Contradictions and possibilities. In *School talk.* Urbana, IL: National Council of Teachers of English.

Hollins, E. R. (1996). *Culture in school and learning: Revealing the deep meaning.* Mahwah, NJ: Lawrence Erlbaum.

Irvine, J. J. (1990). *Black students and school failure: Policies, practices, and prescriptions.* New York: Greenwood.

Irvine, J. J. (2003). *Educating teachers for diversity: Seeing with a cultural eye.* New York: Teachers College Press.

Kelly, T. E. (1994). Democratic empowerment and secondary teacher education. In J. M. Novak (Ed.), *Democratic teacher education: Programs, processes, problems, and prospects* (pp. 63–88). Albany, NY: SUNY Press.

Kohn, A. (2000). *The case against standardized testing: Raising the scores, ruining the schools.* Portsmouth, NH: Heinemann

Kruse, M. (2001). Escaping ethnic encapsulation: The role of multicultural children's literature. *The Delta Gamma Bulletin, 67*(2), 26–32.

Ladson-Billings, G. (1994). *The dreamkeepers: Successful teachers of African American children.* San Francisco: Jossey-Bass.

Ladson-Billings, G. (1995). Reading between the lines and beyond the pages: A culturally relevant approach to literacy teaching. *Theory into Practice, 31,* 312–320.

Lee, C. (1993). *Signifying as a scaffold to literacy interpretation: The pedagogical implications of a form of African American discourse* (NCTE Research Report No. 26). Urbana, IL: National Council of Teachers of English.

Lee, C. (2007). *Culture, literacy and learning: Taking bloom in the midst of a whirlwind.* New York: Teachers College.

Lewison, M., Leland, C., & Harste, J. (2008). *Creating critical classrooms: K-8 reading and writing with an edge.* New York: Lawrence Erlbaum.

Lipson, M. Y., & Wixson, K. K. (1997). *Assessment and instruction of reading and writing disability: An interactive approach* (2nd ed.) New York: Longman.

Louie, B. Y. (2006). Guiding principles for teaching multicultural literature. *The Reading Teacher, 59,* 438–448.

Macphee, J. S. (1997). That's not fair: A white teacher reports on white first graders' responses to multicultural literature. *Language Arts, 74*(3), 33–40.

McCarthey, S., & Raphael, T. (1992). Alternative perspectives of reading/writing connections. In J. W. Irwin, & M. A. Doyle (Eds.), *Reading writing connections: Learning from research* (pp. 2–30). Newark, DE: International Reading Association.

McGovern, A. (1997). *The lady in the box.* New York: Turtle Books.

McIntyre, E., Rosebery, A., & González, N. (2001). Introduction. In E. McIntyre, A. Rosebery, & N. González (Eds.), *Classroom diversity: Connecting curriculum to students' lives* (pp. 1–17). Portsmouth, NH: Heinemann.

Nieto, S. (2003). *What keeps teachers going?* New York: Teachers College Press.

Nieto, S., & Bode, P. (2008). *Affirming diversity: The sociopolitical context of multicultural education.* Boston, MA: Allyn & Bacon.

Oakes, J., & Lipton, M. (2003). *Teaching to change the world* (2nd ed.). Boston, MA: McGraw-Hill.

Oakes, J., & Lipton, M. (2007). *Teaching to change the world* (3rd ed.). Boston, MA: McGraw-Hill.

Peterson, B. (2009) in W. Au (Ed.), *Rethinking multicultural education: Teaching for racial and cultural justice* (pp. 361–367). Milwaukee, WI: Rethinking Schools.

Powell, R. (1999). *Literacy as a moral imperative.* Lanham, MD: Rowman and Littlefield.

Powell, R. (2009). Introduction. In L. A. Spears-Bunton and R. Powell (Eds.), *Toward a literacy of promise: Joining the African American struggle* (pp. 1–19). New York: Routledge.

Risko, R. J., & Walker-Dalhouse, D. (2007). Tapping students' cultural funds of knowledge to address the achievement gap. *The Reading Teacher, 61,* 98–100.

Tharp, R. G., & Gallimore, R. (1988). *Rousing minds to life: Teaching, learning, and schooling in the social context.* Cambridge: Cambridge University Press.

Wolfram, W., Adger, C. T., & Christian, D. (1999). *Dialects in schools and communities.* Mahwah, NJ: Erlbaum Associates.

Chapter 7

Pedagogy/Instruction: Beyond "Best Practices"

Susan Chambers Cantrell and Tiffany Wheeler

We need to view all approaches and methods with a critical eye, even with skepticism, because no method will solve learning problems for all students. This is the problem with any pedagogical approach that is uncritically elevated to the level of "best practice" as if a particular practice is appropriate for all students in all contexts.

(Nieto & Bode, 2008, p. 136)

Ms. Faith Brown and her kindergarten students are studying about African American leaders. Ms. Brown works diligently to help students apply the concept of leadership in their own lives. She emphasizes to the children that while the African American historical figures that we often study lived long ago and are now deceased, leaders do not have to be dead. She gives the children several examples of leaders in their own lives. She tells the children that she and her instructional assistant are leaders. She reminds children of the leaders who have come to their classroom throughout the school year, many of whom are African American. She knows that several children attend church and asks them to state the names of their pastors. When many of the children name their pastors quite easily, Ms. Brown enters into the following exchange with her class and one African American female student in particular:

> Mrs. Brown: Your pastors are leaders. Many leaders are right here, not dead. You don't have to be dead to be a famous leader.
> [Mrs. Brown asks Charity to name a leader that she knows.]
> Charity: My Uncle Anthony's a leader.

Mrs. Brown: What does he do?

Charity: He helps me.

[Mrs. Brown validates Charity's response and also informs the children that they are leaders as well. As they are preparing to read a book about George Washington Carver, the conversation continues.]

Mrs. Brown: You're all leaders. Children, say, "I am a leader."

Class: I am a leader.

[Ms. Brown tells her class that being a leader "starts right here and right now."]

This scenario comes from the actual classroom of Faith Brown (pseudonym), an African American culturally responsive teacher highlighted in a study by Tiffany, one of the authors of this chapter, in her doctoral dissertation (Wheeler, 2007). Ms. Brown wanted her students to see leadership as related to their own lives, and she built on her students' knowledge and prior experiences with the concept of leadership.

SUPPORTING RESEARCH

In focusing on her students' own lives and relating instruction to their experiences, Ms. Brown exhibited key characteristics of culturally responsive instruction and pedagogy. Much is known about effective classroom literacy instruction. A rich body of research and practical applications of literacy theories point to a number of "best practices" for helping students reach proficiency in reading and writing (Biancanrosa & Snow, 2004; National Institute of Child Health and Development, 2000; Zemelman, Daniels, & Hyde, 2005). However, in spite of an extensive emphasis on improving literacy instruction over the years, many students from diverse cultural, linguistic, and socioeconomic backgrounds do not reach high levels of literacy achievement. These persistent achievement gaps suggest traditional literacy instruction is not sufficient for improving literacy in diverse classrooms and schools. To ensure all students achieve high levels of literacy, teachers must implement instruction that responds to the diverse backgrounds and learning styles of the students in their classrooms. While this entire book focuses on creating classrooms that support the learning of students from diverse cultural and linguistic backgrounds, this chapter focuses specifically on how teachers can best serve culturally diverse student populations through engaging literacy instruction.

What is missing from a discussion of "best practices" is the idea that literacy learning is a *social* process. Instruction is mediated within a "social space"— within a "zone of proximal development"—in which the teacher helps students to make connections from the known to the yet-to-be-learned (Vygotsky, 1978).

While literacy instructional methods provide specific ideas for scaffolding young learners within their "zone," they generally ignore the sociocultural context within which learning occurs. More specifically, a discussion that is limited solely to appropriate methodology fails to acknowledge the crucial importance of the student–teacher relationship in student learning, and the critical need to affirm students as learners by validating the cultural knowledge that they bring to learning.

Thus, we maintain that the national discussion on literacy instruction is limited, not only because "best practices" can never be appropriate for all students (as Nieto and Bode, 2008, suggest in the introductory quote), but also because this discussion fails to consider the social dimension of learning. Even the best of practices will fail us in our attempts to close the literacy achievement gap if we ignore the sociocultural and political dimensions of literacy and language acquisition.

In a culturally responsive classroom, the teacher's position is that of a learner who investigates her students' cultural backgrounds and accommodates instruction to students' learning styles and diverse perspectives (Montgomery, 2001). First, culturally responsive teachers learn *about* their students' cultures, communities, interests, and lives. They use this knowledge to contextualize instruction within the real-world concerns of students and to create relevant learning events for students (Gay, 2000). Next, culturally responsive teachers learn *with* their students. They engage their students in multi-perspective investigations that challenge the status quo and raise students' socio-political consciousness (Ladson-Billings, 1994). In this way, culturally responsive instruction (CRI) is not a collection of strategies, but is a consistent mindset that influences a teacher's planning and lesson implementation. CRI requires that teachers know and understand the cultural backgrounds of their students and that they possess openness to multiple perspectives and ways of knowing. Culturally responsive teachers value the knowledge and experiences that students bring to the classroom and build on students' strengths. In addition, they have a sociocultural consciousness that enables them to understand the inequities in society, including the ways in which schools perpetuate those inequalities, and engage their students in meaningful instruction that addresses those inequities (Villegas & Lucas, 2007).

Matching Instruction to Students

In planning and implementing instruction, culturally responsive teachers understand the cultures of their students and the ways in which those cultures influence students' learning styles or preferences. Children from many ethnic groups are raised in cultural contexts that are very different from the contexts in which middle-class European American children are raised and in which most middle-class, White teachers raise their own children. These differences in behavioral norms and expectations between home and school can greatly influence the learning of students of color. For example, Shade's (1994) research indicates that the cultural contexts or behavioral norms that are accepted in homes of many African American children are in conflict with norms that are often associated with acceptable school behavior. Whereas interpersonal interactions are central to the learning process of many African American children, this often conflicts with the expectation of students' passive receptivity to teachers' transmission of knowledge that is often inherent in school contexts. In culturally responsive classrooms, teachers work to construct learning events which more closely match students' learning styles and cultural norms. By creating cultural congruity, teachers ensure that instruction capitalizes on the learning processes of diverse students (Gay, 2000). In addition, learning styles are multidimensional and dynamic tendencies do not apply equally to all members of an ethnic group; thus, while it is important to consider shared ethnic group characteristics when planning and implementing instruction, culturally responsive teachers recognize individual differences among students as they engage students in literacy instruction.

Cultural congruity is especially important in classroom interactional processes (Gay, 2000). Instructional interactions between teachers and students and among students can facilitate students' access to content and can improve the participation levels of students in diverse classrooms. Research conducted in the early 1980s at Kamehameha Early Education Program (KEEP), a demonstration school for native Hawaiian children, indicated that student achievement is positively influenced when classroom interaction patterns and participation structures are adapted to match the cultural patterns and structures of the students (Au, 1980; Au & Mason, 1983). Student engagement and literacy learning were increased when teachers at KEEP intentionally established discourse structures that utilized "talk story," a conversational practice that involves joint performance and turn-taking patterns with more than one speaker. Valuing and incorporating students' home and community interaction structures into the classroom support students' cultural identities and build on what students know and can do. (A more comprehensive discussion of effective classroom discourse practices can be found in Chapter 8.)

Not only are interactions between teachers and students central to effective instruction, but interactions among students facilitate learning, especially for students of color. Collaboration is an important instructional component in culturally responsive classrooms. While European Americans value individuality and competition, students from African American, Latino, and Native American

155

backgrounds value cooperation, interdependence, and "group-ness" (Gay, 2000; Shade, 1994). Thus, culturally responsive instruction includes many varied opportunities for students to work together. When students are assigned to work in heterogeneous groups on specific lessons, they can learn content and skills from each other and at the same time have the opportunity to identify with peers from different cultural backgrounds. In the KEEP program, students spend half of their day in learning centers, working with other students on similar assignments, with permission to help each other complete their work (Tharp & Gallimore, 1988). In Ladson-Billings' (1994) study of successful teachers of African American students, she found that effective teachers encouraged students to learn collaboratively and to take responsibility for one another. The teachers created a family-like culture, and provided opportunities for students to work together to achieve common goals.

A number of studies have documented the benefits of engaging students in cooperative tasks around text. Dill and Boykin (2000) compared the text recall and task engagement of African American students who participated in one of three learning contexts: individual, peer tutoring, and communal learning. Students in the communal learning context performed significantly better on the recall test and exhibited higher levels of task engagement than did students in the other two conditions. Other researchers have examined the use of small-group literature discussions in diverse classrooms and have found that such discussions, with teacher scaffolding, support the literacy learning of student participants (Fairbanks, Cooper, Masterson, & Webb, 2009; Kong & Fitch, 2002–2003; Maloch, 2005). In these studies, cooperative discussions enabled students to use their prior knowledge and background experiences to construct meaning.

Collaborative learning contexts are especially beneficial for students with limited English proficiency. Calderón, Hertz-Lazarowitz, and Slavin (1998) evaluated the impact of a cooperative learning program, Bilingual Cooperative Integrated Reading and Composition (BCIRC), on the literacy achievement of second- and third-grade English learners in bilingual programs and found positive outcomes in writing and reading when compared to students in a matched comparison group. Students who participated in BCIRC for two years significantly outperformed comparison students on measures of reading and language. While studies such as this illustrate the benefits of cooperative learning in helping students develop English proficiency, other research has pointed to complex contextual factors that influence the effectiveness of collaboration. Jacob and colleagues (1996) investigated the impact of cooperative learning on English learners in a sixth-grade social studies classroom. This observation study indicated that cooperative learning was beneficial in helping students learn the meaning of academic terms, but the researchers noted contextual features (students' definitions of the task, features of the task, and participant structures) which resulted in missed opportunities for learning. Thus, while collaborative tasks are often associated with higher levels of learning for students, culturally responsive teachers pay attention to the contextual factors that can influence students' learning in cooperative learning events.

Teachers must use care to ensure that cooperative learning structures are effective. Johnson, Johnson, and Holubec (1993) assert that the essential components of cooperation are positive interdependence, face-to-face interaction, individual and group accountability, interpersonal and small group skills, and group processing or reflection. Students must know that their group's success is dependent on the success of the individuals in the group, and they must be taught to rely on and support one another in the task. Often, issues of social status and peer expectations can interfere with effective collaboration and can further marginalize students from diverse backgrounds. Thus, teachers must work to ensure that status differences among groups in society are not re-created in cooperative group structures and must attempt to equalize existing status differences among students (Slavin & Cook, 1999). This might be accomplished by identifying students' strengths and assigning them to specific roles that use those strengths, making lower-status students group "experts" in areas in which they have strengths, and publicly acknowledging the competencies of lower-status students (Cohen, 1994).

Another important aspect of culturally responsive instruction is the extent to which it supports students' cultural identities, builds on students' cultural knowledge and experiences, and is relevant to students' lives. Lee (1995, 2001, 2006, 2007) has identified a framework, called cultural modeling, for designing instruction which enables students to use everyday knowledge and "non-standard" language to learn content material. In a cultural modeling framework, teachers build on the cultural knowledge that students possess by structuring learning events that integrate students' existing knowledge with new academic content. New content is connected directly to students' prior knowledge and language use. For instance, Lee has documented the use of signifying, a form of talk in African American English that uses figurative language, to enhance students' interpretations of narrative texts in diverse classrooms. In Lee's studies, the use of signifying was associated with increases in students' reading comprehension and written production of narrative texts.

This and other research suggest that teachers can meet the needs of students in diverse classrooms by building on the cultural traditions of the students in those classrooms, thereby capitalizing on students' rich funds of knowledge (Moll, Amanti, Neff, & Gonzalez, 1992; Moll & González, 1994). Culturally responsive teachers create bridges between the cultures, traditions, and languages of school and the home and community (Gay, 2000). Some research has

157

explored ways in which teachers create learning events in which home and school discourses are combined to create "hybrid" classroom cultures in which a "third space" is created in the intersection of home- and school-based learning (Gutiérrez, 2008; Gutiérrez, Baquedano-Lopez, & Tejeda, 1999; Gutiérrez, Baquedano-Lopez, & Turner, 1997; Gutiérrez, Rymes, & Larson, 1995). In one such study, Gutiérrez and colleagues (1999) illustrated how a unit on human reproduction was initiated in a culturally and linguistically diverse second- and third-grade classroom when students engaged in sexuality-specific name calling. With the blessing of school administrators and parents, the teacher used school language and practices (the official script) and students' language and behaviors (the unofficial script) to create a third space where students constructed meaning through collaborative literacy events. In this example, the teacher used the knowledge and language that students brought to the learning situation and extended that learning through collaborative talk.

Other studies have pointed to the importance of using students' existing knowledge and experiences. Ladson-Billings (1994) identified teachers' perceptions about students' knowledge as central to instruction that is culturally relevant. She found that successful teachers viewed each student as knowledgeable and that those teachers valued students' knowledge and incorporated it into classroom instruction. The teachers legitimized students' out-of-school experiences and created lessons that used those experiences. Similarly, in Lynn's (2006) study of three African American male teachers who implemented culturally relevant practices, all three teachers were characterized as connecting instruction to students' lives and concerns. They used literature and materials that were relevant to students' lives and encouraged students to make personal connections to what they read.

Explicit Teaching

To effectively close the achievement gap between White students and students of color, instruction in diverse classrooms must include a rigorous focus on students' academic development. In addition to implementing instructional practices that build on students' cultural knowledge and experiences, culturally responsive teachers provide explicit instruction in the skills and strategies that students need to be successful in the classroom and in the dominant culture. Through modeling, explanation, and appropriate scaffolding to extend students' knowledge, culturally responsive instruction ensures that students develop the necessary competencies for multiple settings. While students maintain their cultural identities through instruction that connects to their funds of knowledge, they learn the strategies and discourses of the dominant culture as well (Delpit, 1995).

Some perspectives on diversity hold that students of color need direct instruction and extensive practice in basic literacy skills often delivered through scripted methods (Bereiter & Engelmann, 1966; Shade, 1994). These notions are grounded in the belief that students of color come to school with serious learning deficits that must be remedied before they can successfully engage in higher-level literacy activities. Such perspectives are not consistent with theories that undergird culturally responsive literacy instruction. In culturally responsive classrooms, teachers hold high expectations for students' thinking and learning (Ladson-Billings, 1995). In a study of effective teaching in schools serving students from high-poverty backgrounds, Taylor and colleagues (1993) documented the practices of the most effective teachers. In nine schools across the nation, the researchers found that teachers who emphasized higher-order thinking promoted the greatest gains on measures of students' reading achievement. The teachers who were most successful with students in this study asked higher-level questions and involved students in tasks that required high levels of cognitive engagement. Taylor and colleagues also found that routine practice exercises were not effective in helping students develop reading abilities. In their study, the more researchers observed these practice exercises, the less students exhibited growth on reading assessments. This study illustrates the importance of rigorous and engaging instruction for all students, regardless of their cultural or ethnic backgrounds.

The National Reading Panel (2000) identified five areas in which students must develop competence to learn to read effectively: phonemic awareness, phonics, fluency, vocabulary, and comprehension. The panel acknowledged the importance of other aspects of reading as well, but their work was limited in terms of time and available research from which to draw conclusions. Other comprehensive examinations of reading implored attention to issues related to students' motivation and cultures in developing students' early reading proficiency (Snow, Burns, & Griffin, 1998). In culturally responsive classrooms, teachers develop students' competencies in meaningful and engaging contexts that bridge new learning with students' existing knowledge and experiences (Gay, 2000).

Explicit instruction in the processes of literacy is essential for all students, but may be particularly important for students from underrepresented groups. Effective literacy teachers directly teach the strategies that students need to be successful, and they do so through demonstrations, explanations, and applying appropriate scaffolds as students practice in meaningful contexts (Duffy, 1993; Morrow, Tracey, Woo, & Pressley, 1999; Wharton-McDonald, Pressley, Ranking, & Mistretta, 1997). For instance, certain strategy interventions have been shown to be effective in improving students' comprehension abilities. Strategy-training programs such as reciprocal teaching (Palinscar & Brown,

1984), Informed Strategies from Learning (Paris, Cross, & Lipson, 1984; Paris & Jacobs, 1984; Paris & Oka, 1986), and Transactional Strategies Instruction (Brown, Pressley, VanMeter, & Schuder, 1996; Pressley et al., 1992) have proven successful with readers at various age levels. In these approaches, teachers make their own thinking visible to students and provide extended opportunities over several weeks for students to integrate strategies on their own. These programs engage students in active processing of texts in which students are equipped to monitor and control their comprehension.

Extensive research reviews have indicated that English learners benefit from the same kinds of explicit skill and strategy instruction as monolingual students. Shanahan and Beck's (2006) meta-analysis of research on effective strategies for English learners indicates that these learners benefit from reciprocal teaching, explicit instruction of comprehension strategies, and paired reading for the improvement of students' fluency. However, the authors point out that successful teachers often use extensive scaffolding to support students' comprehension development. The research suggests that the teachers' scaffolding may be as important as the comprehension strategies themselves. Gersten and Jiménez (1994) have developed a model for effective instruction for language minority students which emphasizes the importance of teacher scaffolding of students' cognitive strategies. In this model, teachers scaffold students' thinking through: (1) thinking aloud, building on, and clarifying student input; (2) using visual organizers/story maps or other aids to help students' organize and relate information; and (3) providing background knowledge to students.

One of the most important aspects of children's literacy development is vocabulary acquisition, particularly for students with low socio-economic status and limited English language proficiency (Coyne, Simmons, & Kame'enui, 2004; Taffe, Blachowicz, & Fisher, 2009). Differences in exposure to vocabulary, depending on families' economic circumstances, are evident early in children's lives, and these differences tend to persist across the grades (Biemiller, 2001; Juel, Biancarosa, Coker, & Deffes, 2003). To ensure that children acquire rich vocabularies that enable them to access and construct meaning from a wide range of texts, teachers must provide strong vocabulary instruction. For students who are less familiar with academic discourses, instruction must be more extensive, must begin earlier, and must include the kinds of supports and scaffolds that ensure students will be successful in acquiring new vocabulary (Taffe, Blachowicz, & Fisher, 2009).

Taffe, Blachowicz, and Fisher (2009) reviewed the research on vocabulary instruction for economically disadvantaged students and for English Language Learners and found that exemplary vocabulary instruction includes three categories: (1) the classroom environment is concept rich, language-rich, and word rich; (2) instruction focuses on word meanings with "a focus on deep understanding and lasting retention," (p. 322); and (3) students learn strategies for figuring out the meanings of words on their own. All students develop vocabulary knowledge from extensive text reading (Nagy, Anderson, & Herman, 1987), and this is true for English learners as well, particularly when reading is accompanied by appropriate teacher scaffolding and follow-up (Sénéchal, Thomas, & Monker, 1995). Research has demonstrated the effectiveness of such scaffolding as highlighting words in literature, manipulating, sorting, and writing words, and applying words in a variety of contexts (Beck & McKeown, 2007). For English Language Learners, it is important to create a language-rich environment in which students can first express themselves in their native language and then experiment with English vocabulary (Jiménez & Gersten, 1999; Martinez-Roldan, 2003).

In addition to creating a classroom environment in which students develop rich vocabularies, teachers need to provide explicit instruction in the meanings of words. This includes telling students the meanings of new words in student-friendly ways and teaching the spellings and pronunciations of the words in addition to the meanings (Beck & McKeown, 2007; Ehri & Rosenthal, 2007). For students to internalize new vocabulary words, they need to practice using targeted vocabulary repetitively and in a number of different contexts (Shanahan & Beck, 2006; Graves, 2006).

Not only should teachers help students learn new words through explicit instruction, but they should also develop students' independent word learning strategies. Students can learn to use morphology (word structure) and contextual information to learn new vocabulary on their own during independent reading (Graves, 2006; Taffe et al., 2009). For English Language Learners, using cognates, or words in the native language that are similar to English forms of the word, is an especially useful form of morphological analysis (Jiménez, Garcia, & Pearson, 1996; Taffe et al., 2009). Equipped with strategies for word learning, students can learn many more words than a teacher might be able to teach through explicit instruction.

Balanced Instruction

Over the past decade, many authors have advocated for a balanced approach to literacy instruction (Farris, Fuhler, & Walther, 2004; Fitzgerald, 1999; McIntyre & Pressley, 1996; Tompkins, 2005; Zemelman, Daniels, & Hyde, 2005). A balanced literacy approach includes meaning-centered and literature-based instructional activities as well as explicit instruction in specific skills such as phonics (Farris, Fuhler, & Walther, 2004). Fitzgerald (1999) noted that in a balanced literacy perspective, three broad categories of children's knowledge

161

need to be considered as equally important: local knowledge about reading, global knowledge about reading, and love of reading or affective knowledge about reading. Local knowledge about reading includes areas such as phonological awareness, sight word vocabulary, phonics, and word identification strategies. Global knowledge refers to comprehension elements, such as understanding, interpretations, and response to reading. Affective knowledge involves feelings, positive attitude, motivation, and the desire to read. These forms of knowledge are interrelated, and teachers should arrange instruction and literacy opportunities so that children can acquire as many kinds of reading knowledge as possible in an integrated way. Specific instructional components that support this view of reading include: (1) a balance between student-centered and teacher-directed instruction; (2) flexible grouping practices (a combination of homogeneous and heterogeneous instructional groups); and (3) the use of a mixture of classic literature books, trade books, easy readers, and predictable books.

Classroom research has indicated that the most effective teachers emphasize both skills and meaning through balanced instruction (Cantrell, 1998; 1999; Morrow, Tracey, Woo, & Pressley, 1999; Wharton-McDonald, Pressley, & Hampston, 1998). These studies describe the characteristics of classrooms in which students reach high levels of literacy achievement:

1   Teachers focus on particular reading strategies and skills but do so to enhance the construction of meaning as part of meaningful reading and writing.
2   There is an emphasis on comprehension of text and children are provided multiple opportunities to respond to texts through discussion, writing, and art.
3   Teachers read aloud high-quality literature and students read literature independently.
4   Teachers model the use of reading and writing strategies and provide extensive scaffolding for students as they learn to use strategies on their own.
5   Teachers foster self-regulation and develop students' metacognitive abilities.

Although the effective practices described here are important for all children's literacy development, such practices alone are not sufficient for addressing the needs of students in diverse classrooms. To close achievement gaps, these best instructional practices must be extended to consider and respond to the social and cultural contexts in which classrooms are situated. Culturally responsive literacy instruction moves beyond standard definitions of literacy to emphasize the social worlds and cultural identities of students, and views literacy as the construction of meaning within a social context (Au, 1993; Cazden, 1988; Hammerberg, 2004; Pérez, 1998). In this sociocultural view, literacy is "not always about reading in the traditional sense of decoding a text and extracting meaning from it" (Hammerberg, 2004, p. 649). Instead, literacy involves all that students bring to the reading or writing event and the context in which that event is situated. Thus, to ensure that students from diverse backgrounds achieve at high levels, teachers need to consider the social and cultural context in which instruction occurs (Villegas & Lucas, 2007). Explicit and balanced instruction is effective when it is contextualized within a framework that honors students' ways of learning and when literacy events are relevant to students' lives and concerns. In culturally responsive classrooms, students apply literacy skills and strategies in ways that are consistent with their cultural backgrounds and in work that is important to them.

Beyond Balanced Instruction

While challenging and explicit instruction in literacy skills and strategies is important for all learners, instruction must engage students from all cultural and linguistic backgrounds. Research suggests that student engagement in reading is strongly associated with reading achievement and that reading engagement is comprised of cognitive, social, and motivational dimensions (Guthrie & Wigfield, 2000). In addition to possessing the knowledge and strategies that facilitate successful literacy experiences, engaged students are motivated to read and write for a variety of purposes, and their literacy practices are socially interactive (Guthrie, McGough, Bennett, & Rice, 1996). When literacy tasks are not motivating and are completely removed from a social context, students may actively resist learning and even disrupt the learning of others (Powell, McIntyre, & Rightmyer, 2006). Thus, to promote students' engagement in literacy, teachers must attend to students' cognitive literacy processes, the social context in which literacy occurs, and students' motivations for fulfilling their personal literacy goals.

Students' motivations, or the reasons they do the things they do, are determined in large part by the histories, values, and worldviews of their cultural or ethnic groups. Because learners are socialized according to their cultural norms, the circumstances which elicit motivation for culturally and linguistically diverse students are often different from those which motivate students from dominant cultural backgrounds (Ginsberg & Wlodkowski, 2000). For instance, while students from dominant backgrounds have been socialized to pursue extrinsic rewards such as grades, prizes, or college entrance, many students of color do not see direct links from their efforts to these rewards, due to historical patterns of societal discrimination. Thus, it is essential that teachers' instructional practices match the norms, beliefs, and values of students from diverse

163

groups so as to elicit students' intrinsic motivation to succeed at academic literacy tasks.

Based on the notion that learning depends on the social context in which students are situated, Wlodkowski and Ginsberg (1995; Ginsberg and Wlodkowski, 2000) developed a motivational framework for instruction which includes four conditions. The first condition is *establishing inclusion*, or creating a learning atmosphere in which students and teachers feel respected by and connected to one another. In an inclusive environment, students feel safe to be themselves and to take risks with academic tasks. Students and teacher learn from one another and appreciate differences in values, points of views, and ways of interacting. A second condition for motivation is *developing a positive attitude* through personal relevance and choice. When students can relate to the content and can make decisions about what they learn and how they will be assessed, they develop positive dispositions toward their learning. The third condition is *enhancing meaning*, which involves creating challenging and engaging learning experiences that include students' cultural values and points of view. The fourth condition is *engendering competence*, or developing students' understanding that they are gaining competence toward a goal that they value and is valuable to the larger society. When teachers plan and implement instruction that considers the social and cultural aspects of motivated engagement, students from all cultural and linguistic backgrounds benefit in ways that promote higher levels of learning and achievement.

Meaningful instruction that supports intrinsic motivation and student engagement is instruction that actually *responds to* the topics and issues that concern students (Gay, 2000). Compton-Lilly (2004) provides examples by documenting her work as a first-grade teacher in a diverse, high-poverty school. She engaged her students in inquiry projects centered on topics that were drawn from students' lives and communities, including controversial or challenging issues such as gun violence and the dangers of lead in children's homes. To link instruction to students' home experiences and personal concerns, Compton-Lilly used familiar jump rope rhymes to develop students' early reading skills and engaged students in interviewing their family members about their own reading behaviors. While Compton-Lilly's young students were motivated by inquiry-based learning, using inquiry projects as the basis for instruction is important in engaging older students as well (Smith & Wilhelm, 2006). Through mutually respectful relationships that support students' developing competence toward shared goals, culturally responsive teachers support students' motivation to learn and engage in personally relevant and meaningful literacy tasks.

Researchers have focused on the types of tasks in which teachers engage students and the extent to which these influence motivation. Turner (1995) studied the effects of literacy tasks in first grade through extensive observations in 12 elementary classrooms and interviews of 84 children. Results of her study indicate that the type of literacy tasks provided for first-grade students was the single best predictor of students' motivation. Turner found that "open" tasks which allow students to have control over their learning promoted higher levels of motivation than more "closed" tasks which are tightly controlled by the teacher. During open tasks, students engaged in more strategy use, persisted longer with the task, and paid better attention during literacy instruction. Students were motivated when they were permitted to make choices in the learning process and have control over their learning. An example of providing choice and control to students in vocabulary instruction is the Vocabulary Self-Collection Strategy (VSS), in which the class develops its own spelling and vocabulary word lists based on what words students find interesting and want to know. Ruddell and Shearer (2002) used this strategy with a group of struggling adolescent readers and demonstrated significant improvements in students' spelling and vocabulary test scores.

In addition to engaging students in tasks that enable students to control their own learning, culturally responsive teachers structure tasks that are active. They incorporate drama, rhythm, music, and movement into lesson formats and include performance-based ways for students to demonstrate what they know (Gay, 2000). Activities such as Readers' Theater, in which students practice and perform oral readings of texts, is one strategy that has shown to be successful in increasing students' reading fluency (Griffith & Rasinski, 2004; Martinez, Roser, & Strecker, 1999). Hands-on activities grounded in the dramatic and visual arts are effective in developing students' vocabularies as well. In her study of middle school English learners, Short (1994) identified several successful strategies for developing academic vocabulary that incorporated drama, drawing, graphic organizers, and collaborative work. These active learning strategies enabled students to make sense of the academic language in content area textbooks and acquire higher levels of content knowledge. Further, they allowed students to use language in purposeful ways, which is essential for language acquisition.

Purposeful Learning in Meaningful Contexts

For literacy instruction to be truly motivating for all students, they must be engaged in meaningful uses of oral and written language. In his book *Results Now: How We Can Achieve Unprecedented Improvements in Teaching and Learning*, Schmoker (2006) points to the importance of authentic literacy for all students, and particularly those students who are at risk of school failure. He laments the current lack of meaningful in-class reading, writing, and talking in favor of

165

"literature-based arts and crafts" in which students spend extensive time in activities such as cutting, pasting, and coloring:

> Generous amounts of close, purposeful reading, rereading, writing, and talking as underemphasized as they are in K-12 education, are the essence of authentic literacy. These simple activities are the foundation for a trained, powerful mind—and a promising future. They are a way up and out—of boredom, poverty, and intellectual inadequacy. And they're the ticket to ensuring that record numbers of minority and disadvantaged youngsters attend and graduate from college. We have yet to realize how much is at stake here.
>
> (p. 53)

Schmoker contends that students should be learning how to read deeply and strategically, analyze and interpret texts, frame an argument considering multiple perspectives, and write in powerful ways. Such high-level, meaningful literacy activity is central to a culturally responsive instructional program.

Teachers can make literacy instruction more meaningful to students by using an integrated approach to literacy instruction. Students from many cultural and linguistic backgrounds learn in ways that are holistic, intuitive, and integrative (Hale, 1982; Shade, 1994). Students with this learning style benefit from connected lessons that enable them to apply literacy to real situations (Hanna, 1988; Heath, 1983). Thematic instruction, inquiry learning and project-based activities provide opportunities for students to develop competence in more integrated and applicable ways. In these holistic approaches to literacy instruction, students read for authentic purposes, write for real audiences, and engage in the kinds of academic dialogue and social interaction that support the transfer of skills and strategies to other learning situations (Powell, Cantrell, & Adams, 2001; Smith & Wilhelm, 2006).

Meaningful literacy learning involves the development of students' critical thinking skills. Culturally responsive teachers help students view knowledge critically, and they often do so in ways that raise the socio-political consciousness of their students. While this aspect of culturally responsive instruction is addressed in depth in Chapter 9, it is useful to mention it here since culturally responsive teachers frame their pedagogical decision-making within a socio-political context. Culturally responsive teachers contextualize their literacy instruction to help their students understand the world and they challenge their students to become positive agents of change. Whether it is engaging students in a critical examination of views of beauty as did the teacher in Ladson-Billings' (2004) study of African American female teachers, or empowering students to confront the ways in which African Americans are disenfranchised in American society as did the teacher in Lynn's (2006) study of African American male teachers, culturally responsive teachers teach their students to think about important issues.

PRACTICAL APPLICATIONS

In the pages that follow, we present suggestions for implementing instructional practices that are culturally responsive. At the outset, we believe it is important to reiterate the role of "best practices" within a culturally responsive framework. Recently, a former elementary school principal shared an illustrative story about a new, White, upper-middle class teacher working in a diverse classroom that included many students from low-income families. The teacher was exasperated that she had used "best practices" to teach her students to write a narrative about their summer break, but the quality of students' narratives was disappointing. Her students had not written much at all. The teacher had modeled for students by writing her own narrative on the overhead projector, thinking aloud as she wrote. She had shared photographs to help students visualize and had provided plenty of explanations about the characteristics of good writing she wanted her students to include in their narratives. She told the principal she just did not understand why the students did not respond positively to her efforts. When the principal inquired further, the teacher shared that the topic of her modeled narrative was her family's three-week vacation to Europe. The principal gently asked if he might give it a try with her students, and the teacher agreed.

When the principal first talked about his own summer break with students, he told them he had not done much over break but that in many ways, it was his best summer ever. He had gardened, spent time with his family, and relaxed. The principal then modeled and explained good writing strategies as he composed his narrative on the overhead projector. The students responded by writing high quality narratives about their own experiences on summer break. Why the difference? We have concluded that the students could not connect the teacher's model of world travel to their own lives and experiences, but they could relate well to spending relaxing time with family. As this example illustrates, explicit, balanced instruction is insufficient for many children if the texts and tasks are not relevant to their experiences. Applying principles of culturally responsive pedagogy to actual classroom practice involves using students' own lives and strengths as the focal point.

Creating a Culturally Responsive Environment for Instruction

In talking with teachers about culturally responsive instruction, many will ask, "What does culturally responsive teaching look like in the classroom?" While culturally responsive teaching cannot be reduced to a particular set of strategies, there are instructional practices and approaches that teachers can utilize to create a more culturally relevant classroom environment for their students. As noted in Chapter 2, culturally responsive teachers exhibit genuine caring for their students, get to know them as individuals, and respect their cultural differences (Gay, 2000; Ladson-Billings, 1994). Culturally responsive teachers demonstrate high expectations for their students' learning and create opportunities to acquire the necessary knowledge required for school success. Culturally responsive teachers communicate their expectations for their students to help them monitor their academic success. For example, teachers can begin the day by asking their students to set goals for success in instructional and non-instructional endeavors, and at the end of the day, students can reflect on their successes and areas for improvement (Ladson-Billings, 1994).

As noted previously in Chapter 3, one way that culturally responsive teachers display caring for their students is through the type of classroom environment that they create. Gay (2000) notes that culturally responsive environments can be created through the use of symbols and visual imagery. Culturally responsive classrooms often feature pictures and posters reflecting people from a variety of cultures, as well as ethnic cloths, art work, and artifacts (Gay, 2000; Perry, 2003; Shade, Kelly, & Oberg, 1997). They include bright reading corners that feature a wide range of reading materials that highlight a variety of cultures and ethnicities (Callins, 2006; Gay, 2000; Montgomery, 2001). Gay (2000) shares a description of this type of book area in a kindergarten classroom:

> The room's "Reading Center" is a prototype of multicultural children's literature—a culturally responsive librarian's dream! Many different ethnic groups, topics, and literary types are included. Books, poems, comics, song lyrics, posters, magazines, and newspapers beckon the students to discover and read about the histories, families, myths, folktales, travels, troubles, triumphs, experiences, and daily lives of a wide variety of Asian, African, European, Middle Eastern, Latino, Native American, and Pacific Islander groups and individuals . . . These resources invite students to explore the past, to reflect on the present, and to imagine the future.
>
> (pp. 39–40)

In Tiffany's research conducted in culturally responsive classrooms, she noted that teachers communicated high expectations through visual imagery by featuring motivational signs and posters in their classroom, such as "You are above average," "You never know what you can do until you TRY," and "Believe you can" (Wheeler, 2007).

Because social activity and collaboration are essential elements of instruction that is culturally responsive, teachers need to help students develop respect for one another (Cartledge & Kourea, 2008; Ford, Howard, Harris, & Tyson, 2000; Haley & Capraro, 2001; Ladson-Billings, 1994; Montgomery, 2001). Many culturally responsive teachers take time at the beginning of the school year to create communal experiences where students can learn to appreciate each other's differences and similarities. One strategy that we have found effective for helping students learn to appreciate their classmates' cultural diversity and personal experiences is by asking them to create "Me Museums." Students bring items from home to represent themselves in a variety of categories (e.g. family, clothing, hobbies, food, housing, art, music) and tell the class why they chose the items and how they reflect their interests and personality. Students then might write an autobiography, memoir, or personal narrative. This activity enables students to learn more about each other and become more connected to one another, as well as strengthening students' verbal and written communication skills.

Incorporating Students' Prior Knowledge into Instruction

Culturally responsive teachers find ways to connect instruction to students' prior knowledge and experiences to make learning more relevant for them (Gay, 2000; Ladson-Billings, 1994; Villegas & Lucas, 2007; Wheeler, 2007). Villegas and Lucas (2007) describe teachers who use students' experiences as the basis for curricular units and topics. For instance, one group of teachers taught a unit based on the topic of immigration and used the students' personal experiences with immigration to guide the unit. Another example included an African American male teacher who used hip-hop songs to help students interpret the meaning of lyrics and then asked students to apply similar principles when analyzing more "traditional" literary texts, such as poems by Robert Frost. In the Introduction to this chapter, the African American kindergarten teacher used her students' prior knowledge and experiences to help students relate to the concept of leadership. She regularly invited community leaders, parents, and family members to her classroom to serve as guest speakers and role models.

An effective way to use students' existing knowledge to motivate their learning and enhance literacy skills is to introduce students to texts that relate to their lives and experiences. Tatum (2009) urges teachers to use "enabling" texts in their literacy instruction, particularly for African American male

169

students. Enabling texts are those that allow African American male students to identify with their particular social contexts and help them form positive relationships. In his study of African male adolescent students, Tatum found that enabling texts were texts that the students found significant and meaningful and generally contained the following four characteristics:

1 The texts promoted a healthy psyche.
2 They reflected an awareness of the real world.
3 They focused on the collective struggle of African Americans.
4 They served as a road map for being, doing, thinking, and acting. (p. 76)

Tatum also recommends asking students to map out their "textual lineage" to help them make connections between their lives and what they're reading. When he asked African American male middle and high-school students to identify books that they would always remember and write about why these texts resonated with them, the students identified texts that have been influential across several decades such as *The Autobiography of Malcolm X* (Haley, 1965), *Black Boy* (Wright, 1945), *A Raisin in the Sun* (Hansberry, 1958), *The Bible*, and *Up from Slavery* (Washington, 1919). These texts were powerful for students because they provided guidance for living life, reflected real-life family situations, and depicted African American challenges to which students could relate. Tatum noted that books African American males find meaningful and significant are often not included in the canonical texts that students are required to read. Culturally responsive teachers need to take time to identify books that will advance students' literacy skills and help them make connections to their own lives.

Exposing Students to Multiple Language Varieties

In addition to building on students' prior experiences, culturally responsive teachers incorporate children's language and culturally influenced communication styles into instruction. Culturally responsive teachers recognize that some students use language variations that may differ from Standard English, but they find ways to allow students to have opportunities to speak using their home discourse *and* learn standard conventions of English that will be expected in mainstream settings such as school and the workplace. This approach also helps students to know when to "codeswitch" and use language in ways that are appropriate in different contexts.

Many culturally responsive teachers use instructional materials that feature a variety of dialects and languages. An instructional approach called "contrastive analysis" helps students make connections between different types of language varieties (Heath, 1983; Hollie, 2005; Wheeler & Swords, 2004). Contrastive analysis involves the close examination of the similarities and differences of Standard English and other language varieties. One way a teacher might engage students in contrastive analysis is by using a poem or text that features a dialect other than Standard English to help students analyze and appreciate the dialect. A poem such as "Harriet Tubman" by Eloise Greenfield (Hudson & Hudson, 1993) might be used to help students explore differences in language varieties. With the teacher's guidance, students could translate a poem such as this into Standard English and discuss how the translation changes the mood, voice, or emphasis of the poem.

Another way that teachers can conduct contrastive analysis is to allow students to analyze the variations in their own vernacular, as well as to compare their vernacular with standard linguistic forms (Hollie, 2005; Rickford, 1999; Wheeler & Swords, 2004). For instance, teachers can encourage children to explore how language differs between formal and informal situations, and help them to realize that they need to "codeswitch" accordingly. In their study of a third-grade classroom, Wheeler and Swords (2004) found that contrastive analysis helped children to become more aware of rules across language varieties. For example, the teacher noticed that her students, who spoke African American Vernacular English (AAVE), did not follow conventional Standard English patterns to show possession. Students would say things like "Taylor cat is black" and "The boy coat is torn" (Wheeler & Swords, 2004). The teacher demonstrated a lesson on possessive patterns and compared the differences in the AAVE and Standard English forms. In so doing, the teacher affirmed the students' language while helping them to have a greater command of language variation so they would learn how to use language appropriately in different social contexts. The researchers found that teachers who conducted explicit lessons like these helped African American students who had previously scored lower on standardized tests, to improve their achievement and score at the same benchmark levels as White students.

In her ethnographic study, Heath (1983) provides examples of teachers who employ contrastive analysis during their instruction. One of the teachers, Mrs. Pat, asked her students to become language "detectives" in their school and community. During the first week of school, Mrs. Pat asked parents, community members, and school personnel to come to the class to talk about their ways of talking, as well as to explain what they read and wrote and how they used reading and writing. The students also listened to the speech used on radio and television broadcasts. The students discussed the linguistic diversity displayed by their classroom guests and the broadcast announcers. Also, Mrs. Pat introduced terms such as *dialect, casual, formal, conversational,* and *standard* to discuss the different

171

varieties of speech that people use in various situations. Mrs. Pat allowed students to learn about and value their own home language while introducing them to other language forms to help them appreciate linguistic diversity and develop communicative competence (Diller, 1999; Hymes, 1972). Helping students to develop linguistic competence is discussed in greater detail in the next chapter.

Providing Explicit Instruction

Culturally responsive teachers recognize that students of color, students who live in poverty, and English Learners benefit from explicit instruction of literacy skills and processes. As noted earlier, culturally responsive teachers help students understand when certain types of linguistic forms are expected. Another aspect of literacy instruction where explicit instruction is valuable is through vocabulary development. Many culturally responsive teachers explicitly address academic vocabulary development during instruction to enhance their students' understanding of key concepts and terms. Faith Brown, who was highlighted in the Introduction to this chapter, was a culturally responsive teacher who did this routinely during instruction. As a kindergarten teacher, Ms. Brown explicitly discussed vocabulary words and concepts during literacy instruction. For instance, during one lesson, Ms. Brown was reading the book, *Look for the Wheels*. She showed the students a picture of a steering wheel in the text, and one of the students called it a driving wheel. Ms. Brown went on to explain that "a driving wheel in a car or vehicle is called a steering wheel. A steering wheel. And what a steering wheel does is it determines the direction that the car is going in and whether it will go straight or to the left, to the right." Ms. Brown believed that emphasizing vocabulary development would help her students, especially her African American male students, develop more knowledge about Standard English and function better in middle-class, mainstream settings like school. She felt that this emphasis in her instruction was "raising the bar and exposing them to rich vocabulary because we need to be able to speak in that language."

An excellent example of how to expand students' vocabularies through culturally responsive teaching is found in the *Teachers' Voices* vignette included in this chapter. The teacher, Mr. Malo-juvera, uses many creative strategies to expand students' word knowledge. Despite the fact that he teaches in a middle school that is in a high poverty neighborhood, his students scored fourth on the Florida state assessment—a powerful testament to the use of culturally relevant vocabulary instruction.

TEACHERS' VOICES

Vocabulary Instruction in Diverse Classrooms

Victor Malo-juvera

EIGHTH GRADE LANGUAGE ARTS TEACHER, REDLAND MIDDLE SCHOOL, MIAMI, FL

These students can't learn this. *Where* do you think you are teaching?

These are the kinds of statements I heard as I started teaching language arts at a Title I middle school in Miami in 2004. My school was rated a "D" school by the state of Florida. Our student demographics are 60% Hispanic and 30% African-American; 84% of the school receives free/reduced lunch. When I looked around at some classes, I was stunned. They looked nothing like the English classes I had during my time in middle school, not because of the students, but because of the curriculum. The most glaring differences were the lack of novels and the complete absence of weekly vocabulary words. Vocabulary words formed the cornerstone of all of the English classes I had as a student, and I decided that in the classes I taught, vocabulary would play a pivotal role.

I was faced with a group of students who yearned to learn, but who essentially had been trained to hate school. The curriculum that a majority of teachers followed was geared toward practice for the state-administered standardized tests, and students had become accustomed to withholding their assent to learn. Therefore, I needed to do two things to get my students interested in learning vocabulary: (1) I had to choose vocabulary words that they could use regularly during each day; and (2) I had to get them excited about learning and using the vocabulary words.

The first step was to pick words. I decided to teach two different sets of words each week. The first 20 words were groups of synonyms for four words students were already familiar with. For example, the first week of school I start out with *a lot* as it relates to quantity (myriad, cornucopia, plethora, copious, profuse), *a lot* as it relates to frequency (perpetually, relentlessly, interminably, constantly, eternally), *good* (priceless, precious, splendid, outstanding, celestial) and *bad* (vile, vicious, pathetic, atrocious, disastrous). Because not all of the words are exact synonyms, students are shown the nuances between the definitions.

In addition to what I call the synonyms (sometimes cinnamons), I give my students what I call my Funky Fly Fresh words. These are words that many people would consider high level, and I get my kids excited by telling them that they are going to get to learn some words some that adults might not know. For the first

173

week, the words are *halcyon days, draconian, diatribe, vituperative* and *lambaste*. I always try to choose words that my students can easily use or identify in school or at home. For example, most of my students on the first day of school realize their *halcyon days* of summer are over when they are *lambasted* with a *vituperative diatribe* by a *draconian* teacher for not paying attention. I also teach the etymology of words, such as the tale of Ceyx and Alcyone for *halcyon days*, the story of Alexander the Great for *Gordian knot*, or even connecting Morpheus from *The Matrix* to his Greek father, Somnus, to teach *somniferous*.

Students promptly started to fail my tests. After discussions with students, I realized that most of them did not have adequate study skills to achieve in secondary school, so instead of lecturing them, I decided to teach the skills to them. I showed students how to make double-sided index cards for studying, and any student who brought their study cards on test day would get extra credit on the test. I also showed students how to use acronyms to memorize word lists. I gave them some acronyms and they came up with some on their own, some of them too creative for publication.

I also started doing cumulative reviews in different formats to engage students. One of my favorites is to let students pick teams. Team captains are based on vocabulary grade point average, and then the teams compete against each other in contests. Teams can also be rows of boys versus girls. The contests can be in "hockey style shootout" format, where one student shoots a word at another, or in team "horse race" reviews, where teams get points based on the difficulty of the words and move their horse around a track. The first to reach the finish line is the winner and gets a 10% bonus on the test, the second gets 5%, and third 2.5%. No matter what the contest, I always give the winners extra credit toward the cumulative exam. This works well as it motivates the students to study for the review and creates active learning.

Infusing the vocabulary into the culture of my class is equally critical. If students want to use the bathroom, their request must contain at least one vocabulary word for each week in the semester. (Yes, that means around the winter holidays students need to put about 14 words into a request.) Students are allowed to use their notebooks and sometimes to get help from classmates. Needless to say, students who have mastered vocabulary become immensely popular. It also makes for some hilarious requests. Because I have a supportive administration, I also give students extra credit if they can "teach" visitors a word they do not know. This means every time an administrator or visitor from the district or state comes by, my students literally leap at the opportunity to teach them words. Many times educators will sit and "spar" with my students on vocabulary, and my administrators love that my students are so aggressive about their learning.

My favorite assignment with vocabulary is for students to make a 40-line poem, song, or rap (their favorite), using at least one vocabulary word per line. Students read their poem or perform their rap in front of the class, and this is always one the best days of the year. Students will regularly challenge me to rap with them, and I have been schooled on more than one occasion by students who are deemed failures by others.

Here's one example of a student's rap:

I'm **loquacious** with my bros,
intimidate my foes,
I usually look tight
augmented by my fro
I'm the new Santana, **cherished** by the pros
If you want my story, here is how it goes
Haters **abhor** me
Ladies **adore** me
If you mess with me
get ready to pay the fee
I'll bust my **arcane** knowledge of geometry.

Juan J. Rodriguez, 8th Grade, Redland Middle School

Explicit instruction in literacy skills and strategies supported by teacher scaffolding is particularly important for English Language Learners (Shanahan & Beck, 2006). Avalos, Plasencia, Chavez, and Rascon (2007–2008) recommend an approach called modified guided reading (MGR) to support English Language Learners' literacy development. Guided reading is an important part of a balanced literacy program that helps to provide differentiated instruction to small groups of students several times a week (Fountas & Pinnell, 1996). During guided reading instruction, teachers provide explicit instruction about reading strategies and skills, often using leveled readers that are appropriate for students' instructional levels. In traditional guided reading instruction, the teacher leads a guided discussion about the features of the text, encouraging the students to use strategies such as taking "picture walks" and predicting before they read a text. Students usually read the text on their own silently, and teachers prompt students to use problem solving strategies when they come to words that they don't know. MGR builds upon these guided reading components and provides additional scaffolding for English Language Learners by incorporating culturally relevant texts that relate to students' lives (Avalos et al., 2007–2008). MGR differs from typical guided reading lessons in that the teacher reads the text aloud to students to generate discussions to support comprehension and vocabulary, and vocabulary journals and writing assignments are connected to the guided reading text. Teachers use the text to provide explicit demonstrations of reading strategies and engage students in "word work" that focuses on morphological awareness, phonemic awareness, or phonics.

Promoting Collaborative Learning

In addition to explicit instruction that is contextualized in students' lives and experiences, students from diverse backgrounds also benefit from opportunities to engage in collaborative and inquiry-based learning. Collaborative learning is particularly beneficial for English Language Learners because it gives them an opportunity to learn from their peers and feel more comfortable as they adapt to an English-speaking classroom environment (Gersten et al., 2007). Christian (2001) suggests that teachers engage students in instructional units that allow them to interact as a community of learners. For instance, Christian documents how middle school students involved in an inquiry-based, interdisciplinary unit learned about their own community of Nikiski, Alaska. The unit integrated math, science, social studies, and language arts, and students acted as "historians, scientists, statisticians, and writers" (p. 60). Students chronicled their community by writing poetry, conducting oral history interviews, and analyzing statistics and worked collaboratively in many aspects of the project. Projects like these allow students to learn how to compromise and work together as a community and acquire higher-level thinking skills.

Tatum (2009) highlighted the importance of collaborative writing for African American male adolescents. He designed a five-week African American Adolescent Male Summer Literacy Institute (AAAMSLI) for the reading clinic at the University of Illinois in Chicago in which African American males from various public schools in the Chicago area worked collaboratively to write poetry, short stories, children's literature and other texts to become more aware of social justice issues. Tatum found consistently that young African American males at various ages learned more by working together and thought that the institute should be extended, because they wanted more time to read and write together. Examples like this indicate that teachers should provide opportunities in the classroom for students to critique and analyze texts collaboratively and write together so that they can see the relevance of literacy in their lives.

The Power of Inquiry-Based Learning

Collaborative and inquiry-oriented instruction can raise students' socio-political consciousness in addition to supporting students' literacy skills and competencies. Inquiry-based learning reflects Wlodkowski and Ginsberg's (1995) framework for motivation, as this type of learning helps to establish inclusion, develop positive attitudes about learning, enhance meaning for students and engender student competence. Powell, Cantrell, and Adams (2001) documented a year-long inquiry project in which fourth-grade students examined the issue of strip mining, a controversial topic in the state in which they lived, and considered the issue from multiple perspectives. Students conducted research using books, articles, newspapers and the internet to investigate the advantages and disadvantages of strip mining. They invited coal advocates to the classroom to discuss the importance of strip mining to communities and the economy. They wrote letters to the editor of their newspaper to express their views about the issue. They even visited a community in another part of the state in which the highest peak in the state was slated to be strip mined and visited with members of the local community. When the students decided to join forces with children in that community to stop strip mining of that mountain, they learned that they could use literacy to effect powerful change in the world. Their efforts, which included testimony before the state legislature, contributed to an agreement by coal operators to preserve a significant portion of the mountain. In this inquiry project, even students who were typically disengaged in literacy found motivation for strengthening their skills for acquiring knowledge and communicating to others.

The current emphasis on standards and accountability for teaching specific and sometimes discrete knowledge and skills does not preclude providing students with choice and engaging them in project-based inquiry learning. Through a "backward planning" process, teachers can identify what students need to know and be able to do, provide explicit instruction in those concepts and processes, and scaffold students' competence in the context of authentic and meaningful literacy activities (Smith & Wilhelm, 2006). In the strip mining project described above, teachers mapped potential project activities on to the state standards for accountability to ensure that all standards were addressed through the project. This ensured that students learned the content they were expected to learn, and students performed well on the state assessment.

Inquiry projects do not have to include such lofty goals, however. For instance, Powell and Davidson (2005) describe a project with kindergarteners that used literacy that was situated in children's play. The project began with a "field study" to the local donut shop. During their visit, the children took notes and recorded the steps in making donuts. They subsequently created books and charts and used what they learned to create their own "Donut House" in the classroom. The project included visits from local bankers to acquire a loan, personal letters from shareholders, and an inspection of their enterprise by the city's building inspector. Children were engaged in numerous literacy experiences, including reading signs, experience charts, materials lists, letters from shareholders, picture charts, and labels; and writing thank-you letters, lists, stock certificates, building permit forms, loan applications, invitations, signs, and labels. Children acquired sophisticated vocabulary and grew in their development of print concepts, and many were able to read words such as "building inspector" and "vice president" when they were presented within a meaningful context.

In their book *Ladybugs, Tornadoes, and Swirling Galaxies: English Language Learners Discover Their World through Inquiry* (2006), Buhrow and Garcia provide detailed accounts of how they guide their young students in the inquiry process. For instance, a study of insects begins with reading numerous texts about the topic, such as information books, big books, and posters. The children then go outside to collect their own insects, which are placed in jars for a classroom "insect museum." Together, they begin to generate questions about insects, which are written on sticky notes and organized according to topics. They also develop a word wall of academic vocabulary related to their study. Once the class has studied about and observed insects, the children come up with individual topics for further research. The authors write that: "Some of [the students] might start by taking notes, and others start with their illustrations and art—it's all good. It is a cyclical process, and each of them will work in his or her own way" (p. 83). During this time of individual research, the teachers confer with the children and carefully observe their use of language and skills. The insect study culminates with a "mind map," which begins with a main idea ("insects") and has various "stems" that represent important connections ("insects that fly, and ones that don't"). Together, they fill in the mind map with important details that they have acquired through their inquiry.

Inquiry-based methods can be used with virtually any subject area. The main difference between inquiry and more traditional learning is that an inquiry study begins with students' questions. Reading, writing, and research skills are taught as students are engaged in purposeful learning. Publication can take a variety of forms, from posters and student-created books, to PowerPoint presentations, museum displays, and drama productions.

Inquiry-based learning projects allow students to enhance their literacy skills *and* help teachers get a sense of their students' social contexts. McGinnis (2007) found that inquiry-based learning projects are particularly beneficial in that they foster a caring and supportive classroom environment and draw upon "the multilingual and multimodal nature of students' literacy and language practices" (p. 571). During a summer program in an urban community of the northeastern United States, the middle-school students, who had recently come from China, Vietnam, and Cambodia, came up with questions that they wanted to study, such as exploring the origins of rap music in the United States and learning more about fruit from their native countries. They used different modes of learning, including visual images, written text, and music, to investigate their topics and share their research findings. The students were at varying levels of English acquisition, but the inquiry-based projects allowed them space to use their understandings of literacy in their native languages to connect to new under-standings of English. These projects also allowed the students in this program to investigate their own interests, collaborate with their peers to form a bond, and reflect on their cultural identities. Further resources for inquiry learning are given on p. 189.

Inquiry-based learning can be an integral part of pedagogical reform for teachers in urban settings. Peck (2010) found that a school called "Quest" (a pseudonym), with a low-achieving and diverse student population located in a large northeast city, experienced much success when it implemented more inquiry-based learning in its instructional program. Before it began using inquiry-based learning, the school had used traditional types of materials such as basal readers and textbooks during instruction, but the students had low levels of achievement. When the school began utilizing more innovative approaches such as inquiry-based learning to reform its instructional program, student achievement soared and teachers worked more collaboratively to create an engaging curriculum to help their students achieve academic success. Teachers and students worked together to select problems to study based on interests and curriculum standards, and teachers in this school began to use a wide variety of resources to engage students' learning, such as children's literature, online resources, magazines, museum displays, podcasts, and videos. In one sixth-grade class at Quest, students participated in a study of leaders in which they compared contemporary leaders, including President Obama, to those in early Greece. During the study, the students read a variety of texts, including online resources, and interacted with various leaders in their community. Culminating projects included letters on the nature of leadership and comic books that focused on heroes. Through inquiry-based learning, the teachers at Quest learned what made students passionate and developed instruction that was interesting and relevant. This example of school-wide pedagogical change certainly fits well with the principles of culturally responsive teaching that we present in this chapter and that are presented throughout this book.

CONCLUSION

Classrooms in the United States are becoming increasingly more diverse, and this provides both challenges and opportunities for teachers to implement engaging, rigorous, and meaningful literacy instruction. Culturally responsive teachers possess a sociocultural consciousness that enables them to make

179

thoughtful instructional decisions to maximize students' learning. They begin with solid instructional practices, understanding that explicit instruction of literacy strategies is especially beneficial to culturally and linguistically diverse students, who are often navigating both a new culture and a new language. While what researchers have deemed "best practices" for literacy instruction provide an important foundation for increasing students' literacy achievement, closing the gap requires that we extend these practices and consider the sociocultural parameters for literacy teaching and learning. Culturally responsive teachers embrace the varied backgrounds of their students by building upon their students' prior knowledge and incorporating texts that relate to students' lives. They work diligently to provide culturally congruent instruction to make learning more relevant and meaningful. Teachers who utilize culturally responsive instructional practices create classroom settings that allow for rich collaborative learning experiences and rigorous inquiry-based approaches. Culturally responsive teachers also understand the role of language in students' literacy development, and help students to make connections between their home language and the standard discourse and to acquire academic vocabulary.

Implementing culturally responsive literacy instruction can be challenging, but it can also be extremely rewarding work. We have found that culturally responsive classrooms are invigorating. Students are excited about learning and are confident in their ability to learn. It is important to note, however, that such classrooms are often characterized by a much higher activity level than in more traditional classrooms. As discussed throughout this chapter, social activity and collaboration are essential elements in culturally responsive instruction. Thus, students are often "in motion"; they are actively engaged in inquiry; they are having regular conversations with peers. Conceptualizing literacy as a *social* construct requires that we acknowledge that authentic uses of literacy are communal; that is, they always involve communication or the active sharing of ideas.

While teaching in a culturally responsive way may take many of us "outside of our comfort zones," we argue that teachers and schools need to begin adapting instructional practices to make them more culturally appropriate for the students we serve. Becoming culturally responsive is an achievable goal for teachers from all backgrounds, and we hope that this chapter has provided some insights about how teachers can enhance their literacy instruction to make literacy learning a reality for all students.

Table 7.1 Summary of CRIOP Component: Pedagogy/Instruction

Element	What you would expect to see in a classroom where CRI practices are occurring	What you would expect to see in a classroom where CRI practices are not occurring
Instruction is contextualized in students' lives and experiences.	Literacy tasks and texts relate directly to students' lives outside of school; classroom interaction patterns and communication structures match those found in students' homes and communities; the teacher builds on students' existing cultural knowledge in literacy lessons and activities.	Literacy tasks and texts reflect the values and experiences of dominant ethnic and cultural groups; only interaction patterns and communication structures of the dominant group are deemed acceptable.
The teacher learns with students.	The teacher learns about diverse perspectives along with students; s/he engages students in the inquiry process and learns from students' investigations.	The teacher is the authority; students are not encouraged to challenge or question ideas presented or to engage in further inquiry.
The teacher allows students to collaborate with one another.	Students work in pairs and small groups to read, write, and discuss texts; the teacher works to equalize existing status differences among students.	Students read and write in isolation; students are not permitted to help one another or to work together in pairs or groups.
Students engage in active, hands-on literacy tasks.	Literacy tasks allow students to be physically active.	Students work passively at their seats on teacher-directed tasks.
The teacher gives students choices based on their experiences, values, needs and strengths.	Students have multiple opportunities to choose texts, topics, and modes of expression based on preferences and personal relevance.	The teacher selects reading texts, writing topics, and modes of expression for students.
The teacher balances instruction using both explicit skill instruction and reading/writing for meaning.	Instruction is rigorous and cognitively challenging for students from all ethnic, linguistic, and socio-economic backgrounds; the teacher models and explains skills and strategies and provides appropriate scaffolding for students; students apply skills and strategies in the context of meaningful and personally relevant literacy activities.	Instruction focuses on low-level skills; students engage in isolated and repetitive tasks that are disconnected from each other; students practice skills in ways that are not meaningful or personally relevant to students.

181

Table 7.1 Continued

Element	What you would expect to see in a classroom where CRI practices are occurring	What you would expect to see in a classroom where CRI practices are not occurring
The teacher focuses on developing students' vocabularies.	The teacher provides explicit instruction in the meaning of words and students practice using new words in a variety of meaningful contexts; students learn independent word learning strategies such as morphology, contextual analysis, and cognates.	Little attention is paid to vocabulary instruction or new words are taught outside of meaningful contexts; students are not taught independent word learning strategies.

REFLECTIVE ACTIVITIES

1 Think of the various cultural, linguistic, and socio-economic groups that are represented by the students in your classroom. Research the cultural norms of those groups that might be different from your own. Consider how cultural norms might influence students' learning styles, and list some ways that you might adapt your instruction to accommodate the learning styles of all of the students in your classroom.
2 Take an inventory of your classroom library. How many of the books reflect diverse cultural experiences? How do the books reflect the lives of your students?
3 List examples of culturally responsive instructional practices that you currently utilize. How can you incorporate more culturally responsive practices into your instruction?
4 Make a list of topics that you currently teach that could incorporate inquiry-based learning. How do you (or will you) integrate students' interests into your curriculum planning?
5 What opportunities do students currently have to collaborate with their peers in your classroom? What are some additional ways that your students could work collaboratively?

REFERENCES

Au, K. H. (1980). Participation structures in a reading lesson with Hawaiian children: Analysis of a culturally appropriate instructional event. *Anthropology and Education Quarterly, 11*, 91–115.

Au, K. H. (1993). *Literacy instruction in multicultural settings*. Orlando, FL: Harcourt Brace.

Au, K. H., & Mason, J. M. (1983). Cultural congruence in classroom participation structures: Achieving a balance of rights. *Discourse Processes, 6*, 145–167.

Avalos, M. A., Plasencia, A., Chavez, C., & Rascón, J. (2007). Modified guided reading: Gateway to English as a second language classroom. *The Reading Teacher, 61*(4), 318–329.

Beck, I. L., & McKeown, M. G. (2007). Increasing young low-income children's oral vocabulary repertoires through rich and focused instruction. *Elementary School Journal, 107*, 251–271.

Bereiter, C., & Engelmann, S. (1966). *Teaching disadvantaged children in the preschool*. Englewood Cliffs, NJ: Prentice-Hall.

Biancanrosa, G., & Snow, C. (2004). *Reading next: A vision for action and research in middle and high school literacy: A report to Carnegie Corporation of New York*. Washington, DC: Alliance for Excellent Education.

Biemiller, A. (2001). Teaching vocabulary: Early, direct, and sequential. *American Educator, 25*, 24–28, 47.

Brown, R., Pressley, M., Van Meter, P., & Schuder, T. (1996). A quasi-experimental validation of transactional strategies instruction with low-achieving second-grade readers. *Journal of Educational Psychology, 88*, 18–37.

Buhrow, B., & Garcia, A. U. (2006). *Ladybugs, tornadoes, and swirling galaxies: English Language Learners discover their world through inquiry*. Portland, ME: Stenhouse.

Callins, T. (2006). Culturally responsive literacy instruction. *Teaching Exceptional Children, 39*(2), 62–65.

Calderón, M., Hertz-Lazarowitz, R., & Slavin, R. E. (1998). Effects of Bilingual Cooperative Integrated Reading and Composition on students making the transition from Spanish to English reading. *Elementary School Journal, 99*, 153–165.

Cantrell, S. C. (1998). Effective teaching and literacy learning: A look inside primary classrooms. *The Reading Teacher, 52*, 370–378.

Cantrell, S. C. (1999). The effects of literacy instruction on primary students' reading and writing achievement. *Reading Research and Instruction, 39*(1), 3–26.

Cartledge, G., & Kourea, L. (2008). Culturally responsive classrooms for culturally diverse students with and at risk for disabilities. *Exceptional Children, 74*(3), 351–371.

Cazden, C. B. (1988). *Classroom discourse: The language of teaching and learning*. Portsmouth, NH: Heinemann.

Christian, S. (2001). *Writing to make a difference*. New York: Teacher's College Press.

Cohen, E. G. (1994). Restructuring the classroom: Conditions for productive small groups. *Review of Educational Research, 64*, 1–35.

Compton-Lilly, C. (2004). *Confronting racism, poverty and power: Classroom strategies to change the world*. Portsmouth, NH: Heinemann.

Coyne, M. D., Simmons, D. C., & Kame'enui, E. J. (2004). Vocabulary instruction for young children at risk of experiencing reading difficulties: Teaching word meanings during shared storybook readings. In J. F. Baumann & E. J. Kame'enui (Eds.), *Vocabulary instruction: Research to practice* (pp. 41–58). New York: Guilford Press.

Delpit, L. (1995). *Other people's children: Cultural conflict in the classroom.* New York: The New Press.

Dill, E., & Boykin, A. W. (2000). The comparative influence of individual, peer tutoring, and communal learning on text recall of African American children. *Journal of Black Psychology, 26,* 65–78.

Diller, D. (1999). Opening the dialogue: Using culture as a tool in teaching young African-American children. *The Reading Teacher, 52*(8), 820–828.

Duffy, G. G. (1993). Teachers' progress toward becoming expert strategy teachers. *The Elementary School Journal, 94,* 109–120.

Ehri, L. C., & Rosenthal, J. (2007). Spellings of words: A neglected facilitator of vocabulary learning. *Journal of Literacy Research, 29,* 289–409.

Fairbanks, C., Cooper, J., Masterson, L., & Webb, S. (2009). Culturally responsive instruction and the impact on reading comprehension. In S. E. Israel & G. G. Duffy (Eds.), *Handbook of research on reading comprehension* (pp. 587–606). New York: Routledge.

Farris, P. J., Fuhler, C. J., & Walther, M. P. (2004). *Teaching reading: A balanced approach for today's classrooms.* New York: McGraw-Hill.

Fitzgerald, J. (1999). What is this thing called balance? *The Reading Teacher, 52,* 100–107.

Ford, D. Y., Howard, T. C., Harris, J. J., & Tyson, C. A. (2000). Creating culturally responsive classrooms for gifted African American students. *Journal for the Education of the Gifted, 23,* 397–427.

Fountas, I. C., & Pinnell, G. S. (1996). *Guided reading: Good first teaching for all children.* Portsmouth, NH: Heinemann.

Gay, G. (2000). *Culturally responsive teaching.* New York: Teachers College Press.

Gersten, R., Baker, S., Shanahan, T., Linan Thompson, S., Collins, P., & Scarcella, R. (2007). *Effective literacy and English language instruction for English learners in the elementary grades: A practical guide* (No. NCEE 2007-4011). Washington, DC: National Center for Education, Evaluation and Regional Assistance, Institute for Education Sciences, U. S. Department of Education.

Gersten, R., & Jiménez, R. T. (1994). A delicate balance: Enhancing literature instruction for students of English as a second language. *The Reading Teacher, 47,* 438–449.

Ginsberg, M.B., & Wlodkowski, R.J. (2000). *Creating high motivating classrooms for all students: A schoolwide approach to powerful teaching with diverse learners.* San Francisco, CA: Jossey-Bass.

Graves, M. F. (2006). *The vocabulary book: Learning and instruction.* New York: Teachers College Press.

Griffith, L. W., & Rasinski, T. V. (2004). A focus on fluency: How one teacher incorporated fluency with her reading curriculum. *Reading Teacher, 58,* 126–137.

Guthrie, J. T., McGough, K., Bennett, L., & Rice, M.E. (1996). Concept-Oriented Reading Instruction: An integrated curriculum to develop motivations and strategies for reading. In L. Baker, P. Afflerbach, & D. Reinking (Eds.), *Developing engaged readers in school and home communities.* (pp. 165–190). Mahwah, NJ: Lawrence Erlbaum Associates.

Guthrie, J. T., & Wigfield, A. (2000). Engagement and motivation in reading. In M. L., Kamil, P. B., Mosenthal, P. D. Pearson, & R. Barr (Eds.) *Handbook of reading research* (Vol. 3, pp. 403–421). Mahwah, NJ: Erlbaum.

Gutiérrez, K. (2008). Developing a sociocritical literacy in the third space. *Reading Research Quarterly, 43,* 148–164.

Gutiérrez, K., Baquedano-Lopez, P., & Tejada, C. (1999). Rethinking diversity: Hybridity and hybrid language practices in the Third Space. *Mind, Culture, and Activity, 6,* 286–303.

Gutiérrez, K., Baquedano-Lopez, P., & Turner, M. G. (1997). Putting language back into language arts: When the radical middle meets the Third Space. *Language Arts, 74,* 368–378.

Gutiérrez, K., Rymes, B., & Larson, J. (1995). Script, counterscript, and underlife in the classroom: James Brown versus *Brown v. Board of Education. Harvard Educational Review, 65,* 445–471.

Hale, J. E. (1982). *Black children: Their roots, culture, and learning style.* Provo, UT: Brigham Young University Press.

Haley, A. (1965) *The autobiography of Malcolm X* (1st ed.). New York: Grove Press.

Haley, A., & Malcolm X. (1999). *The autobiography of Malcolm X: As told to Alex Haley.* New York: Random House.

Haley, D. L., & Capraro, R.M. (2001). Strategies for teaching in heterogeneous environments while building a classroom community. *Education, 122*(1), 80–86.

Hammerberg, D. D. (2004). Comprehension instruction for socioculturally diverse classrooms: A review of what we know. *The Reading Teacher, 57,* 648–658.

Hanna, J. L. (1988). *Disruptive school behavior: Class, race, and culture.* New York: Holmes & Meier.

Hansberry, L. (1958). *A raisin in the sun.* New York: Random House.

Heath, S. B. (1983). *Ways with words: Language, life, and work in communities and classrooms.* Cambridge: Cambridge University Press.

Hollie, S. (2005). Acknowledging the language of African American students: Instruction that works. In B. Hammond, M. E. R. Hoover, & I. P. McPhail (Eds.), *Teaching African American learners to read: Perspectives and practices* (pp. 189–199). Newark, DE: International Reading Association.

Hudson, W., & Hudson, C. (1993). *Pass it on: African American poems for children.* New York: Scholastic.

Hymes, D. (1972). Models of the interaction of language and social life. In J. Gumperz & D. Hymes (Eds.), *Directions in sociolinguistics: The ethnography of communication* (pp. 35–71). New York: Holt, Rinehart & Winston.

Jacob, E., Rottenberg, L., Patrick, S., & Wheeler, E., (1996). Cooperative learning: Context and opportunities for acquiring academic English. *TESOL Quarterly, 30,* 253–280.

Jiménez, R. T. (1997). The strategic reading abilities and potential of five low-literacy Latina/o readers in middle school. *Reading Research Quarterly, 32,* 224–243.

Jiménez, R. T., Garcia, G. E., & Pearson, P. D. (1996). The reading strategies of bilingual Latina/o students who are successful English readers: Opportunities and obstacles. *Reading Research Quarterly, 31,* 90–112.

Jiménez, R. T., & Gersten, R. (1999). Lessons and dilemmas derived from the literacy instruction of two Latino/a teachers. *American Educational Research Journal, 36,* 265–301.

185

Johnson, D. W., Johnson, T. R., & Holubec, E. J. (1993). *Cooperation in the classroom* (6th ed.). Edina, MN: Interaction Book Company.

Juel, C., Biancarosa, G., Coker, D., & Deffes, R. (2003). Walking with Rosie: A cautionary tale of literacy instruction. *Educational Leadership, 60*(7), 12–18.

Kong, A., & Fitch, E. (2002–2003). Using book clubs to engage culturally and linguistically diverse learners in reading, writing, and talking about books. *The Reading Teacher, 56,* 352–362.

Ladson-Billings, G. (1994). *The dreamkeepers: Successful teachers of African American children.* San Francisco: Jossey-Bass.

Ladson-Billings, G. (1995). Toward a theory of culturally relevant pedagogy. *American Educational Research Journal, 32,* 465–491.

Ladson-Billings, G. (2004). Landing on the wrong note: The price we paid for *Brown. Educational Researcher, 33,* 3–13.

Lee, C. D. (1995). A culturally based cognitive apprenticeship: Teaching African American high school students skills in literary instruction. *Reading Research Quarterly, 30,* 608–603.

Lee, C. D. (2001). Is October Brown Chinese? A cultural modeling activity system for underachieving students. *American Educational Research Journal, 38,* 97–142.

Lee, C. D. (2006). Every good-bye ain't gone: Analyzing the cultural underpinnings of classroom talk. *International Journal of Qualitative Studies in Education, 19,* 305–327.

Lee, C. D. (2007). *Culture, literacy, and learning: Taking bloom in the midst of the whirlwind.* New York: Teachers College Press.

Lynn, M. (2006). Education for the community: Exploring the culturally relevant practices of Black male teachers. *Teachers College Record, 108,* 2497–2522.

Maloch, B. (2005). On the road to literature discussion groups: Teacher scaffolding during preparatory experiences. *Reading Research and Instruction, 44,* 44–64.

Martinez, M., Roser, N., & Strecker, S. (1999). "I never thought I could be a star": A Reader's Theatre ticket to reading fluency. *The Reading Teacher, 52,* 326–334.

Martinez-Roldan, C. M. (2003). Building worlds and identities: A case study of the role of narratives in bilingual literature discussions. *Research in the Teaching of English, 337,* 491–526.

McGinnis, T. A. (2007). Khmer rap boys, X-men, Asia's fruits, and Dragonball Z: Creating multilingual and multimodal classroom contexts. *Journal of Adolescent and Adult Literacy, 50*(7), 570–579.

McIntyre, E., & Pressley, M. (Eds.). (1996). *Balanced instruction: Strategies and skills in whole language.* Norwood, MA: Christopher Gordon.

Moll, L., Amanti, C., Neff, D., & González, N. (1992). Funds of knowledge for teaching: Using a qualitative approach to connect homes and classrooms. *Theory into Practice, 31,* 132–141.

Moll, L. C., & González, N. (1994). Lessons from research with language-minority children. *Journal of Reading Behavior, 26,* 439–456.

Montgomery, W. (2001). Creating culturally responsive, inclusive classrooms. *Teaching Exceptional Children, 33*(4), 4–9.

Morrow, L. M., Tracey, D. H., Woo, D. G., & Pressley, M. (1999). Characteristics of exemplary first-grade literacy instruction. *The Reading Teacher, 52,* 462–476.

Nagy, W. E., Anderson, R. C., & Herman, P. A. (1987). Learning word meanings from context during normal reading. *American Educational Research Journal, 24,* 237–270.

National Institute of Child Health and Human Development (NICHD) (2000). *Report of the National Reading Panel. Teaching children to read: An evidence-based assessment of the scientific research literature on reading and its implications for reading instruction* (NIH Publication No. 00-4769). Washington, DC: U.S. Government Printing Office.

National Reading Panel (2000). *Report of the National Reading Panel: Reports of the subgroups.* Washington, DC: National Institute of Child Health and Human Development Clearinghouse.

Nieto, S., & Bode, P. (2008). *Affirming diversity: The sociopolitical context of multicultural education* (5th ed.). Boston, MA: Allyn & Bacon.

Palinscar, A. S., & Brown, A. L. (1984). Reciprocal teaching of comprehension-fostering and comprehension-monitoring activities. *Cognition and Instruction, 1,* 117–175.

Paris, S. G., Cross, D. R., & Lipson, M. Y. (1984). Informed strategies for learning: A program to improve children's reading awareness and comprehension. *Journal of Educational Psychology, 76,* 1239–1252.

Paris, S. G., & Jacobs, J. E., (1984). The benefits of informed instruction for children's reading awareness and comprehension skills. *Child Development, 55,* 2083–2093.

Paris, S. G., & Oka, E. R. (1986). Children's reading strategies, metacognition, and motivation. *Developmental Review, 6,* 25–56.

Peck, S. M. (2010). Not on the same page but working together: Lessons from an award-winning urban elementary school. *The Reading Teacher, 63*(5), 394–403.

Pérez, B. (1998). *Sociocultural contexts of language and literacy.* Mahwah, NJ: Erlbaum.

Pérez, E., (1994). Spanish literacy development: A descriptive study of four bilingual whole-language classrooms. *Journal of Reading Behavior, 26,* 75–94.

Perry, T. (2003). Up from the parched earth: Toward a theory of African-American achievement. In T. Perry, C. Steele, & A. Hilliard (Eds.), *Young, gifted, and Black: Promoting high achievement among African American students.* Boston, MA: Beacon Press.

Powell, R., Cantrell, S., & Adams, S. (2001). Saving Black Mountain: The promise of critical literacy in a multicultural democracy. *The Reading Teacher, 54,* 772–781.

Powell, R., & Davidson, N. (2005). The donut house: Real world literacy in an urban kindergarten classroom. *Language Arts, 82*(5), 248–256.

Powell, R., McIntyre, E., & Rightmyer, E. C. (2006). Johnny won't read, and Susie won't either: Reading instruction and student resistance, *Journal of Research in Early Childhood Literacy, 6*(1), 5–31.

Pressley, M., El-Dinary, P. B., Gaskins, I., Schuder, T., Bergman, J. L., Almasi, J., & Brown, R. (1992). Beyond direct explanation: Transactional instruction of reading comprehension strategies. *Elementary School Journal, 92,* 513–555.

Rickford, J. R. (1999). Language diversity and academic achievement in the education of African American students: An overview of the issues. In C. T. Adger, D. Christian, & Y. O. Taylor (Eds.), *Making the connection: Language and academic achievement among African American students* (pp. 1–29). Washington, DC: Center for Applied Linguistics.

Ruddell, M. R., & Shearer, B. A. (2002). "Extraordinary," "tremendous," "exhilarating," "magnificent": Middle school at-risk students become avid word learners with the

Vocabulary Self-Collection Strategy (VSS). *Journal of Adolescent and Adult Literacy, 45,* 352–363.

Schmoker, M. (2006). *Results now: How we can achieve unprecedented improvements in teaching and learning.* Alexandria, VA: Association for Supervision and Curriculum Development.

Sénéchal, M., Thomas, E., & Monker, J. (1995). Individual differences in four year olds' acquisition of vocabulary during storybook reading. *Journal of Educational Psychology, 87,* 218–229.

Shade, B. J. (1994). Understanding the African American learner. In E. R. Hollins, J. E. King, & W. C. Hayman (Eds.), *Teaching diverse populations: Formulating a knowledge base* (pp. 175–189). New York: State University of New York Press.

Shade, B. J., Kelly, C., & Oberg, M. (1997). *Creating culturally responsive classrooms.* Washington, DC: American Psychological Association.

Shanahan, T., & Beck, I. L. (2006). Effective literacy teaching for English-language learners. In D. August, & T. Shanahan (Eds.), *Developing literacy in second-language learners: Report of the National Literacy Panel on Language-Minority Children and Youth* (pp. 415–488). Mahwah, NJ: Erlbaum.

Short, D. J. (1994). Expanding middle school horizons: Integrating language, culture, and social studies. *TESOL Quarterly, 28,* 581–608.

Slavin, R. E., & Cook, R. (1999). Improving intergroup relations: Lessons from cooperative learning programs. *Journal of Social Issues, 55,* 647–663.

Smith, M. W., & Wilhelm, J. D. (2006). *Going with the flow: How to engage boys (and girls) in their literacy learning.* Portsmouth, NH: Heinemann.

Snow, C. E., Burns, M. S., & Griffin, P. (1998). *Preventing reading difficulties in young children.* Washington, DC: National Academy Press.

Taffe, S. W., Blachowicz, C. L. Z., & Fisher, P. J. (2009). Vocabulary instruction for diverse students. In L. M. Morrow, R. Rueda, & D. Lapp (Eds.), *Research on literacy and diversity* (pp. 320–337). New York: The Guilford Press.

Tatum, A. W. (2009). *Reading for their life: Re-building the textual lineages of African American adolescent males.* Portsmouth, NH: Heinemann.

Taylor, B. M., Pearson, P. D., Peterson, D. S., & Rodriguez, M. C. (1993). Reading growth in high-poverty classrooms: The influence of teacher practices that encourage cognitive engagement in literacy learning. *Elementary School Journal, 104,* 3–28.

Tharp, R. G., & Gallimore, R. D. (1988). *Rousing minds to life: Teaching, learning, and schooling in social context.* Cambridge: Cambridge University Press.

Tompkins, G. E. (2005). *Literacy for the 21st century: A balanced approach* (4th ed.). Upper Saddle River, NJ: Pearson.

Turner, J. C. (1995). The influence of classroom contexts on young children's motivation for literacy. *Reading Research Quarterly, 30,* 410–441.

Villegas, A. M., & Lucas, T. (2007). The culturally responsive teacher. *Educational Leadership, 64*(6), 28–33.

Vygotsky, L. (1978). *Mind in society.* London: Harvard University Press.

Washington, B. T. (1919). *Up from slavery: An autobiography.* Garden City, NY: Doubleday, Page & Co.

Wharton-McDonald, R., Pressley, M., & Hampston, J. M. (1998). Literacy instruction in nine first-grade classrooms: Teacher characteristics and student achievement. *The Elementary School Journal, 99,* 101–128.

Wharton-McDonald, R., Pressley, M., Ranking, J., & Mistretta, J. (1997). Effective primary-grades literacy instruction = balanced literacy instruction. *The Reading Teacher, 50,* 518–521.

Wheeler, R. S., & Swords, R. (2004). Codeswitching: Tools of language and culture transform the dialectically diverse classroom. *Language Arts, 81*(6), 470–480.

Wheeler, T. R. (2007). Making the connection: An investigation of the literacy instructional practices of two culturally responsive African American teachers. (Unpublished doctoral dissertation). University of Kentucky, Lexington.

Wlodkowski, R. J., & Ginsberg, M. B. (1995). A framework for culturally responsive teaching. *Educational Leadership, 53,* 17–21.

Wright, R. (1945). *Black boy.* New York: Harper.

Zemelman, S., Daniels, H., & Hyde, A. (2005). *Best practice: Today's standards for teaching and learning in America's schools* (3rd ed.). Portsmouth, NH: Heinemann.

FURTHER RESOURCES FOR INQUIRY LEARNING

Buhrow, B., & Garcia, A. U. (2006). *Ladybugs, tornadoes, and swirling galaxies: English Language Learners discover their world through inquiry.* Portland, ME: Stenhouse.

Compton-Lilly, C. (2004). *Confronting racism, poverty and power: Classroom strategies to change the world.* Portsmouth, NH: Heinemann.

Harste, J. C., Short, K. G., & Burke, C. (1995). *Creating classrooms for authors and inquirers* (2nd ed.). Portsmouth, NH: Heinemann.

Pappas, M. L., & Tepe, A. E. (2002). *Pathways to knowledge and inquiry learning.* Santa Barbara, CA: Libraries Unlimited.

Smith, M. W., & Wilhelm, J. D. (2006). *Going with the flow: How to engage boys (and girls) in their literacy learning.* Portsmouth, NH: Heinemann.

Chapter 8

Discourse/Instructional Conversation: Connecting School and Personal Discourses

Sherry W. Powers

The war will be won when she who is the marginalized comes to speak more in her own language, and people accept her communication as valid and representative . . . In such a time, mothers will no longer have to force their children to act like strangers among their elders. They will hold hands with generations and celebrate the community experience that makes language sensible to all those who are members of the group. Their children will join them in their quest to preserve the ancestral tones and images that represent centuries of love, hope, and success. This is when we will all be able to speak "clearly," not just enunciate, and put our soul's reality out in the open.

(Dowdy, 2002, p. 13)

Ms. Neel's [pseudonym] fourth grade classroom is located in rural Appalachia. One of her students, 9-year-old Zane [pseudonym], speaks with a pronounced Appalachian dialect. Zane is a European-American who lives with his grandmother who is also native to Appalachia. He spends a great deal of time engaging in oral storytelling activities.

Zane does not like school, and he fails to see the relevance of school learning to his everyday life. In spite of his negative feelings about school, he expresses positive feelings and respect for his teacher, Ms. Neel. According to Zane, "Ms. Neel is a good teacher because she cares about you." The majority of teachers and administrators in the school view Zane as slow and unmotivated as a learner. However, Ms. Neel believes that Zane is a very capable thinker and learner. Therefore, during classroom conversation and instruction, she tries to identify and build upon his specific areas of interest. Throughout the day, she provides a variety of opportunities for Zane to tell family stories, share personal experiences, and explain the meaning of colloquial words and phrases used in his home and community (Powers, 2002).

At the same time, however, Ms. Neel frequently conveys the message that there are particular styles of writing and communicating—styles that are reflective of the dominant society—that are more acceptable than the nonstandard discourse style of Zane's home and community. For instance, Ms. Neel encounters the following phrase in Zane's written narrative: "I will clean up the bottom so you can come to the PTO meeting at school." Ms. Neel asks Zane to explain the meaning of "clean up the bottom." Zane explains that this is the flat ground behind his house. In response, Ms. Neel states that when speaking with her family, she refers to this area as the backyard. In a later interview, Ms. Neel expresses the frustration involved in teaching children like Zane to use formal Standard English in oral and written contexts. Although she values Zane's native language use, she acknowledges that she has to lower Zane's scores on writing assignments when he does not use the forms of Standard English that are expected in formal written discourse.

In research comparing the written compositions of Appalachian versus mainstream students, Eller (1989) found that the Appalachian students tended to use a less formal writing style than the non-Appalachian students. Their writing conveyed a more personal tone, evidenced by the more frequent use of *you/your*, greater use of colloquial vocabulary, and the utilization of "linear-linking" in which arguments were connected by conjunctions. She writes: "The Appalachian students seemed to use a discourse style which is more typically 'oral' and is discouraged in educational settings, whereas the non-Appalachian students used a style which is more typically 'written' and is encouraged in educational settings" (p. 355). Zane's writing contained many of the characteristics that Eller identified in her research—elements that are considered "less literate" than the more formal discourse style endorsed by the education establishment.

In oral interviews, Zane indicated that he had made a decision not to change or adjust his oral or written language practices to match the teacher's expectations for his work. Thus, while Zane frequently demonstrated the ability to produce descriptive and lengthy oral and written episodic narratives, he chose not to do so. In assigned writing tasks by the teacher, Zane continually produced brief and nondescript pieces of writing, reflecting his deliberate rejection of the expected school standard. Zane sensed that Ms. Neel valued Standard English over nonstandard variations of English. Therefore, by refusing to comply with the oral and written literate expectations of the school, Zane felt that he validated the language and literacy traditions of his home (Powers, 2002).

Instead of providing situated contexts in which Zane's home language could be affirmed, Ms. Neel unintentionally silenced his voice by soliciting only a formal style of writing that to him was disconnected from real life. Allowing Zane opportunities to write about his experiences in the same episodic manner that he talked—while simultaneously teaching him the "language of power"—would have validated his use of language as well as his style of writing. Yet as a result of school practices that devalue and even denigrate different languages and discourse styles, Zane made the conscious choice to be disengaged in classroom writing activities and to produce limited pieces of writing.

As observed in Zane's story, language is inherently social, and social settings involve relationships of power. Classrooms are social spaces with their own particular patterns of language use and power structures. Schools privilege certain forms of discourse, such as mainstream Standard English, over non-standard forms of discourse. As a social setting, the classroom reinforces the dominant ideology and privileges the language of the elite. It is important to recognize that language is part of one's identity, and to devalue a student's language is to devalue his identity. Thus, many students are silenced and disempowered when the dominant discourse is exclusively promoted over other, non-mainstream discourses.

Knowing when, where, and how to use different styles of discourse gives students the power to converse in many different situations, including in school. When this type of instruction is not provided, students like Zane conclude that their language—their discourse, and hence their identity—is inferior to the "dominant" language promoted within the culture of the school. Furthermore, many children from diverse backgrounds find themselves in situations where they must choose between their home language and the oral and written literate expectations of the school in order to be successful. Students like Zane may decide to sabotage their academic success rather than assimilate into the culture of the school and comply with language expectations. The unique and rich language features of students from diverse backgrounds are often misunderstood and tragically erased by well-meaning educators, state assessment systems, and national policy-makers.

SUPPORTING RESEARCH

B. Smith (1971) explains that "teaching is, above all, a linguistic activity" and "language is at the very heart of teaching" (p. 24). Vygotsky (1962) focused on the reciprocal relationship between language, thought, and culture. He acknowledged that "thought development is determined by language" as well as the "socio-cultural experience of the child" (p. 51). From Vygotsky's (1978) perspective, learning takes place within the context of social relationships. Hence, learning and failure to learn occur within socially organized experiences and activities (McDermott, 1977, 1987).

Classroom Discourse Rules and Cultural Discontinuity

The dynamics of classroom discourse are shaped by the culture of the school and classroom. Who participates in communicative interactions, under what conditions, and how students and teachers interact are all influenced by cultural socialization (Gay, 2000). Typically, conventional classroom discourse is of a passive-receptive nature: teachers talk; students listen. Teachers ask questions; students answer. Some ethnic groups, however, have communication styles that are of a participatory-interactive nature (Kochman, 1985). In these instances, the speaker expects listeners to actively engage by responding vocally or through movement and motion. Therefore, for many students from diverse backgrounds (e.g., Latinos, African Americans, and Native Hawaiians), the stereotypical passive-receptive classroom discourse practices do not align with their familiar participatory-interactive communication style (Hymes, 1985).

A key to successful student participation in classroom discourse is the teacher's ability to adapt discourse practices to make them culturally congruent with the students' expectations for language use (Au, 1993; Delpit, 1988, 1995; Heath, 1983; Philips, 1983). Heath (1983) notes that literacy events have social interactional rules which regulate the type and amount of talk that is produced in the classroom. The traditional interactional rules that govern classroom language use tend to be common to many mainstream middle-class homes and communities (Au, 1993; Delpit, 1995; Heath, 1983; Philips, 1983; Purcell-Gates, 1995). Essentially, children who do not know the school language and rules for talking are usually marginalized and may eventually become silenced in the classroom (Delpit, 1988). Research shows that when teachers adapt their discourse practices in literacy instruction to be more culturally appropriate to the students they teach, students tend to be more successful (Au, 1993; Delpit, 1988; Heath, 1983).

For instance, some students benefit from creating a "stage" or "setting," or engaging in what Gay (2000) terms "stage setting" behavior prior to the performance of a task. Stage setting involves making connections with others in the group prior to addressing a task. These common practices are a means for individuals to ready themselves for "work." These culturally contextual stage setting practices have been observed in African American speakers who inform the audience of their ideology and values underlying the positions they will take in a speech (e.g., "where they are coming from"). Students in classrooms may engage in stage setting practices as a means of preparing for a learning task (e.g., clearing desks, sharpening pencils, discussing procedures, reading prompts aloud, drawing pictures, physical flexing and movement). Latino adults frequently begin task interactions by inquiring about the wellbeing of family members of other participants. Frequently, however, classroom teachers believe that stage setting behaviors of students are unnecessary and interpret them as socializing with peers rather than attending to tasks (Gay, 2000). These behaviors, however, are a part of the linguistic practices of particular cultural groups, and thus are an integral part of their identity. Therefore, accommodating students' preferences for stage setting can contribute to student learning.

In addition to different stage setting practices, research shows that various groups prefer particular types of interactive or communicative styles. For example, many African Americans prefer the dialogic feature of call and response, which involves dialogue in which the audience responds actively to a speaker to complete a shared "community text" (Moss, 2001). Teachers who expect students to participate aloud in this way are equipped to nod, comment, and/or continue their instructional presentation instead of bogging down in behavioral admonitions. Another example of interactive style is found in Pang's research on Asian Pacific American (APA) students, who may be reluctant to participate in discussions and debates because of learned patterns of communication that teach them that it is disrespectful to question the teacher or to make their views known (Pang, 1998). Culturally responsive teachers, therefore, provide these students with opportunities to interact in small groups prior to engaging in large group discussions. Some Asian Americans prefer small group "collaborative and negotiated problem solving" (Gay, 2000), in which the ideas of individuals within the group are critiqued and negotiated. Au (1993, 2006) notes that Hawaiian children are more engaged when teachers use an interactive talk story participation structure, whereby students work together to create a story or an idea. Learners are well served when teachers use preferred modes of interaction in the classroom, and hence it is important that teachers examine the interaction patterns of the group(s) being served.

Because classroom instruction and assessment are largely conducted through the medium of language, classroom contexts which do not accommodate these varied communicative practices force many students to acquire new styles or procedures of linguistic performance while at the same time learning substantial content. To enhance student achievement, the procedures for learning and the processes for demonstrating learning require that teachers change their instructional practices to make them more culturally responsive to students from ethnically and culturally diverse backgrounds (Delpit, 1988, Gay, 2000).

Teachers' Perception of Students' Home Language

Educators and researchers observe noticeable differences when comparing the successful school experiences of children from mainstream backgrounds who do not experience language discontinuity with the unsuccessful school experiences of children from diverse backgrounds (Au, 1993; Delpit, 1988, 1995; Heath, 1983; Phillips, 1983). Many anecdotes of children learning to use regional language variations across and within local groups show that they are able to use oral and written language proficiently in multiple home and community settings (Heath, 1983; Purcell-Gates, 1995). However, the teachers of these same children frequently find themselves asking why children who demonstrate such proficient language skills within their home and other social contexts experience such difficulty using oral and written language in the classroom (Delpit, 1995).

How teachers view the home language of students and their families plays a significant role in teacher expectations and teacher respect for a student's culture. Unfortunately, speaking a different dialect or language can prejudice a teacher's attitude toward a child's ability to achieve. Many teachers fail to recognize the vernaculars of diverse populations as anything other than sub-standard linguistic forms. As a result, they may view these children as ignorant, lazy, or subordinate, although these value judgments may be couched in more acceptable terms such as "disadvantaged," "at risk," or "in need of language remediation" (Delpit, 1997; Purcell-Gates, 2002; Stubbs, 2002).

Such concerns point to the need for a full description and analysis of the primary face-to-face discourse interactions occurring between teachers and students in culturally diverse classroom settings. The way language is used by the teacher and the student during whole group, small group, and individual instruction, as well as during formal and informal conversations, creates the milieu in which the processes of learning take place (Au, 1993; Cazden, 2001; Heath, 1983; Hymes, 1996; Philips, 1983). Many aspects of language use in the classroom are the result of non-deliberate, usually unconscious choices at the moment of use. This raises the question, therefore, of how these unconscious uses of language affect student performance and learning (Cazden & Mehan, 1989; Heath, 1983; Hymes, 1996). There are rules or codes for participating in power structures which relate to linguistic forms, communication strategies, and presentation of self. These rules are a reflection of the norms of the culture of those who have power in the larger society. This means that success in school and the workplace is predicated upon acquisition of the cultural knowledge of those who are in power, that is, upon knowing the ways of talking, writing, dressing, and interacting that are "appropriate." Research suggests that children from dominant groups tend to do better than children from underrepresented populations when the culture of the school is based on dominant cultural norms, which include privileging the language of power. (Au, 1993; Cummins, 1994; Delpit, 1995, 1997; Gay, 1994; Giroux, 1987, 1988).

Sociolinguist Michael Stubbs suggests that, even if the teacher does not overtly convey disapproval of a child's language, the child may nevertheless perceive his home language to be inferior simply because it is "different." He writes:

> The teacher may (rightly or wrongly) regard the child's language as *inappropriate* in the classroom. The child's language may also provoke negative *attitudes* in the teacher, perhaps because the child speaks a low prestige dialect. These attitudes may be transmitted to the child. Even if the teacher expresses no overt disapproval of the child's language, the teacher's own language may still be different from the child's in the direction of prestige varieties, and this in itself may be an implicit condemnation of the child's language. The child will be aware that people with more prestige and authority than him speak differently, and may draw his own conclusions. Such a complex of sociolinguistic factors may lead cumulatively to educational problems for a child.
>
> (2002, pp. 78–79; italics in original)

The dominant ideology perpetuates the idea that certain discourses are "more literate" than other discourses, and therefore they are inherently superior. Classroom discourse practices reflect these dominant norms for language use. Further, these discourse practices have become so embedded in "the way we do school," that they are rarely seen as problematic. Because most teachers are members of the dominant group and have been socialized to accept the dominant ideology, the rules governing discourse expectations in the classroom often go unchallenged. Helping students to examine the language of the dominant ideology, however, can be liberating for both teachers and students, in that this critique can lead to the recognition that appropriate language use is *situational*, and hence students' home language and discourse practices have value. More will be said on this topic in a later section of this chapter.

The Dominant Ideology and Subtractive Language Policies

Perhaps nowhere are our hegemonic notions about language more prevalent than with the current emphasis on "English-only" policies in schools. Such policies are subtractive in nature in that they limit, rather than enhance, students' linguistic competence. There is a rather large body of research that suggests that bilingual programs that promote dual-language development have a positive effect on students' academic achievement and cognitive growth, and that learning done in a student's first language transfers to learning in the second language (Crawford, 1999; Cummins, 1996, 2000; Krashen & Biber, 1988; Thomas & Collier, 2002).

The passage of English-only policies such as Proposition 227 in California and Proposition 203 in Arizona, however, are indicative of the pervasiveness of the dominant ideology. Rather than perceiving bilingualism as a strength and promoting students' development of both languages, such policies act to subtract the linguistic resources that students bring with them to school. The English-only movement has been found to be particularly damaging to students' language development when combined with reductionist literacy instructional practices that focus on the "pieces" of written language (such as learning individual letters and sounds) versus meaningful applications of language in authentic social contexts. In their research on the effects of English-only when used in conjunction with highly scripted phonics programs, Gutiérrez, Baquedano-López, and Asanto (2000) report that the percentage of students reading at or above grade level in one large district dropped significantly on the statewide assessment. Indeed, a number of theorists have warned against the negative ramifications for English Language Learners (ELLs) resulting from such scripted literacy programs (Freeman & Freeman, 1999; Gutiérrez, Baquedano-López, & Asanto, 2000; López-Reyna, 1996; Mora, 2002). Gándara (2000) provides a glimpse into what this instruction "looks like" in classrooms:

> Ms. P. stood at the front of the class and had just read the first problem on the worksheet. She instructed students that they were supposed to circle each long vowel sound in each of the sentences and write this word in the long vowel column. Ms. P. completed the first three sentences with the students. During the first three sentences, a few students were calling out without being officially recognized. When this happened on the 4th sentence, Ms. P. said, "Since you seem to have no problem with this activity you can do it on your own."
>
> Ruben and Miguel rubbed their hands together excitedly when they were told that they would be doing the activity on their own:
>
> Miguel: (Reading "Will Pat go to the store?" in a flat tone with no questioning intonation.) "Will Pat go to the store?" (Pauses for a moment.) "Will Pat go to the store?" (Still no raised intonation.) Will Pat. . . Pat go to the store? (An almost raised but unnatural intonation on "store.") Miguel raises his head from the text. "That doesn't make any sense." "Don't matter." He picks up his pencil and writes the words *go* and *store* in the Long O column.
>
> Thus, Miguel could write words with long O's in a column, but he had no idea what the words meant.
>
> (pp. 6–7)

Excerpts like this one from actual classrooms provide evidence of how reductionist instructional practices can inhibit students' academic and linguistic development. Importantly, the presence or absence of authentic uses of language and literacy is what is significant here, and not whether students use English or their native languages in their discussions. Montero and Kuhn (2009) write that "[t]he most effective and efficient way to teach language-minority students to read and write in English is to take advantage of their oral proficiency in their home languages" (p. 162). What is crucial for such development to occur is that students be engaged in meaningful conversations and dialogue (Goldenberg, 1991). It is to this topic that I now turn.

The Importance of Student Talk

Research indicates that opportunities for genuine conversation are rare in classrooms, and students are generally afforded few opportunities to talk. Most classroom discourse is dominated by the teacher, and when students are given an opportunity to talk, typically it is to reply to a teacher's prompt using short and simplistic responses (Cazden, 2001). This pattern of teacher–student interaction not only limits a student's opportunity for language development, but also limits the student's ability to engage in more complex learning. McIntyre, Kyle, Chen, Kraemer, and Parr (2009) write that:

> Teachers seem hard-wired to ask questions, wait for a student to answer the question (usually with one word or a short phrase), and then evaluate the response in some way (e.g., "Good! Correct!"). But this form of talk is extremely limiting for students because so little talk is actually done by the students. It is most detrimental to English language learners because they need many opportunities to practice speaking about ideas.
>
> (p. 98)

To develop linguistic competence, more student talk is needed in classrooms. Student talk is particularly important for students who are acquiring English in order to provide them with opportunities to develop academic language (Cummins, 1979). The form of student talk, however, seems to make a difference. In their review of research on effective teaching practices for ELLs, Waxman and Tellez (2002) suggest that to be effective, classroom discourse needs to focus less on "cooperative learning" and more on the concept of "collaborative learning communities" that emphasize the importance of social relationships in learning language. Citing several ethnographic studies that examined the language development of ELLs in classrooms, the authors conclude that student interaction when engaged in collaborative tasks enhances language acquisition, even when no student in the group has strong English proficiency. Within the classroom social context, the teacher serves as an important language model, but the teacher "is merely one model of many." Rather, "These studies suggest that inviting students who are learning English to engage in academic conversations with their peers is the primary tool of language learning" (p. 12).

Tharp and Gallimore (1991) coined the term "instructional conversation" to describe this type of social discourse. Instructional conversation is characterized by natural and spontaneous use of language and extended discussion that involves a high level of student participation. To invite conversation, teachers provide questions and prompts that can have more than one answer, and encourage students to build on the utterances of their peers. The instructional conversation involves shared interaction, i.e., ideally no individual—including the teacher—dominates the discussion.

The findings of the National Literacy Panel on Language-Minority Children and Youth confirm the importance of the instructional conversation. In summarizing the research, August and Shanahan (2008) note:

> To learn literacy with maximum success, students need to have command of the various literacy skills and strategies, as well as sufficient knowledge of oral English. It is not enough to teach reading skills, but instruction must teach these skills while fostering extensive oral English-language development. That the oral English development provided in most programs is insufficient can be seen in studies that show that second-language learners with adequate word recognition, spelling, and decoding skills still may lag behind their first-language peers in reading comprehension and vocabulary. The more promising of the complex literacy instruction routines that have been studied (such as instructional conversations) provide instructional support of oral language development in English along with high-quality instruction in literacy skills and strategies.
>
> (p. 10)

In addition to the need to scaffold students' oral language development in English, research confirms that allowing students to converse in their home language during instructional conversations can increase student learning and understanding (Gutiérrez, Baquedano-López, & Alvarez, 2001; Moll & Díaz, 1987). For instance, Martinez-Roldan's (2005) study in a second grade classroom investigated the effect of children's first language as a mediational tool for thinking and talking about text written in English. During literature circles, the ELLs were observed engaging one another in an attempt to understand the English text. Students used English, Spanish, and code switching in order to combine linguistic resources to create a useful repertoire of codes and forms to deepen understanding and comprehension of text. In another study, ELLs who were learning English achieved more sophisticated and higher levels of understanding English text when they were allowed to discuss the text in Spanish (Moll & Dworin, 1996). It has also been shown that ELL students can benefit from activities involving paraphrasing and translating text when coupled with opportunities for them to summarize text ideas in their own words. These learning activities prove to be powerful comprehension tools for understanding English text (Orellana & Reynolds, 2008). Other investigations have supported these conclusions. Allowing for equitable opportunities for ELL students to talk, initiate topics, change the direction of a discussion, and relate learning to prior experiences increases their performance, reading comprehension, and overall achievement (Iddings, Risko, & Rampulla, 2009).

Learning the Language of Power

When teachers are unaware of their own culturally-based assumptions about language and literacy, they often fail to recognize the need to adapt their discourse practices to the students they serve and to apprentice their students into the "language of power." Because power-associated practices and discourses generally are not explicitly taught in schools, educational institutions serve to maintain inequitable access to "power literacy" (Delpit, 1988; Gee, 1990). In this view, children who come from families and communities that do not share in the power of the mainstream groups require explicit instruction about the conventions and strategies of these powerful literacies and discourses in order to gain full access to them. Delpit (1988) contrasts process-oriented activities, which she calls "personal literacy," with explicit instruction in "power literacy." The reading, writing, and speaking experiences children bring to school are the elements of their own unique "personal literacy." On the other hand, "power literacy" utilizes the rules or codes of the culture of power. These codes are acquired by students from mainstream backgrounds through interactions within standard English-speaking families and communities. "Power literacy" is frequently not acquired by students of diverse backgrounds since their families are usually outside the culture of power.

In Delpit's (1988) analysis, conventions of literacy, such as written and spoken grammar that is representative of Standard English, are part of mainstream American culture, or what she refers to as the culture of power. She contends that children of diverse ethnic and linguistic groups are well served by "power literacy" instruction that gives them access to the language of power dictated by the mainstream group (Delpit, 1988; 1995). She also argues that teachers should recognize the linguistic and cultural forms students bring to school.

For ELLs, the instructional task becomes one of teaching the rules and conventions of Standard American English while simultaneously affirming their native language. As with other underrepresented populations, students' native languages are an essential part of their identity, and thus students who are acquiring English are often "caught between two worlds"—the world of the school, with its expectations for using formal Standard English, and the expectations of the home community for preserving their cultural identities. When individuals entering a new discourse community are expected to give up their old identities (i.e., assimilate) rather than add new identities to those they already possess, tensions can arise between students and their families and communities (Valenzuela, 1999; Wong Fillmore, 1991). Yet current foundational practices and policies that influence the culture of schools in the United States are based upon expectations for student assimilation.

Further, immigrant students may feel competent as learners in their countries of origin, but confused, bewildered, and uncertain about what counts as literacy, learning, and linguistic competence when attending U.S. schools. Within-school tracking and cross-school segregation can drastically reduce the extent to which the majority of students from diverse backgrounds have access to different types of instruction, opportunities to interact, chances to gain multiple perspectives, and occasions to meaningfully understand personal literacy and power literacy (Darling-Hammond, 2010). Creating circumstances in which teachers and students are free to discuss issues, interests, and personal literacy narratives among individuals from diverse backgrounds discourages separation and silence where communication and connections are needed.

In conclusion, students from marginalized groups have fewer opportunities to engage in student–teacher discourse that favorably focuses on their ethnicity, potential, language, achievements, and personality traits than mainstream White students (Darling-Hammond, 2010). Too frequently these students are given few opportunities for sharing their voice and personal literacy in the classroom. Students need to feel and know that their home language (their "personal literacy" or primary discourse, and hence, their cultural identity) is affirmed. Teachers can do this by: (1) allowing students to use their native language and personal discourse in the classroom, and building on students' preferred interaction structures; (2) allowing students to use different styles of discourse in a variety of situational contexts that assist them in identifying when and where to use various discourse forms (e.g., informal classroom group discussions versus speaking with an employer); (3) providing opportunities for students to share their stories and personal responses to experiences; (4) promoting more equitable opportunities for talk (e.g., developing an environment that encourages authentic discussion and instructional conversation); and (5) examining their own views, behaviors, and perceptions that potentially silence the voices of specific students in the classroom.

PRACTICAL APPLICATIONS

Typically, teachers attempt to curb alternative forms of student discourse by controlling classroom communication, enforcing rules of individualistic turn-taking, and imposing didactic passive-receptive forms of discourse that predominate in schools (Goodlad, 1984). Teachers who reject students' home languages and alternative discourse patterns may cause irreversible damage to students' academic achievement and willingness to engage in instructional processes. Negative attitudes toward students' language may cause them to feel alienated, resentful, and ashamed, and as we saw with Zane, may eventually lead them to refuse to participate in school literacy activities (Au, 1993; Delpit, 1995; Fairchild & Edwards-Evans, 1990; Labov, 1972; Powers, 2002). In rejecting a student's language, we are essentially rejecting his or her identity (Gay, 1994; Gee, 1992). By creating settings for discussions that focus on differences in individuals' ways of speaking, valuing, being, and behaving, students are given meaningful opportunities to develop positive self-concepts related to their ethnic identities.

Typical of the individualistic, didactic forms of discourse found in schools is the Initiate, Respond, Evaluate (IRE) discourse pattern found in most classrooms (Cazden, 2001), whereby the teacher poses a direct question and individual students are called on to respond. Consider that IRE discourse generally promotes truncated responses with limited opportunities for extended conversation or divergent thought. Thus, the typical discourse pattern found in most classrooms does not give voice to students or allow them to demonstrate their linguistic competence. Because students are rarely asked to use explanatory or descriptive language, teachers' knowledge of students' linguistic performance is limited, and they may begin to view their students through a deficit lens. Further, such restricted discourse practices fail to provide opportunities for genuine social exchanges that would promote the development of important social relationships in the classroom. If students are not permitted to speak and engage in authentic classroom discussion, it is difficult, if not impossible, for teachers to assess their linguistic competence and to get to know them as individuals in order to teach effectively.

To become truly literate, students need opportunities to learn what Gee (1992) calls "secondary discourses"—those discourses we acquire as we interact within various institutions such as schools, workplaces, and businesses. Acquiring secondary discourses develops linguistic competence for learners, as they learn how to communicate and negotiate meaning within different social settings. Being able to use language appropriately in a variety of settings and with a variety of audiences provides individuals with social and political power. Contrary to popular notions about language use, power is more than just demonstrating the ability to communicate using Standard English; rather, power is having the linguistic repertoire to be able to control one's language use in diverse social contexts. Thus, the challenge for teachers like Ms. Neel is to teach children like Zane standard linguistic forms, which is part of her job, and also to teach them when and where it is situationally appropriate to use their "home languages."

We all possess a "home language" or "primary discourse." Therefore, acquiring "secondary discourses," as well as "secondary languages" or bilingualism, ought to be a goal for every student. Rarely are students from historically privileged backgrounds viewed as being linguistically incompetent, yet many are essentially monolingual, due largely to the hegemonic language policies in the United States that privilege English over other languages. Consider too that even students whose primary discourse is consistent with the dominant discourse can be viewed as linguistically incompetent if they do not possess the capacity to vary their language to fit the social context or to communicate with those outside of their own particular speech community.

Therefore, it is important that we re-define what is meant by "linguistic competence," and establish goals that support the language development of all students. Every language arts program ought to include the acquisition of secondary discourses, as well as bilingualism and even trilingualism, as goals for student learning. Expecting students to meet state and national education standards for the language arts that simply promote the acquisition and proficient use of Standard English linguistic forms does not support or develop the linguistic competence of all students. To learn language and develop competence, students must actually practice it in various social settings. While research suggests that it is important to provide ELLs with numerous opportunities to use language (Lapp, Fisher, Flood, & Moore, 2002), the CRIOP authors believe that it is important for *all* students to engage in authentic uses of language. Indeed, we would argue that this ought to be a primary responsibility of the language arts program. There are many strategies and techniques that teachers can use to enhance the linguistic competence of their students. A few of these are listed below, and several more are suggested in the *Teachers' Voices* section of this chapter.

Affirming Students' Language

Although discourse is an abstract concept (Janks, 2010), texts become the material form of discourse. Texts are not neutral. Linking students' primary discourse to academic discourse through the curriculum requires finding and using classroom materials and resources that represent the cultures and identities of students. However, even when they choose culturally relevant texts, many teachers are unprepared or underprepared to work with students whose cultural backgrounds differ from their own. For example, an African American student was reprimanded by a teacher for using "call and response" during first-grade reading time. The teacher thought the student was rude because he interrupted her while reading aloud, responding to the story with comments such as "That is so funny!" (Ford, Howard, Harris, & Tyson, 2000). Therefore, using culturally diverse materials in the classroom is not enough to promote the learning of students from diverse backgrounds; the teacher must also understand and value students' home languages. In culturally responsive classrooms, students are at the center of teaching and learning; students experience a sense of membership and ownership; teachers address real-world issues, multicultural education is a core component of the curriculum, and teachers take responsibility for the learning and well-being of their students.

This belief system is foundational for building upon the language of students and their families. Culturally responsive teachers intentionally utilize strategies and philosophies that affirm students' dialects and languages, and hence, affirm their identities. Children have a right to their own language as well as their own culture, and should be allowed to express themselves using their own discourse style. Schools must change so that children can be empowered to understand themselves as learners, understand teacher expectations, and build upon personal experiences and knowledge (Delpit, 1988).

Recognizing children as experts in the classroom requires that educators know their students and become familiar with the students' cultures and communities in order to respect and address their languages and discourses. Culturally responsive teachers create learning opportunities and assignments that allow students to share family and community experiences and to use their home language. For example, I observed one elementary school teacher who used photographs and family artifacts to introduce herself to students on the first day of class (Powers, 1999). During the presentation, she showed a pecan grown from a tree in her grandmother's backyard in South Carolina. The teacher talked about the different pronunciations used for the word "pecan," and how she felt when others had laughed at the way she talked. She stopped and asked the students if they had ever had a similar experience. One child eagerly raised his hand and said that he had encountered a similar experience when pronouncing the word "peony." Other students jumped into the conversation sharing similar types of experiences.

The next day, students brought their own box of personal artifacts to share with classmates. After much discussion, the teacher and the students decided that they would each pick a favorite artifact from their boxes, draw a picture of the item, and write about the significance of the artifact. The teacher modeled the writing of her own narrative, and provided a "think aloud" experience for children as she told them why she included specific words and information in the writing. She told the students that she liked to use the "southern" pronunciation for "pecan" to honor her grandmother. In response, students engaged in conversations with classmates while composing their narratives to explain reasons for including specific words and information in the text. When students read their narratives to the class, one child said that he used the Spanish word for "toy drum" in his narrative since that was the familiar word used in his home. This example illustrates one way that teachers can build upon student interests and experiences to give students voice as well as to value the identity of each student in the classroom. Using students' own lives and experiences positions them as experts.

In another elementary classroom, I observed a teacher who shared her own personal rendition of the poem *Where I'm From* (Lyon, 1999) with students. Her poem included language representative of her own southern roots (e.g., *ya'll, hey there, how-dee*). In response, the students created their own versions of the poem that included words, dialect, artifacts, people, places and Spanish words that were representative of their own personal literacy. When sharing their poems, the children discussed the specific meanings and importance of selected areas in their writings. The teacher highlighted similarities and differences in the language used in the poems to demonstrate the variety of ways that writers tell about themselves. Through this activity, students were given the opportunity to share their voice and feel validated by the teacher and their classmates. At the same time, students learned new language forms which can be utilized in specific social contexts.

Affirming students' home languages is also important for ELLs. As noted previously, research demonstrates the value of allowing students to discuss ideas and new concepts in their native languages. All students benefit when educators understand and appreciate student differences as demonstrated through their diverse discourses. Furthermore, it is essential that teachers identify entrenched attitudes and stereotypes toward language use that impact student access to high quality instruction. Culturally responsive teachers are very intentional in providing opportunities for all learners to engage in meaningful classroom discourse.

Expanding Students' Linguistic Knowledge

It is our view that language policies in schools ought to be additive rather than subtractive. That is, we should strive to make the ultimate goal of the language arts program to increase students' linguistic repertoires by providing opportunities for students to develop linguistic flexibility. Students need to learn when and where it is appropriate to use various linguistic forms, based upon the situational context, and they need opportunities to practice using language within various social settings. Stubbs (2002) notes:

> To say that a piece of language is "wrong" is therefore to make a judgment relative to a social situation. It may be felt just as inappropriate to use collo-quialisms and regional dialect forms in a job interview, as it is to use very formal language over a drink with some friends in a pub.
>
> (p. 76)

Thus, teachers must help students determine *situational appropriateness* in language use. Teaching situational appropriateness acknowledges that no linguistic form is superior to another; what is important is that students learn when to use the "language of power" and when to use their "home language."

Teaching students when and how to "code-switch" can help students to develop this linguistic flexibility. For example, teachers can have conversations with students about when it would be appropriate to use their home language, and when it would be appropriate to use more formal forms of Standard English. At a recent visit to the Culture and Language Academy for Success, we noted an example of instruction in code-switching. Students were asked to give examples of what would be appropriate to say at home, and what would be appropriate to say at school. Students wrote statements like these: "At home I can say *I ain't got no homework*, but at school I must say *I do not have homework*." "At home I can say *What up?* but at school I must say *How are you doing?*"

Codeswitching is one means for assisting students in identifying the use of language that is appropriate for different contexts. Teachers who encourage students to explore how language differs in formal and informal settings assist them in identifying reasons as well as opportunities for code switching. Williams (1982) found that African Americans who were conscious of their own language as a legitimate communication system were more accepting and willing to acquire secondary discourses. By affirming the legitimacy of non-mainstream language variations and the native languages of ELLs, students are more receptive to learning the languages of a wider community and sharing in multiple discourses (Gee, 1996; Williams, 1982).

Teachers can also help students to develop linguistic competence by developing their metacognitive knowledge about language and language differences (Hollie, 2005). For example, as discussed in Chapter 7, Wheeler and Swords (2004) observed that contrastive analysis of vernacular variations with standard linguistic forms helped children become aware of the linguistic rules across language varieties. A teacher noted that students who spoke African American

Vernacular English (AAVE) did not follow the rules of conventional Standard English patterns to show the possessive case. One student said: "Taylor cat is black." Later, the teacher taught a lesson that demonstrated possessive patterns and compared the differences between AAVE and the forms of Standard English. Throughout the lesson, the teacher showed that she valued the students' home language while helping them to acquire dominant discourse forms. The researchers found that engaging students in contrastive analysis helped close the achievement gap between African American students and their White peers.

Heath (1983) provides additional examples of teachers who engage students in contrastive analysis during instruction. One teacher invited parents, school personnel, and community members to visit the classroom to discuss their ways of talking, reading, and writing. Students also listened to radio and television programs and discussed the linguistic diversity of all of these speakers. Children were allowed to learn about their own language while exploring other language forms, which helped them develop communicative competence and appreciate linguistic diversity (Hymes, 1985).

It is possible and desirable to make the study of oral and written language diversity part of the curriculum for all students. Involving younger children in discussions about the differences in the ways television characters from different regions and/or cultural groups speak can provide a starting point. Exposing students to a collection of the many children's books written in the dialects of various cultural groups can also provide learning opportunities about linguistic diversity, as can audio-taped stories narrated by individuals from different cultures, including audio books read by members of the children's home communities. Children can learn that there are many different ways of saying the same word or concept, and that certain contexts suggest particular kinds of linguistic performances. Teachers could use a variety of poetry written in students' vernaculars and translate the work into Standard English to illustrate how translation changes meaning, mood, emphasis, voice, and tone of a text.

Activities that allow children to engage in role play, conduct interviews, and participate in dramatic play events provide opportunities for children to practice using and playing with language in a variety of contexts. For instance, students can dramatize various events to show how language use varies with the situational context. Helping students negotiate the numerous discourses they bring to school from their home and community through group discussions and role playing can provide explicit instruction as well as modeling of the expected use of language in a variety of contexts. This also provides opportunities for students to acquire new styles or procedures of performing while learning substantial content.

Just as importantly, students need to understand the social construction of the "language of power." Making explicit the hegemonic system that privileges some languages and discourses over others gives students the personal power that comes from "knowing the game." Teachers provide this type of learning opportunity when they guide students through an exploration of the negative attitudes held toward specific dialects and vernaculars based on who speaks those dialects. Furthermore, having students explore the pros and cons of code switching in specific social contexts can provide opportunities for learners to identify and address feelings, as well as reasons, for choosing whether or not to comply with oral and written literate traditions of those in power (e.g., schools, employers, and teachers).

Providing for Cultural Continuity

Since the home language is the authentic, accepted voice of a speech community, educators must increase their repertoire of practices to meet the needs of all learners in the classroom. For example, Lee (1995) found that signifyin(g), a popular discourse pattern in the Black community that uses the verbal art of indirect put-downs, can be used to scaffold Black students' acquisition of skills in literacy interpretation. When teachers used signifyin(g) along with prior knowledge, Black students' literacy interpretations improved. Research shows that students also become more engaged when teachers use "morning circle" events to provide opportunities for learners to describe their day and out-of-school experiences. African American students become more involved in the classroom when storytelling is a part of the curriculum, because these skills are highly valued in the Black community (Boykin, 1994).

Also highly effective for engaging students of color is the technique of call and response, defined as a "spontaneous verbal and non-verbal interaction between speaker and listener in which all of the speakers' statements ('calls') are punctuated by expressions ('responses') from the listener" (Smitherman, 1977, p. 104). For example, during a recent visit to the Culture and Language Academy for Success (CLAS), we witnessed an excellent example of call-response during a class discussion of *Charlotte's Web* (White, 1952). Consistent with culturally responsive instruction, the first grade teacher, Dr. Davis, had asked the students to dramatize a section of the text. She used call and response to get them back on task.

Teacher: When I say "Wilbur," you say "pig." Wilbur—
Students: Pig.
Teacher: Wilbur—
Students: Pig.
Teacher: Back into academic position.

This was a highly effective way of getting students back into their seats using a discourse style that was familiar to the children. Teachers at CLAS often invite their students to suggest other call and response patterns that can be used to gain their attention following group work. For instance, Mr. Russell's sixth graders chose this as a call–response pattern:

Teacher: Sixth grade—
Students: What's up? (using "intonational contouring" [Redd & Webb, 2005] whereby the word "up" is pronounced as two syllables with a raised pitch on the second syllable).

Another effective use of call and response is through a form of "oral cloze," whereby the teacher makes a statement and allows the "audience" to complete the statement. For instance, in reviewing a text that was read the previous day, the teacher might say something like this:

Teacher: Let's review the character traits that we discussed yesterday. We decided that Alex was really ____
Students: Clever.
Teacher: Because he tricked the ____
Students: Shopkeeper.

Note that this type of overlapping interaction is consistent with many culturally responsive discourse practices that encourage students to contribute to and build on the ideas of others.

It is important for teachers to examine carefully the preferred interaction structures of their students and their students' communities, so that they can build on those structures in the classroom. For instance, in her book *Teaching Other People's Children* (1999), Ballenger describes how she was able to learn and mimic the "control talk" of the Haitian teachers in order to improve her relationships with her Haitian children. Rather than using the more typical school management discourse that emphasizes individual emotions and consequences, Ballenger learned to use the Haitian style of reprimand, which assumes that the children have a shared knowledge with adults about what constitutes good and bad behavior. Adopting the "control talk" of Haitian adults enabled her to feel more connected to her young Haitian students and resulted in improved student behavior.

As noted previously, using small group and interactive talk structures can have positive results for many students from underrepresented groups. These structures, however, may not be appropriate for all student populations. For instance, these same structures have been found to be ineffective when used with Navajo children (Vogt, Jordan, & Tharp, 1987). Native students, however, may benefit from "talking circles," whereby students are seated in a circle and each has an opportunity to express his or her ideas without interruption from others. Often the speaker holds an artifact (such as a feather) while she speaks, and then passes it on when she is done speaking. Contrary to the "talk story" discourse pattern of native Hawaiian children whereby responses are cooperatively produced (Au, 1980, 1993), with talking circles, only the person holding the artifact is permitted to speak. Thus, talking circles are very different from the overlapping interaction patterns that are preferred by some groups in that students are prohibited from contributing to the conversation until it is their turn to speak.

The important point to be made here is that teachers must learn the language patterns of their students' speech communities. To assure that their classroom discourse practices are culturally compatible, they need to observe their students and their families as they interact with one another both in school and in their home communities. Visiting local places of worship and community centers and making note of various interaction patterns being used, observing individuals as they communicate with one another at various athletic and social events, or otherwise becoming familiar with their students' sociocultural background can help teachers to determine discourse practices that are culturally relevant for their students.

Promoting Instructional Conversation

As noted previously, a large body of research supports the notion that students must be engaged in meaningful conversations in the classroom in order to develop literacy and conceptual understanding. In summarizing the characteristics of an instructional conversation, Goldenberg (1991) suggests that it is a discussion that is "interesting and engaging:"

> It is about an idea or a concept that has meaning and relevance for students. It has a focus that, while it might shift as the discussion evolves, remains discernible throughout. There is a high level of participation, without undue domination by any one individual, particularly the teacher. Students engage in extended discussions—conversations—with the teacher and among themselves. Teachers and students are responsive to what others say, so that each statement or contribution builds upon, challenges, or extends a previous one. Topics are picked up, developed, elaborated.
>
> (pp. 5–6)

Throughout this book, we have emphasized the critical importance of having students work collaboratively and converse with one another regularly in pairs

210

and/or small groups, with the teacher serving as a language model and guide. Such collaborative discussion is important for developing a supportive classroom community, for assessing student understanding throughout instruction, and for promoting students' development of academic discourse. Research on English language learners shows that these students are in particular need of more opportunities to converse using both English and their native languages in order to develop social and academic language (August & Shanahan, 2008). In summarizing the research, Brock, Lapp, Salas and Townsend (2009) write: "Best practices for English learners include providing myriad meaningful opportunities for effective language-based social interactions in the classroom" (p. 19).

There are several discourse structures that have been shown to be effective in promoting authentic student interaction, three of which are presented below. These formats can be useful to facilitate peer interaction so that students are given the opportunity to converse with one another around a specific topic. All students should have many occasions for purposeful talk that allows them to pose questions and talk through their ideas, and discourse structures such as these can encourage rich conversations that help students develop language and conceptual understanding. These structures can be used throughout the various content areas as well as in the English language arts classroom.

Tea Party

The tea party is a protocol usually used to introduce the characters of a text. Christensen (2000) states that when she uses the tea party with works of fiction, she provides a card on each character that presents their point of view. On these cards may be written passages taken directly from the novel or the teacher may write the card describing the character's perspective. Each student is provided with one of the character cards. They are then directed to write down the character's name and other information that would be important for their peers to know, such as their problem and what has happened to them in the past. The students then assume their character roles and "get up, walk around, and introduce themselves to other characters" (p. 115). Students take notes on the various characters that they meet before returning to their seats.

The tea party can be used with historical texts to introduce important players during a particular time period. For instance, prior to studying about the Vietnam War, students can take on the roles of individuals such as Ho Chi Minh, Daniel Berrigan, Lyndon Johnson, Lieutenant William Calley, and Daniel Ellsberg. Introducing the "characters" that were involved in various time periods personalizes the study of history, while also teaching important concepts prior to reading the text. The tea party can be followed with another conversational activity in which students work together to jot down on sticky notes what they already know about the particular historical time period. Students group their sticky notes on a poster using whatever categories make sense to them. The students later share their posters with the entire class. All of these activities provide opportunities for students to collaborate while they are engaged in meaningful learning. Asking students to articulate what they already know about a topic also leads to inquiry, as students' own questions emerge from this process.

Read-Around

Christensen writes: "The read-around is the classroom equivalent to quilt making or barn raising . . . During our read-arounds, we socialize together and create community, but we also teach and learn from each other" (2000, p. 14). With the read-around, students sit in a circle and share their writing. Students are encouraged to listen carefully to "what works" in the papers of their peers, and to respond to the author's content and style. Students are allowed to "pass" if they prefer not to share. Christensen suggests that in order to create a "safe space" for sharing at the beginning of the year, she asks students to write down at least one compliment on a blank strip of paper as a student reads, and to sign their names so the student knows who praised them. They later hand out their compliments to one another.

The read-around is an effective tool for jump-starting dialogue in any class. For instance, students can read a persuasive text and write down their opinions in their journals. The classroom is arranged in a circle so that everyone can partake in the discussion. Students are asked to share their journal entries or to "pass." They are then encouraged to respond and build on the thoughts of their peers. A typical dialogue might go something like this:

Teacher: Who would like to begin?
Brianna: I will. (She reads or shares her journal entry.)
Teacher: Thank you, Brianna.
Teacher (to the other students):   Respond to her ideas. Do you agree? Do some of you have a different opinion?

In read-around, the teacher sits in the circle with her students and guides the conversation; her voice does not dominate but facilitates the conversation so that students interact and are given voice.

To enhance student conversation, the class can be divided into small "read-around" groups. Having strong English speakers in these groups who can serve as language models can help other students develop their linguistic competence. At the same time, it is important to scaffold students' interactions within these groups to assure equitable participation.

Like the tea party, the read-around can be used to introduce important vocabulary and concepts prior to engaging in a thematic study in nearly every content area and at nearly every grade level. For instance, to begin a science unit on "living things," elementary students can be asked to examine the characteristics of the various creatures that exist in the classroom and to share what they observed during a read-around. Older students can be asked to read about a specific event that occurred during a particular time period, to respond to that event through writing, and to share their ideas in a read-around. The value of the read-around is that all students are provided with the opportunity to offer their thoughts and opinions and to respond to the ideas of their peers; no student is marginalized.

Discussion Web

The discussion web is a structure that is specifically designed to encourage students to examine an issue from various perspectives. In using the discussion web, students work in pairs and groups to provide "yes" and "no" responses to a prompt, and are then required to reach consensus and provide a single answer. Originally developed by Alvermann (1991), one version of the Discussion Web is shown in Figure 8.1.

The teacher begins by posing a question such as "Are sharks bad?" Working in pairs, students propose reasons why sharks are considered bad or why they are not considered bad, and they write those responses in the appropriate columns ("Yes" or "No"). They then reach a decision and write a rationale for their response. Next, each pair of students joins another pair and they compare and add to their responses. Finally, this group of four must reach consensus by choosing "yes" (sharks are bad) or "no" (sharks are not bad) and defending their response.

The discussion web can be used with both literary and informational texts. For instance, when used with a literary text, students can be asked to defend the actions of a particular character. Using the discussion web structure with students encourages rich conversation and promotes a high level of engagement. Further, students are required to use academic language in conversing with their peers, thereby reinforcing essential vocabulary and concepts.

DISCUSSION WEB

YES   NO

_____   _____

_____   _____

_____   _____

_____   _____

_____   _____

Discussion Question

Decision and Rationale:

_____

_____

_____

_____

_____

_____

Large Group Consensus:

_____

_____

_____

_____

_____

_____

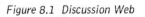

Figure 8.1 Discussion Web

TEACHERS' VOICES

Our Favorite Discourse Protocols

Graffiti

Darell Rickmers

P-5 SPANISH TEACHER

A protocol that my students really like is called "Graffiti." Here is the way it works. I list a topic, statement, or idea on the top of several pieces of chart paper, using one topic per chart. Then I divide the class into the same number of groups. Each group is assigned to one of the charts. The group discusses the topic and then they write on the chart paper what they discussed that answers the question or pertains to the topic. They are given a specified amount of time and a specific color of marker to use. Then each group rotates from chart to chart until they have written their responses on each chart paper in the room. They are not permitted to replicate what is already on the chart. If they choose, they can note inaccuracies and write and explain their correction, or they can write a new response, answer or statement that is not already on the chart. Once every group has had a chance to work on every "graffiti wall," we discuss them as a group to validate or make corrections as necessary.

Floor Buddies

Amy Baker

THIRD GRADE TEACHER

This is one of my favorites for my third graders. I love having my babies sitting on the floor near me during whole lesson time. I present the lesson and then we practice. I found out early on though that the same few students catch on quickly and give the answers, leaving the same other few students able to hide and not give answers. So, I take popsicle sticks, (craft sticks) and have half with yellow stickers and the other half with green. Then I number them. Each child gets one stick. They partner up with the person who matches their number. Green and yellow 1s go together, green and yellow 2s go together, and so on. Now we have floor buddies. (The first and second time through it takes a few minutes to explain and then after that it is so easy. It gives them different partners to work with each time. It is random and there is no choosing who gets to sit by whom.)

215

Now when we are settled in our places with our floor buddies, dry erase boards, erasers, and markers, we can begin. The lesson usually goes like this:

1. Whole lesson.
2. Examples worked together as a whole group.
3. Examples worked as partners.
4. Examples worked as individuals and checked by your partners. If the partners did not reach the same answer, they try to figure out why and come up with the right answer. (This is where the teacher steps in. In the beginning of the year you have to teach students how to work it out if you come to different answers.)

This floor buddy system is fun because is breaks up those little cliques and the kids work with others. You see friendships bloom and you see kids really start to shine in areas that they have never been able to shine before because others have never given them a chance.

Songs and Rhymes

Rebekah Pascucci

KINDERGARTEN TEACHER

In my classroom I use songs and rhymes to teach literacy skills that reinforce language development. I have found that using this strategy allows all students to participate in the classroom discourse and no student is singled out to carry the conversation. Through this method, each student gains confidence in using the literacy skill as they practice the skill correctly. The repetition of the songs and rhymes allows my students to master literacy skills and then build upon that foundation as they learn new skills. I most often use this discourse pattern because I have found that all students are engaged, practice the skill correctly, and gain confidence as we use the songs to review and introduce new literacy skills.

Musical Shares

Megan Bechard

7TH GRADE LANGUAGE ARTS TEACHER

This discourse protocol gets students moving, it involves music, and students will think it's a game! Students stand up with whatever you want them to share (journals or open-ended questions work best) and a pencil. You start the music and students move around the room. When you stop the music, students pair with the person closest to them. They read their work to their partner. After they share, they initial each other's papers so that they find a new partner the next round. After a few minutes, start the music again.

This game works best if you lay down some ground rules before playing. My rules are: (1) When the music is on, you must be walking, not running or standing still; (2) when the music stops, you get two giant steps (only) to find your partner (this keeps them from running to their friends); (3) both partners share and initial each other's paper. Try this protocol out the next time your students need to get some energy out!

Thanks to the teachers of the Culture and Language Academy for Success (CLAS) for sharing this protocol with us.

Peer Collaboration

Angelia Howard

MIDDLE SCHOOL SPECIAL EDUCATION TEACHER

I find that the more engaged and hands-on an activity is, the more my students can relate. Some of the simple discourse methods I frequently use are "elbow partner" sharing, free conversation, role play, interviews, drama, and presentations in various forms. I think that peer collaboration is the key when using any method. When students are allowed to drive the discussion, engage in finding the answer and analyze their opinions in order to draw conclusions, they are actively engaged and learn from each other. For example, to better understand a concept in math or science, I have students do the following:

1. Draw models of a topic.
2. Write or verbalize explanations of their models.
3. Critique their peers' models.
4. Revise their models based on this feedback.
5. Discuss their own questions in an open forum.

I also use a vocabulary wall that is like a "graffiti wall." The students work in groups to find synonyms, draw pictures, and/or define the "word of the day" across the curriculum and write these on the wall.

Inside/Outside Circle

Megan Bechard

7TH GRADE LANGUAGE ARTS TEACHER

When I want students to share open-ended responses, I like using the inside/outside circle. First, you split the class into two *equal* groups (jump in yourself if you have to). The two groups make circles, one inside the other. The inside circle faces the outside circle, with pairs of students standing face-to-face. I instruct students to share their answers, and give them a time limit in which to do so. I make sure to tell them that both circles need to share in the time allotted! When the time is up, either the inside or outside circle moves one person to the left or right. Make sure the same circle moves the same way each time, or students may end up talking to the same person twice. Instruct students what to share next and start the process over. I find this protocol works best outside on a pretty day. There's more space to make the circles, and kids love getting outside for a bit. This discourse protocol makes something simple like sharing answers more fun.

Line Dancing

Laura Hampton

KINDERGARTEN TEACHER

This year, I decided to try something new with my students to encourage them to share their journal entries, so I invented "line dancing." This protocol is similar to "inside/outside circle," except students sit in two lines and face each other. Once they share with their partner, one student gets up and goes to the end of the line, and the entire line shifts. My students know to go to the rug and form their lines when I give them the cue "Let's go dancing!"

Discussion Web

Sue Ellis

6TH GRADE LANGUAGE ARTS TEACHER

I tried out the discussion web this year with my sixth grade students. I used an article in the May 10th issue of *Scope Magazine* entitled "Should Orcas Be Kept in Captivity?" We read the article orally (with some portions being read chorally), and then I handed the students the discussion web with the question about orca whales and whether they should be kept in captivity. Then I asked them to work on their own to complete the "yes" and "no" columns. After working on their own, I assigned them a partner to discuss further their "yes" and "no" rationale. I then asked them to make a decision on how they felt. Those thinking that orcas should be kept in captivity moved to one side of the room, and those thinking that orcas should not be kept in captivity moved to the other side of the room. Students at each side of the room then discussed the question a few minutes more. Finally, I asked them to sit at their desks and write a business letter to Sea World Orlando attempting to persuade the organization to adopt their point of view – either to allow orcas to be free or to continue to be held in captivity.

Call and Response
Madeline Todd

THIRD GRADE TEACHER

In order for all students to contribute to discussions, I use call and response. The majority of my students typically know the answers to short questions. If all students are given wait time to think of the correct response and then call out the response together, most of the students will participate. I truly believe that teaching students to answer and respond with a call and response creates a more engaging atmosphere which results in higher class morale, because each student is able to contribute responses throughout each and every lesson.

Boggle
Darell Rickmers

P-5 SPANISH TEACHER

"Boggle" is a game where I give my students a question about a unit we are discussing. Students are given a specified amount of time to develop a list of descriptions, phrases, and other words that are associated with the topic. Then, in three different rounds, students are asked to "scramble" to find a partner, and are given a specified amount of time to compare lists. (When I have the students "scramble," I give them specific things to use to find their partner, such as same shoes, same color pants, same eye color, same birth month, and so on. This alleviates friends matching with friends all the time.) For every item they have on their list that their partner does not have, they get two points. If both people have the item on their list, they get one point each. At the end of the time period, students "scramble" to find another partner. Once again, they compare their lists. This time, if one student has an item and the other doesn't, they get one point, and if both have the same thing, neither gets a point. Finally, students add up their points. The person with the most number of points gets to lead the next class assessment review session.

CONCLUSION

This chapter has reviewed the various sociolinguistic perspectives about language use, and has provided practical applications for promoting appropriate discourse practices in classrooms. Culturally responsive teachers believe that all students need to develop linguistic competence. Studies indicate, however, that students are rarely asked to use extended talk in classrooms; rather, classroom discourse is generally characterized by teacher control of student talk whereby individual students are asked to respond to teacher prompts in very limited ways. Further, students are rarely provided with opportunities to enhance their linguistic repertoires by exploring the concept of situational appropriateness for language use and by using language in purposeful ways. To develop written and oral language competence, it is essential that students engage in instructional conversation and dialogue. It is also essential that teachers acknowledge and use the communication structures of the students and families they serve.

Research shows that diversity matters, and the deep conflicts that exist between students' home languages and the language of the school impacts students' social status, educational access, and opportunities to construct their identities. As in Zane's case, these conflicts are real and frequently lead to resistance. Even when teachers provide opportunities for students to use their home languages in the classroom, students like Zane do not perceive these experiences as authentic when the teacher consistently lowers scores on assignments, assigns unfamiliar writing topics and communicates low expec-tating for student learning as a result of their failure to comply with expected forms of Standard English. Clearly, affirming student discourse as well as appre-ciating language variations requires more than providing opportunities for learners to use familiar words and phrases in oral discussions and written texts. Instruction that gives value to both "home language" and "school language" while teaching children the concept of situational appropriateness in language use empowers students like Zane.

As discussed in this chapter, the school culture is designed to perpetuate the economic and political status quo. When educational professionals see differ-ence, denigrate it, as well as attempt to correct it, many students face significant challenges as they seek to maintain their self-esteem and cultural integrity. These conflicts in the classroom represent complex and moral challenges for educators. There is inevitable tension in affirming the discourses of students, while also teaching them when, where, why and how to use Standard English forms in expected contexts without fostering the notion of assimilation.

This tension intensifies when coupled with the challenge of providing models of culturally responsive instruction without implying that there is one right way to implement the theory. Developing culturally responsive instructional practices is a life style as well as a process. The journey of becoming a culturally responsive teacher does not have a pre-determined point of arrival, nor should one walk this path without a willingness to experience a certain level of discomfort. Providing culturally responsive instruction for students is a life-long process of learning which involves reflection, honest self-assessment, dis-equilibrium, and the recognition that the majority of educators view the world from a point of privilege. This is a charge for all who have determined that *now* is the time to rid schools of beliefs and practices that perpetuate the oppression of any child. There are numerous children calling out for educators who will remain in the struggle, regardless of the price, to create classrooms filled with rich learning opportunities in which all children thrive.

Table 8.1 Summary of CRIOP Component: Discourse/Instructional Conversation

Element	What you would expect to see in a classroom where CRI practices are occurring	What you would expect to see in a classroom where CRI practices are not occurring
The teacher encourages and responds positively to children's use of home/native language/dialect and culturally-specific discourse styles.	There is peer conversation in the home language or dialect during both free and academic time. Students share stories in their home language/dialect ELL students communicate together in their native language. The teacher accepts students' home languages and dialects, while also teaching the standard vernacular. Students are supported in their use of culturally-specific ways of communicating, such as topic-associative discourse, topic-chaining discourse, and overlapping discourse patterns.	Students are discouraged from using their home language or dialect. ELL students are discouraged from using their native language outside of school. The teacher views topic-associative discourse, topic-chaining discourse, and overlapping discourse patterns as rambling talk. The teacher attempts to control and change student communication styles to match mainstream classroom discourse patterns.

Table 8.1 continued

Element	What you would expect to see in a classroom where CRI practices are occurring	What you would expect to see in a classroom where CRI practices are not occurring
The teacher shares control of classroom discourse with students and builds upon and expands upon student talk in an authentic way.	Students engage in genuine discussions versus "guess what's in the teacher's head." The teacher uses open-ended questions and various discourse protocols to elicit extended student talk. The teacher demonstrates active listening and responds in authentic ways to student comments; s/he encourages the same active listening from students.	There are strict boundaries between personal conversation and instructional conversation. Students rarely have opportunities for genuine discussions. There are few or no opportunities for extended student talk; rather, talk is dominated by the teacher.
The teacher promotes student engagement through culturally responsive discourse practices.	The teacher employs a variety of culturally appropriate discourse protocols to promote student participation and engagement (e.g., call and response, talking circle).	Discourse practices of various cultural groups are not used during instruction.
The teacher promotes equitable discourse practices.	Students use collaborative, overlapping conversation and participate actively, supporting the speaker during the creation of story talk or discussion and commenting/expanding upon the ideas of others. The teacher uses techniques to support equitable participation, such as wait time, feedback, turn-taking, and scaffolding of ideas. All students have the opportunity to participate in classroom discussions. There is a sense of congeniality and consensus building; students build on one another's ideas in a respectful way.	The teacher controls classroom discourse by assigning speaking rights to students. Students follow traditional norms in turn-taking. Not all students have the opportunity to participate in classroom discussions. Some students are allowed to dominate discussions.

Table 8.1 continued

Element	What you would expect to see in a classroom where CRI practices are occurring	What you would expect to see in a classroom where CRI practices are not occurring
The teacher provides structures that promote student collaborative talk.	Structures are used that promote student talk, such as think/pair/share, small group work, and partner work. Students collaborate and work together to solve problems. The teacher encourages the use of a "talk story like" participation structure to allow children to produce responses collaboratively.	Students are discouraged from talking together. Collaborating with other students is discouraged and may be regarded as "cheating." The teacher does not allow students to collaborate in producing answers.
The teacher provides opportunities for students to develop linguistic competence.	The teacher articulates expectations for language use (e.g., "I want you to reply using complete sentences. I want you to use these vocabulary words in your discussion") The teacher develops language objectives in addition to content objectives, having specific goals in mind for students' linguistic performance Students are engaged in authentic uses of language, (e.g., drama, discussion, purposeful writing and communication) Students are taught appropriate registers of language use for a variety of social contexts, and they are provided with opportunities to practice those registers in authentic ways	The teacher does not articulate expectations for language use. The teacher does not have language objectives for students; rather, only content objectives are evident. Students' use of language is limited and they do not use language in authentic ways. Students are not taught how to vary their language use in different social contexts and for different purposes.

REFLECTIVE ACTIVITIES

1 What is the role of schools in the imposition of a Standard English? How do these practices impact students in your classroom who are from culturally and linguistically diverse backgrounds?

2 Explore how the "Ebonics" debate and "English only" controversies demonstrate issues of language and power in schools and communities.

3 Ask students to become "language detectives" in the school, in the community, and at home. Have students listen to broadcasts on the television and radio, podcasts, sermons, school talk and conversations at home. Ask them to identify and discuss the different varieties of language that are used in different social contexts. Follow up with a discussion of why different varieties of languages are used in each context and the consequences for individuals who do not conform with the oral and written language expectations in specific social situations.

4 Observe your own use of language and codeswitching. For example, identify the differences in how you speak when talking with family members and when talking with strangers in a formal setting (e.g., school, doctor's office, job interview). How does the social context determine the language you used in each conversation?

5 Listen to the oral reading of poetry by Paul Laurence Dunbar such as *When Malindy Sings*, http://www.dunbarsite.org/gallery/When MalindySings.asp, which is written in dialect. Translate the work into Standard English. Identify and discuss how the translation changes meaning, mood, emphasis, tone and voice of the text. What did students learn by engaging in this deconstruction and comparison process?

REFERENCES

Alvermann, D. E. (1991). The Discussion Web: A graphic aid for learning across the curriculum. *The Reading Teacher, 45,* 92–99.

Au, K. H. (1980). Participation structures in a reading lesson with Hawaii children: An analysis of a culturally appropriate instructional event. *Anthropology and Education Quarterly, 11*(2), 91–115.

Au, K. H. (1993). *Literacy instruction in multicultural settings.* Belmont, CA: Wadsworth Publishing.

Au, K. (2006). *Multicultural issues and literacy achievement.* New York: Routledge.

August, D., & Shanahan, T. (Eds.). (2008). *Developing reading and writing in second-language learners: Lessons from the report of the National Literacy Panel on Language-Minority Children and Youth.* New York: Routledge.

Ballenger, C. (1999). *Teaching other people's children: Literacy and learning in a bilingual classroom.* New York: Teachers College Press.

Boykin, A. W. (1994). Afrocultural expression and its implications for schooling. In E. R. Hollins, J. E. King, & W. C. Hayman (Eds.), *Teaching diverse populations: Formulating a knowledge base* (pp. 225–273). Albany, NY: State University of New York Press.

Brock, C., Lapp, D., Salas, R., & Townsend, D. (2009). *Academic literacy for English learners: High-quality instruction across content areas.* New York: Teachers College Press.

Cazden, C. B. (2001). *Classroom discourse: The language of teaching and learning* (2nd ed.). Portsmouth, NH: Heinemann.

Cazden, C. B., & Mehan, H. (1989). Principles from sociology and anthropology: Context, code, classroom, and culture. In M. Reynolds (Ed.), *Knowledge base for the beginning teacher.* Elmsford, NY: Pergamon Press.

Christensen, L. (2000). *Reading, writing, and rising up: Teaching about social justice and the power of the written word.* Milwaukee: Rethinking Schools.

Crawford, J. (1999). *Bilingual education: History, politics, theory, and practice* (4th ed.). Trenton, NJ: Crane Publishing Co.

Cummins, J. (1979). Cognitive/academic language proficiency, linguistic interdependence, the optimal age question, and some other matters. *Working Papers on Bilingualism, 19,* 197–205.

Cummins, J. (1994). From coercive to collaborative relations of power in the teaching of literacy. In B. M. Ferdman, R. Weber, & A. G. Ramirez (Eds.), *Literacy across languages and cultures* (pp. 295–331). Albany, NY: State University of New York Press.

Cummins, J. (1996). *Negotiating identities: Education for empowerment in a diverse society.* Ontario, CA: California Association for Bilingual Education.

Cummins, J. (2000). *Language, power, and pedagogy: Bilingual children in the crossfire.* Clevedon: Multilingual Matters.

Darling-Hammond, L. (2010). *The flat world and education: How America's commitment to equity will determine our future.* New York: Teachers College Press.

Delpit, L. (1988). The silenced dialogue: Power and pedagogy in educating other people's children. *Harvard Educational Review, 58,* 280–297.

Delpit, L. (1995). *Other people's children: Cultural conflict in the classroom.* New York: The New Press.

Delpit, L. (1997). Ebonics and culturally responsive instruction. *Rethinking schools: An urban educational journal, 12*(1), 6–7.

Dowdy, J. K. (2002). Ovuh dyuh. In L. Delpit, & J. K. Dowdy (Eds.) *The skin that we speak: Thoughts on language and culture in the classroom.* New York: The New Press.

Eller, R. G. (1989). Ways of meaning: Exploring cultural differences in students' written compositions. *Linguistics and Education, 1*(4), 341–358.

Fairchild, H. H., & Edwards-Evans, S. (1990). African American dialects and schooling: A review. In A. M. Padilla, H. H. Fairchild, & C. M. Valadez (Eds.), *Bilingual education: Issues and strategies* (pp. 75–86). Newbury Park, CA: Sage.

Ford, D. Y., Howard, T. C., Harris, J. J., & Tyson, C. A. (2000). Creating culturally responsive classrooms for gifted African American students. *Journal for the Education of the Gifted, 23*(4), 397–427.

Freeman, D., & Freeman, Y. S. (1999). The California reading initiative: A formula for failure for bilingual students? *Language Arts, 76,* 241–248.

Gándara, P. (2000). In the aftermath of the storm: English learners in the post-227 era. *Bilingual Research Journal Online, 24*(1–2), 1–13.

Gay, G. (1994). *At the essence of learning: Multicultural education.* West Lafayette, IN: Kappa Delta Pi.

Gay, G. (2000). *Culturally responsive teaching: Theory, research and practice.* New York: Teachers College Press.

Gee, J. P. (1990). *Social linguistics and literacies.* London: Falmer Press.

Gee, J. P. (1992). What is literacy? In P. Shannon (Ed.), *Becoming political: Readings and writings in the politics of literacy education* (pp. 21–28). Portsmouth, NH: Heinemann.

Gee, J. P. (1996). *Social linguistics and literacies: Ideology in discourse.* London: Falmer Press.

Giroux, H. A. (1987). Introduction. In P. Freire, & D. Macedo (Eds.), *Literacy: Reading the word and the world.* South Hadley, MA: Bergin and Garvey.

Giroux, H. A. (1988). Literacy and the pedagogy of voice and political empowerment. *Educational Theory, 38,* 61–75.

Goldenberg, C. (1991). *Instructional conversations and their classroom application* (Educational Practice Report 2). Berkeley, CA: The National Center for Research on Cultural Diversity and Second Language Learning.

Goodlad, J. I. (1984). *A place called school: Prospects for the future.* New York: McGraw-Hill.

Gutiérrez, K. D., Baquedano-López, P., & Alvarez, H. H. (2001). Literacy as hybridity: Moving beyond bilingualism in urban classrooms. In M. de la Luz Reyes, & J. J. Halcón (Eds.), *The best for our children: Critical perspectives on literacy for Latino students* (pp. 122–141). New York: Teachers College Press.

Gutiérrez, K. D., Baquedano-López, P., & Asanto, J. (2000). "English for the children": The new literacy of the old world order, language policy and educational reform. *Bilingual Research Journal, 24*(1&2), 87–112.

Heath, S. B. (1983). *Ways with words: Language, life, and work in communities and classrooms.* New York: Cambridge University Press.

Hollie, S. (2005). Acknowledging the language of African American students: Instruction that works. In B. Hammond, M. E. R. Hoover, & I. P. McPhail (Eds.), *Teaching African American learners to read: Perspectives and practices* (pp. 189–199). Newark, DE: International Reading Association.

Hymes, D. (1985). Introduction. In C. C. Cazden, V. P. John, & D. Hymes (Eds.), *Functions of language in the classroom* (pp. xi–xvii). Prospect Heights, IL: Waveland.

Hymes, D. (1996). *Ethnography, linguistics, narrative inequality: Toward an understanding of voice.* Bristol, PA: Taylor & Francis.

Iddings, A. C. D., Risko, V. J., & Rampulla, M. P. (2009). When you don't speak their language: Guiding English-language learners through conversations about text. *The Reading Teacher, 63*(1), 52–61.

Janks, H. (2010). *Literacy and power.* New York: Routledge.

226

Kochman, T. (1985). Black American speech events and a language program for the classroom. In C. B. Cazden, V. P. John, & D. Hymes (Eds.), *Functions of language in the classroom* (pp. 211–261). Prospect Heights, IL: Waveland.

Krashen, S. D., & Biber, D. (1988). *On course: Bilingual education's success in California.* Los Angeles: California Association for Bilingual Education.

Labov, W. (1972). *Language in the inner city: Studies in the Black English vernacular.* Philadelphia, PA: University of Pennsylvania Press.

Lapp, D., Fisher, D., Flood, J., & Moore, K. (2002). "I don't want to teach it wrong": An investigation of the role families believe they should play in the early literacy development of their children. In D. Shallert, C. Fairbanks, J. Worthy, B. Maloch, & J. Hoffman (Eds.), *51st Yearbook of the National Reading Conference* (pp. 275–287). Chicago: National Reading Conference.

Lee, C. D. (1995). Signifying as a scaffold for literary interpretation. *Journal of Black Psychology, 21*(4), 357–381.

López-Reyna, N. A. (1996). The importance of meaningful contexts in bilingual special education: Moving to whole language. *Learning Disabilities Research and Practice, 11*(2), 120–131.

Lyon, G. E. (1999). *Where I'm from: Where poems come from.* Spring, TX: Absey & Co., Inc.

Martinez-Roldan, C. (2005). The inquiry acts of bilingual children in literature discussions. *Language Arts, 83*(1), 22–33.

McDermott, R. (1977). Social relations as contexts for learning in school. *Harvard Educational Review, 47,* 198–213.

McDermott, R. (1987). Achieving school failure: An anthropological approach to illiteracy and social stratification. In G. D. Spindler (Ed.), *Education and cultural processes* (2nd ed., pp. 173–209). Prospect Heights, IL: Waveland Press.

McIntyre, E., Kyle, D. W., Chen, C., Kraemer, J., & Parr, J. (2009). *Six principles for teaching English language learners in all classrooms.* Thousand Oaks, CA: Corwin.

Moll, L. C., & Díaz, E. (1987). Change as the goal of education research. *Anthropology & Education Quarterly, 184,* 300–311.

Moll, L. C., & Dworin, J. E. (1996). Biliteracy development in classrooms: Social dynamics and cultural possibilities. In D. Hicks (Ed.), *Discourse, learning and schooling* (pp. 221–246). New York: Cambridge University Press.

Montero, M. K., & Kuhn, M. R. (2009). English language learners and fluency development: More than speed and accuracy. In L. Helman (Ed.), *Literacy development with English learners* (pp. 156–177). New York: The Guilford Press.

Mora, J. K. (2002). Caught in a policy web: The impact of education reform on Latino education. *Journal of Latinos and Education, 1*(1), 29–44.

Moss, B. J. (2001). From the pews to the classroom: Influence of the African American church on academic literacy. In J. L. Harris, A. G. Kamhi, & K. E. Pollock (Eds.), *Literacy in African American communities* (pp. 195–211). Mahwah, NJ: Lawrence Erlbaum.

Orellana, M. F., & Reynolds, J. F. (2008). Cultural modeling: Leveraging bilingual skills for school paraphrasing tasks. *Reading Research Quarterly, 43*(1), 48–65.

Pang, V. O. (1998). Educating the whole child: Implications for teachers. In V. O. Pang, & L. L. Cheng (Eds.), *Struggling to be heard: The unmet needs of Asian Pacific American children* (pp. 265–304). Albany, NY: SUNY Press.

Phillips, S. U. (1983). *The invisible culture: Communication in classroom and community on the Warm Springs Indian Reservation.* New York: Longman.

Powers, S. W. (1999). The examination of teacher discourse with four Eastern Kentucky fourth-graders during writing conferences. (Unpublished doctoral dissertation). University of Kentucky.

Powers, S. W. (2002). Home and school language connections for a struggling Appalachian writer: Issues of equitable pedagogy for culturally diverse student populations. *Reading Horizons, 43*(2), 85–102.

Purcell-Gates, V. (1995). *Other people's words: The cycle of low literacy.* Cambridge, MA: Harvard University Press.

Purcell-Gates, V. (2002). "... As soon as she opened her mouth!": Issues of language, literacy, and power. In L. Delpit, & J. K. Dowdy (Eds.), *The skin that we speak: Thoughts on language and culture in the classroom* (pp. 121–141). New York: The New Press.

Redd, T. M., & Webb., K. S. (2005). *African American English: What a writing teacher should know.* Urbana, IL: NCTE.

Smith, B. O. (1971). On the anatomy of teaching. In R. T. Hyman (Ed.), *Contemporary thought on teaching* (pp. 20–27). Englewood Cliffs: NJ: Prentice-Hall.

Smitherman, G. (1977). *Talkin' and testifyin': The language of Black America.* Detroit: Wayne State University Press.

Stubbs, M. (2002). Some basic sociolinguistic concepts. In L. Delpit, & J. K. Dowdy (Eds.), *The skin that we speak: Thoughts on language and culture in the classroom* (pp. 63–85). New York: The New Press.

Tharp, R. G., & Gallimore, R. (1991). *The instructional conversation: Teaching and learning in social activity* (Research Report 2). Santa Cruz, CA: The National Center for Research on Cultural Diversity and Second Language Learning, University of California, Santa Cruz.

Thomas, W. P., & Collier, V. P. (2002). *A national study of school effectiveness for language minority students' long-term academic achievement.* Santa Cruz, CA: Center for Research on Education, Diversity and Excellence, University of California-Santa Cruz.

Valenzuela, A. (1999). *Subtractive schooling: U.S.-Mexican youth and the politics of caring.* Albany, NY: SUNY Press.

Vogt, L. A., Jordan, C., & Tharp, R. G. (1987). Explaining school failure, producing school success: Two cases. In E. Jacob, & C. Jordan (Eds.), *Explaining the school performance of minority students* [Theme Issue]. *Anthropology and Education Quarterly, 18,* 276–286.

Vygotsky, L. S. (1962). *Thought and Language.* Cambridge, MA: MIT Press.

Vygotsky, L. S. (1978). *Mind in society: The development of higher psychological processes.* Cambridge, MA: Harvard University Press.

Waxman, H. C., & Tellez, K. (2002). *Research synthesis on effective teaching practices for English language learners.* (Publication Series No. 3). Philadelphia: The Mid-Atlantic Regional Educational Laboratory at Temple University, Center for Research in Human Development and Education.

Wheeler, R. S., & Swords, R. (2004). Codeswitching: Tools of language and culture transform the dialectically diverse classroom. *Language Arts, 81*(6), 470–480.

White, E.B. (1952). *Charlotte's Web.* New York: HarperCollins.

Williams, W. (1982). *Language consciousness and cultural liberation in Black America.* Paper presented at the 6th Annual Conference of the National Council for Black Studies, Chicago, March. Available from: Center for Afro-American Studies, University of Washington, Seattle.

Wong Fillmore, L. (1991). When learning a second language means losing the first. *Early Childhood Research Quarterly, 6,* 323–346.

Part III

Becoming Critical

Chapter 9

Sociopolitical Consciousness and Multiple Perspectives: Empowering Students to Read the World

Yolanda Gallardo Carter

We do not believe in those who state, in hypocritical intonation, that life is really like this—a few having so much, millions having nothing. Our weakness is not a virtue. Let us pretend, however, that we do believe in their discourse . . . We need time to prepare our own discourse that will shake up mountains and valleys, rivers and oceans and that will leave them stunned and fearful. Our different discourse—our action-word—will be spoken by our whole bodies: our hands, our feet, our reflections. All within us will speak a life-bearing language—even the instruments that our hands will use, when, in communion, we shall transform our weakness into our strength.

(Freire, 2007)

Our view of our craft and of our role as teachers can be quite narrow. With the emphasis on federal, state, and local policies, we focus on the task at hand—teaching core content and doing it well. As a new teacher over two decades ago on the border of Arizona with Mexico, I was so excited to meet the new challenge of teaching. All I could think about were my students and how I was going to get them solidly from point A to point B. It took some time, but I got the hang of how to introduce core content to my students and how to make it meaningful. So I thought.

As I began to learn more about "effective teaching," I paid closer attention to the world that my students lived in and how that world was different from my own. I listened to their discourse and that of their parents and was struck by the complexity and beauty of all they had to offer, but also how easily it could be overlooked. I was *already* overlooking their voices. I also paid attention to the issues we faced in Arizona and how they were so intricately connected to, and yet at times, separate from those faced by individuals living just a mile away in another country.

Most of my students came from that "other country," Mexico. Some of them even lived "across the line" as we would say, but it really meant "across the U.S./Mexico border." I soon realized that my "effective teaching" was leaving out an entire story, the story of my students, their families, and the place in which they lived. Was I really being an effective teacher by focusing only on core content? Was I leaving far too many unaddressed gaps in the instruction I provided? Worse yet, was I leaving my own students out of their education by unintentionally silencing them?

The gaps that existed in my teaching resulted from a lack of making important connections for my students, their families, and for me as the facilitator of their learning. The standards that I focused on were the building blocks, or the starting point, of my job as a teacher. They gave me the "what" with regard to the content and materials I put forth each day. I was missing the "how" and the "why." And for all of my good intentions, without these three things, my students were missing out on the kind of education they deserved.

I had the good fortune to work with a phenomenal educator while teaching on the border of Mexico. Her name was Jackie Scott and she was the individual who would travel to the elementary schools in the district to provide instruction for the gifted and talented program. I taught Kindergarten my first two years, and Jackie would come in and do whole group sessions with the students since they were too young to be identified for the accelerated program available to the older students. As Jackie posed questions to my students, she moved them toward critical thinking in a way I had never experienced. With every scenario she took the children through, there was meaningful questioning, and rarely was there ever one right answer or only one way to solve a problem. I noticed a different level of engagement when Jackie facilitated my students' learning. They were excited and unafraid to learn. This, I thought, was the way I needed to teach—unafraid. From this point on, critical thinking became my vehicle of instruction. I took the state standards and presented them in a way that would challenge my students. To this day, I consider Jackie Scott to be one of my greatest teachers. She started my path toward an engaged and critical pedagogy.

I went on to teach second grade after my first two years of teaching at the kindergarten level, and was amazed at the results I was getting from students by ensuring that critical thought was part of our classroom culture. I knew *what* I needed to get done (focus on standards) and *how* it should be carried through (critical thought), but there was an element missing. My students would be the ones to teach me the greatest lesson of all: As teachers, we are ineffective if we don't understand *why* we practice the way we do, and how our practice is connected to a much bigger picture.

That year, I had students who were struggling with many different issues. Some had lost parents, some had been abused by parents, some had parents serving in the Gulf War, and some were struggling with difficult disabilities. The Gulf War had just started and the students were very concerned about what the war meant for them. We began to explore issues that moved us outside of our classroom and into the world in which each of us needed to function. I realized that if I took the vehicle of critical thought to a different level, I could help my students better understand the issues that surrounded them in their communities. By doing so, they could face issues with knowledge and the ability to ask questions as well as be empowered and think about how to empower others. In my third year of teaching I learned to use critical pedagogy, and education took on a whole new dimension for both my students and me. In this chapter, we will discuss the "what," "how," and "why" of teaching and learning through a sociopolitical lens.

SUPPORTING LITERATURE

The literature that supports this domain of the Culturally Responsive Instruction Observation Protocol (CRIOP) infers that utilizing a sociopolitical perspective can move education from a standard traditional experience where the teacher is the "keeper of knowledge," to one that is transformational for everyone within the educational community (students, students' families/caregivers, teachers, administrators, staff, and the surrounding community). As delineated by Darder, Baltodano, and Torres (2009), "all human activity requires theory to illuminate it and provide a better understanding of the world as we find it and as it might be" (p. 13). Practice without consideration of theory is mechanical and fragmented.

Linking theory to practice allows us to move toward *praxis*. As defined by Paulo Freire (1970), *praxis* combines reflective thought, dialogue, and action in order to change or transform society. Sociopolitical consciousness is grounded in the view popularized by Freire (1970) that there cannot be true *praxis* if individuals are taken out of the context of their own learning. That is, students are meant to question, think, talk, and interact with issues and information in a manner that is very different from traditional schooling.

Traditional modes of education emphasize the idea that teachers "fill" students with knowledge, just as an empty jug is filled with water or a blank slate filled with notes. Freire (1970) refers to this kind of education as the "banking model," where teachers "deposit" ideas in the minds of their students. This type of instruction removes the student from his/her learning and thus also inhibits the democratic process within schools that must exist if learning is to be equitable for all. Rather than serving as a means for empowerment, education becomes a means for control.

An individual's life experiences are not universal; instead, they are shaped and mediated by many factors. Such factors as race, ethnicity, language, religion, gender, and social class, can have a profound impact on a person's world-view. The lack of sociocultural consciousness or awareness by teachers regarding how their students may approach life and learning can lead them to rely on their own socialization and world-view, which can result in a misinterpretation of students' abilities (Villegas & Lucas, 2007). *Praxis* cannot be achieved if educators are unaware that their students bring multiple perspectives to the thought, dialogue, reflection, and interaction that occur in democratic classrooms. Teachers of liberating or democratic classrooms have a high level of awareness of the world around them and how they themselves enact agency within that world. Ball (2000) emphasizes that teachers must help raise students' consciousness about life possibilities and prompt them to pose questions about their perceptions of themselves in the world.

Contrary to the commonsense notion that school is the "great equalizer," critical theorists—or those who advocate *praxis* in education—emphasize that schools largely reinforce inequality. This is particularly true for students from marginalized populations, who often lag behind their white, upper-/middle-class peers. Therefore, a commitment to a democratic educational process, where all stakeholders have a voice, is critical if we intend for learning to be equitable. In order for educators to move toward a more liberating form of education, it is important to understand how educational institutions have reinforced a dominant ideology, so that those institutions can begin to be transformed toward equity and justice.

Consideration of how the dominant ideology affects interactions with the school and community is important to understand if students are going to be empowered actors within these contexts. As Macedo, Dendrinos, and Gounari (2003) explain, humans' way of communicating not only reflects, but also produces and/or reproduces, specific ideologies as well as the feelings, values, and beliefs that define their historical and social location (i.e., an individual's race, ethnicity, gender, age, geography, or other attributes). Ideology, as it relates to educational institutions, can be viewed in numerous ways. Referring to ideology from the perspective of critical educational theorists, Hall (1981) sees ideology as the framework of thought that is used in society to give order and meaning to the social and political world. In this way, ideology is used as a point of reference for understanding the outside world and for conceptualizing one's place within that world. Ideology serves the purpose of giving us a way to organize our ideas and values. Because ideologies operate largely at an unconscious level, it becomes difficult to question or resist ideological norms, even if we feel there is something amiss about what drives most of what we do.

The ideology of the dominant social group, that is, White middle-/upper-class, is embedded in our current definition of literacy and our literacy practices. The popular paradigm of literacy instruction, which suggests that literacy can be removed from its sociopolitical context and reduced to a series of sub-skills, is based upon the idea that literacy can be neutral (e.g. that it is "objective"), and hence does not support a particular ideological perspective. Yet every text, which includes everything that can be *read* for the message being communicated, contains certain assumptions about the world.

Even educators, who take part in literacy instruction with their students, cannot be neutral since they themselves cannot be removed from their own thoughts and opinions about matters of life or education. Freire (2007) speaks of the difficulty of being neutral when he points to the notion that teaching in and of itself is a political act. He states that:

> The politicalness of education requires that a teacher know him/herself, in objective terms and on an objective level, on the level of his or her practice . . . the political nature of education requires that the educator be coherent about that choice (what they are for or against).
>
> (p. 60)

In addition, in Freire's view, neither the text nor the facilitator of the text can be neutral. Therefore, the act of engaging in literacy practices cannot be neutral and will always be tied to specific ideologies.

As we have demonstrated in previous chapters, schools are designed to socialize students to accept the values of the dominant culture. This ideology serves as a powerful means of reproducing valued knowledge about the dominant culture and, in essence, silences those who do not have access to it or permission to question it. Consider, for example, the privileged status of Standard American English, and the pervasive acceptance of individual upward mobility versus collective success. Even accepted classroom discourse patterns, such as the expectations for turn-taking and responding, are based upon dominant, Euro-centric norms.

Within this hegemonic structure, the responsibility of success or failure in school is placed upon the individual student. Such cultural knowledge is often abstract and not necessarily reflected in the lived realities of all students. Therefore, students who do not understand the nuances inherent in mainstream cultural behavior are often blamed when they perform poorly in school. The fact that they have a difficult time adapting to mainstream standards is considered to be their fault as opposed to the fault of an institution that does not validate their ways of knowing or allow them to be a part of their own learning. Thus, in many cases, students from underserved populations are set up for failure, thereby perpetuating a social hierarchy of privilege and marginalization. Darder (1991) explains:

> The fact that the opportunities to succeed in the dominant culture are unequally distributed is ignored in the context of a traditional educational discourse. This individualization of responsibility serves effectively to diffuse class and race identity and interclass/race hostility. As such, it effectively provides an acceptable justification for the unequal distribution of resources in American society . . . The class system of education provides an effective vehicle for the dominant culture to civilize bicultural populations to ensure that society remains orderly and safe. As such, the dominant culture is able to maintain its status of privilege and power over society and its institutions.
>
> (pp. 5–6)

Ideology, as central to this hierarchical structure, is an important pedagogical tool when it is used to examine the relationship between dominant school culture and the contradictory lived experiences of some students, particularly those of economically, culturally, and linguistically diverse backgrounds (Darder, 1991). This concept is exemplified in the way students, regardless of cultural and/or linguistic barriers, are taught to read and write (Freire, 1970; Freire & Macedo, 1987). As noted previously, our texts and literacy instructional practices are not neutral; rather, they reflect a particular understanding of what constitutes "literacy" and what is important to know. Thus, it is critical to look at how dominant ideologies shape academic expectations and how the concept of reproducing inequity is exemplified in the literacy instruction provided to all students. Traditional literacy instructional practices, embedded in a dominant ideology, promote a "banking model" of education, thereby encouraging passivity as students become mere "receivers of knowledge." Teachers, too, become reduced to "the specialist in transferring knowledge" (Shor & Freire, 1987, p. 8).

It is important to understand that literacy learning and use always take place within a social context. Literacy is social. Our reductionist model of literacy, which primarily was developed for instructional efficiency and ease of testing, views literacy as a series of discrete skills that can be taught outside of their sociopolitical context. Thus, "comprehension" becomes reduced to identifying the main idea and supporting details, rather than engaging in genuine analysis and critique that might unlock the internal messages of the text. Such skills-based models deny the inherently social nature of literacy and position students as "objects" or as "passive recipients." This position not only leads to passivity, but it is also disempowering for both students and teachers. Students become "empty receptacles" to be filled, and teachers are forced to rely on published materials. Indeed, given the privileged status of achievement tests, which generally are based upon a reductionist model of literacy, teachers are afraid to veer from these materials in order to meet the diverse needs of their students. Removing literacy from the social context in which it is used and produced ignores the critical importance of the student–teacher relationship and the cultural knowledge and resources that students bring to learning. Beyond this, it also ignores the ideological (political) nature of literacy.

Teachers who advocate the use of critical literacy realize there is a relationship between power, knowledge, language, and ideology. They recognize the inequalities that exist, and see literacy as an important tool that can be leveraged for transformative action and social justice (Wallowitz, 2008). As defined by many theorists (Darder, Baltodamo, & Torres, 2009; Freire, 1970; Powell, 1999; Shor, 1992; Wallowitz, 2008), critical literacy is a mindset, not a discrete set of skills. This mindset implies that literacy is seen in the various ways that humans interact with, and in, the world.

> Critical literacy examines texts in order to identify and challenge social constructs, underlying assumptions and ideologies, and power structures that intentionally or unintentionally perpetuate social inequalities and injustices. By employing critical literacy, one questions the construction of knowledge and searches for hidden agendas in school curricula, governmental legislation, corporation policies, and the media.
>
> (Wallowitz, 2008, p. 16)

Critical literacy goes beyond critical thinking that encompasses analysis, evaluation, and creative thought (Paul & Elder, 2005) to questioning established views and structures, thus involving students meaningfully in their own learning.

Thus, the notion of critical literacy suggests that literacy cannot be reduced to the "skill" of critical thinking. Rather, with critical literacy, the whole world becomes a text, i.e., the icons and symbols that represent dominant and subdominant ideologies are "read" as texts. As participants in a media-driven society, we are exposed to a myriad of texts daily. The choices we make in our daily lives — the kinds of toys and video games we enjoy, the type of clothing we wear, how we interact with others, even our notions of beauty — are driven by how we read the texts that are put before us. Billboards, television commercials, movies, advertisements, and other popular media are all "texts" that encode cultural messages about what constitutes "beauty" and "goodness," what we should aspire to, what is considered to be "acceptable" behavior. Hence, these kinds of texts are very powerful vehicles for reading the world, yet they are often overlooked as "texts" when we think about the role that literacy plays in our lives. Fickel (2009) writes:

> What does it mean to engage in a dialogic process that contextualizes and embeds literacy learning in the world of our students? First, it means recognizing that we live in a world of texts . . . We are surrounded on a daily basis by television, magazines, billboards, advertisements, movies, news-papers, and a myriad of other texts. These texts embody and convey important ideas and values that reflect cultural and social perspectives. To contextualize education for our students, we must draw from these sources and then engage with them in a critical examination of these texts. The purpose of this critical examination is to help students come to understand the texts as social, political, and ideological statements that reflect con-ceptions of "right," "good," "truth," and other beliefs about "the way the world does and should work."
>
> (p. 52)

The ultimate goal of a literacy that is critical is to illuminate the ways in which the dominant ideology is reinforced through the material forms and structures of school and society in order to transform "the way the world works."

The practice of critical literacy is inherently tied to culturally relevant pedagogy. For culturally relevant instruction to be realized, teachers must be aware of their own ideological perspectives and how they inform their views, especially their views of their students, and what is important to know (what knowledge is of value). Understanding how the dominant ideology informs our practice is crucial if we are ever to become culturally relevant educators. Yet many of us have received a "banking education." Thus, as teachers, we must first engage in critical literacy in order to "illuminate" our own dominant realities, so that we can acknowledge the ways in which our students and families have been marginalized in our educational institutions and in society. By taking a critical stance on our view of the world, we can, in turn, help students do the same. If we as teachers are not critical, we cannot possibly encourage our students to be critical.

PRACTICAL APPLICATIONS

The only way to engage meaningfully in our learning and with one another is to "pursue inquiry in the world, with the world, and with each other" (Freire, 2009, p. 52). Students need to be led to understand their own agency—to see how their lives can make a difference in their communities and in society. McLaren (2009) reminds us that as individuals, we create and are created by the society in which we are a part. As an important socializing agent in mainstream American society (Bourdieu, 1973, 1977, 1984, 1987), the school must be a place that moves beyond traditional instruction to a place where the cultural and social contexts of students are explored through inquiry (McLaren, 2009). This type of inquiry prompts teachers to expand their notions of literacy to include critiquing and deconstructing the ideological messages found in texts.

Teaching students to read texts critically and to question their social location in the world implies understanding on the teacher's part that such questioning enriches the goals and objectives that must be met in today's educational system. The misconception that allowing students to question takes time away from addressing standards is prevalent. This misconception is particularly unfortunate for students from underrepresented populations, who tend to receive a "watered down" curriculum. Instead, critical literacy should be used

> [to] encourage students to use language to question the everyday world, to interrogate the relationship between language and power, to analyze popular culture and media, to understand how power relationships are socially constructed, and to consider actions that can be taken to promote social justice.
> (Lewison, Leland, & Harste, 2008, p. 3)

Educators of all students must be intentional about the opportunities they present their students to question the way things are in the world around them. Approaching teaching and learning in this way allows students from all backgrounds to see how their stories are connected to the stories of others. In essence, the use of critical literacy enriches instruction in an authentic way as opposed to taking anything away or adding to the work that needs to be done. Teaching students to question—while simultaneously addressing standards—is central to an enriched and meaningful experience for students. As Paulo Freire (1998) states, restless questioning or curiosity moves students toward uncovering elements of the "hidden curriculum" and allows us to be co-learners in our shared contexts. In the remainder of this chapter, I provide examples of how teachers might begin to implement a more critical pedagogy.

Questioning the Way Things Are

Teachers who are culturally responsive take the initiative to explore issues that they and their students deem important. Through this process, culturally responsive educators challenge the traditional way of relating to students, and ultimately involve them in a critically conscious way of learning (Shor & Freire, 1987). Encouraging students to question "the way things are" gives them an opportunity to challenge the status quo. By inviting students to think critically about social issues and to challenge the dominant norms endorsed in schools, they are better able to consider multiple perspectives and ways of viewing the world. Thus, students have the potential to become intellectual leaders within their classrooms and ultimately within their communities.

An example comes from my own teaching. My fourth grade students began a discussion surrounding the fun that the kindergarten students had celebrating Thanksgiving. They talked about how the younger students dressed as Pilgrims and Indians and how they missed doing those kinds of things. This discussion prompted me to engage my students in a dialogue about what they thought Thanksgiving was really like that first year. Together, we jumped into reading about what our school's social studies textbooks told us about that first Thanksgiving and we read about other perspectives that didn't come from textbooks. Once the students were given *permission* to question the traditional history presented to them, they saw things in a different light. It wasn't so much that they found conflicting information and explored the purpose authors and systems rely on to perpetuate hegemonic ideology, they saw that they could indeed question! Questioning information from historical accounts and examining the perpetuation of stereotypes helped students view themselves as pro-actors in their own learning. They didn't have to rely on me or any other educator to "impart" knowledge; they could build knowledge themselves! Students could seek and react to information based upon what they found to be compelling and relevant to their lives. Learning in this way was much more enriching for all of us.

Prompting students to leave the classroom or a lesson with more questions than those they started with is more important than most of us realize. We are accustomed to having answers or finding answers instantaneously, all the while believing that there is only one right answer to any question that may be posed. Putting thinking and learning into a confined space leaves no room for allowing ideas and thoughts to breathe. Looking at the way history is framed is a wonderful way to get students used to questioning the way things are and away from believing there are few questions to be asked or only single answers to be found.

Lewison, Leland, and Harste (2008) offer an example of the kinds of questions students pose when using a critical lens to look at history. They describe a trip that students took to a museum. During their visit to the museum, they viewed an exhibit on the history of war in North America and the conflicts in which Americans played a role. Students looked at the film and still life scenes placed before them and read the placards beneath each one. As they read the written texts, they noted the type of discourse used to convey what they saw in the pictures. They asked questions about how the placards helped them view the scenes in a particular way and why certain quotes were chosen in the descriptions they read. The students left the museum with more questions than they had prior to the field trip, posing questions about the purpose of the texts that were used in the exhibit (both in pictures and words), as well as questions about the funding source for the exhibit. The students had learned enough about questioning at that point to ask questions that went beyond what they saw at the surface level. This example is a very powerful one because it gives us a snapshot of how students grasp critical thinking and acting as they read the world around them, and how doing so empowers them to go deeper with their understanding.

Taking Action on Real-World Problems

Instruction that is culturally responsive makes deliberate connections to the l ives of students and the world in which they live. Teachers who are culturally responsive understand that students ought to be active participants in the democracy to which they have a right (Powell, Cantrell, & Adams, 2001). Powell (1999) delineates the importance of giving students "voice in the active process of deliberation and debate—in determining a common destiny, in defining the common good, in shaping a collective future" (p. 58). Culturally responsive teachers prompt students to identify issues that are relevant to them and their families. Additionally, culturally responsive teachers facilitate student advocacy for their communities by providing opportunities to investigate and take action on issues students have identified as critical. Through helping students write letters to the editor, visit with policy-makers, meet with members of the community, etc., teachers empower students toward advocacy for themselves and others.

Powell, Cantrell, and Adams (2001) discuss the connection between democracy, literacy, and power and the role teachers can play in addressing inequities that exist in society with their students. By focusing on literacy as a means for allowing students to be involved in inquiry, educators can move beyond a reductionist definition that perceives literacy as a discrete set of skills or hoops that children jump through in a systematic and predictable order. Instead, they can focus on using literacy purposefully to involve students in real policy change. The authors describe how students from Kentucky voiced their concern over the destruction of a mountain site in their state by finding out about the issue, interviewing individuals on both sides, organizing a rally, getting in touch with local newspapers in the area, making trips to the mountain site, and preparing a proposal for policy-makers that included recommendations that would save the mountain (see Chapter 7 in this volume). All of these actions demonstrated the students' willingness to learn about this land site and what it meant to local residents, and understand the implications of strip mining. The students weren't just reading and writing about the complexities of tearing down mountains, they were involved in the process of social justice through the use of meaningful, critical literacy. By taking action on this real-world problem, these students saved the mountain from destruction!

The issues addressed by students do not have to be as lofty as saving a mountain, however. Cary (2000) documents how an ESL teacher, Mr. Ledesma, led his students to take action on a dangerous situation near their school. The school where this teacher and his students taught and learned was in the heart of a very populated city. There was a great deal of traffic surrounding the school, and the students noticed how dangerous it was to get from one side of the street to the other. The vehicles of a couple of parents had been struck during that particular school year, and while there were no serious injuries, Mr. Ledesma and his students decided it was time to take action. They discussed the situation and decided that it was necessary to have a traffic light installed that would diminish the danger on the busy street near the school. The students wrote several letters to the mayor of the city, to the office of public works and the police department describing the dilemma their school faced and their proposed solution. As they wrote their letters, they kept their audience in mind and made sure that they were being specific to the individuals who would be reading their writing. In the end, the students never got their traffic light, but they learned a great deal about identifying important issues within their community and writing to specific audiences for specific purposes. They also learned that voicing their concerns was very important, even if they didn't get immediate results.

Using education to change things in small or big ways is true empowerment. Freire (1970) talks about an education that can be liberating instead of alienating, empowering instead of oppressive. Isn't teaching in this way the only choice we have if we are truly interested in demonstrating the belief that all students can learn, and that students can make a difference in the world in which they live? When teachers teach for liberation, they do not do so in a neutral fashion; teaching involves beliefs, values, and ideals, which are never neutral. Edelsky (1999) underscores this point when she states: "Classroom literacy can never be politically neutral. Literacy can be taught as a tool of critical inquiry or of passive transmission. It can be a vehicle for posing and solving important social problems or for accepting official explanations and solutions" (pp. 121–123). By prompting students to take action on real-world problems and issues, we are providing an education that tells them they can take action in their own self-interest. This type of education is particularly important for students and their families who feel that they lack the agency to take action on issues that negatively affect their lives.

TEACHERS' VOICES

"This Land Is Your Land"

Participants in the Summer Institute

CENTER FOR CULTURALLY RELEVANT PEDAGOGY, GEORGETOWN, KY

During our summer institute, we listened to Pete Seeger sing the original version of Woody Guthrie's song "This Land Is Your Land" (Guthrie, 1956). This version includes two controversial verses that are a commentary on poverty in our nation.

We were asked to write our own verses to this song. Here are some of the verses that we created. Exploring the words to the song and writing our own verses caused us to think critically about equity in America, and motivated us to learn more about the time period in which Guthrie produced these lyrics.

As I stood waiting, and the church doors opened,
The people filed out, no words were spoken.
No glances given to the famished ocean.
This land is lost to you and me.

(Darell Rickmers)

This land ain't your land, this land ain't my land
Unless you have money and are a white man.
From the concrete jungles to the oil-filled waters,
This land was made by you and me.

(Kara Ruby, Sarah Carey, & Lauren Cornele)

On the streets I notice all different faces,
Who have come from different places.
Our tolerance is being tested: Are you sure that
This land was made for you and me?

(Madeline Todd)

I heard footsteps in the hallway,
My mom said, "Hurry, get in the closet."
My heart was pounding, don't take my mommy.
This land is not for my family.

(Heidi Hamlyn)

There was no food, the sign displayed.
The people stayed in line anyway.
The hope of my people had slowly faded away.
But they knew they would be back the very next day.

(Leslie Busch)

REFERENCE

Guthrie, W. (1956). *This land is your land*. Retrieved from http://www.arlo.net.

Deconstructing Negative Stereotypes in Instructional Materials

Instructional materials in the classroom can contain many biases. Culturally responsive teachers work against these biases by acting as critical consumers of the materials they use in the classroom (Banks, 1995). Through deconstructing negative stereotypes in instructional materials, teachers refuse to accept negative mainstream definitions given to particular groups (Jones, 2006). Teachers take the opportunity to be purposeful in their instruction to counteract negative stereotypes, and teach their students to do the same.

A few years ago, I asked my graduate students to produce group presentations on literacy practices they were using in their schools. The final group of the evening spoke of the importance of using authentic materials such as story books that one could use to connect to the lives of students. They showed many colorful and beautifully illustrated books about a variety of things. The books were very eye-catching and the stories were age-appropriate for the grade levels they were addressing. One of the books that the group presented was about a young girl and her grandmother taking a trip to visit the young girl's father in prison. The story line did not focus on why the father was in prison, but rather focused on the relationships the little girl had with her family members.

I asked the class what they thought of the book, and they described aspects of the storyline, age-appropriateness, the complexity of the story, and the wonderful illustrations. No one had questioned why the author centered the story around an African-American family. I asked my students if they had noticed the issue of race in the book, and if they hadn't, why not? We had an interesting discussion about the aspects of "life as we know it" and what kinds of things stand out for us as acceptable or "normal" and what do not. Our questioning was in no way a critique of the author's purpose in writing the story in a particular way or having it illustrated in a certain way; it was instead a way for us to notice what we weren't questioning. Knowing that Black males are incarcerated at a rate that is substantially higher than Whites, did the group accept it as "normal" that the father in the story be African American and not from some other racial or ethnic group? As noted previously, we as teachers must first be aware of our own ideological perspectives before we can move toward a critical pedagogy. The goal of the discussion was to help the graduate students be aware of how they themselves accept stereotypes and how they can help their students move toward deconstructing negative stereotypes in the texts they read.

An effective tool in deconstructing negative stereotypes in instructional materials is constructing "counter-narratives." Counter-narratives "encourage people to challenge the unquestioning acceptance of cultural norms that have become more or less invisible over time" (Lewison, Leland, & Harste, 2008, p. 82). Lewison, Leland, and Harste argue that counter-narratives are empowering because they allow us to think about the different realities experienced by others. Counter-narratives can be used to deconstruct all stereotypical social constructions. For example, after students read or view the story of *Peter Pan*, they can dialogue about how the book or film frames Native Americans and can then construct counter-narratives that challenge the popular stereotype of this social group that comes out of the story. Texts that present princesses as young, White and beautiful can be deconstructed for their culturally racist biases, and students can be asked to rewrite these texts to counter gender biases (perhaps using books such as *The Paper Bag Princess* [Munsch & Martchenko, 1999] as a model). Even very young children can detect and participate in a discussion of biases. For instance, children can be asked to respond to a prompt such as "Is this woman like your grandmother?" after listening to a story that depicts an older woman in stereotypically negative ways. Posing questions for students about negative stereotypes is a very powerful way to help them think about materials (text, media, illustrations, advertisements) placed before them and how they can deconstruct these materials in a positive manner.

As a tool for deconstructing negative stereotypes, counter-narratives can be used by teachers and students in many different ways, from simply questioning dominant cultural beliefs, to re-writing stories that counter stereotypical gender, racial, and ethnic roles. Counter-narratives can be used at all levels of education, from pre-Kindergarten through graduate school, and within any genre, both fiction and non-fiction. Using this kind of tool helps interrupt patterns of stereotypical ideology that has become the "normal" way of thinking and learning for most students and teachers (Sumara & Davis, 1999). Aside from promoting social justice, counter-narratives broaden the possibility for dialogue and thought about the common representation of particular groups. As students gain experience and understanding about how to question in this way, they become proficient at identifying negative stereotypes that have been culturally framed as normal.

Uncovering Biases in Popular Culture

The importance of media in society has changed over the past several decades, and the influence of media on students has become a very powerful one. Pierre Bourdieu (1977) once spoke of schools as the greatest socializing agent for students. This statement is still true in many ways, yet the influence of popular culture, particularly as it is played out in the media, arguably overpowers schools in socializing individuals within society. Media such as billboards, TV shows, commercials, magazine ads, and movies are organized in particular ways and "delivered" to particular audiences in order to impart specific messages designed to influence our behavior. Sholle and Denski (1993) suggest that contemporary mass media that has resulted from the expansion of science and technology has "ushered in forms of domination and control that appear to thwart rather than extend the possibilities of human emancipation" (p. 307). Yet despite the huge influence of popular media in society, rarely is it critiqued in schools (Stevens & Bean, 2007).

Consider for a moment, the influence that Disney and other animated movies have had on the youth of America. Young girls dream of becoming princesses saved by a charming prince who is typically White and affluent. There are many messages embedded within these kinds of texts (Cortés, 2000). Body image for women comes into play as the princesses they see in Disney films come in only one shape and size — very slender and petite. Additionally, young girls receive gender information that tells them females are weaker than males and must therefore wait to be "saved" by them. Racial undertones exist in these movies as well, as most protagonists are White, and if they are not, they still carry European features (e.g., small noses, smoothly textured hair). Along with race and gender, messages about social class are also embedded in these movies (Tobin, 2000). "Happily ever after" always involves castles instead of cottages, further promoting the idea that happiness and success always require loads of money.

The images provided by the media have rapidly taken over the appeal of written text (Kress, 2003; Van Leeuwen, 2005). For this reason, it is more important than ever to understand that the whole world is a text and can move far beyond what is seen in the written word. Without exploring the power of popular culture and the media, we ignore the influence of power structures that should and must be questioned. Critical media literacy can be used to carry out necessary critiques of "texts" that exist in our everyday lives. According to Alvermann, Moon, and Hagood (1999), "Print and non-print texts that are a

248

part of everyday life help to construct students' knowledge of the world and the various social, economic, and political positions they occupy within it" (p. 119). In this context, popular culture creates an opportunity for dialogue and expression of multiple viewpoints and interpretations. Thus, there are a variety of ways for students to engage in critical media literacy.

For instance, students can be invited to write counter-narratives to various types of media as described in the previous section. Additionally, students can pose questions for their peers to answer, they can write reflective responses, they can engage in role-play, or they can create media themselves. Stevens and Bean (2007) offer an example of how to use critical media literacy in classrooms through an activity they call the *Resident Critic*. Using popular television shows, the students are taken through the following steps:

1 Create a series of questions or an observation survey provoking a critical stance (i.e., whose viewpoint is most important? What cues are given to help us understand the power relations that are at play? What is the writer's purpose in giving certain people power in a given scenario?).
2 Ask students to provide written responses to the questions and be ready to defend their responses in a classroom discussion.
3 Inform parents about the goals of the lesson and assuage any content concerns.
4 Have students carry out their Resident Critic observations using the questions.
5 Engage students in a follow-up discussion and debriefing where they can raise additional questions.

(p. 51)

Critical media literacy provides a powerful means for questioning that students can carry with them for the rest of their lives. Engaging in this type of questioning is important because of the unparalleled pervasiveness of popular culture and the ideological messages that it conveys. What is deemed as "normal" for most people is defined by popular culture. Thus, it's vital that popular culture be interrogated, lest we accept what appears to be "normal" as fact and truth.

Using Differing Discourse Patterns to Fit the Social Context

Communication provides an avenue for interaction between individuals and groups that is necessary for humans to function effectively on a daily basis. Oftentimes, however, students in the classroom do not feel empowered to communicate with others because their home discourse may differ from the dominant discourse. Miscommunication between students and teachers occurs to the detriment of both when differences in discourse are misunderstood or go unrecognized. As noted in previous chapters, culturally responsive teachers empower students through explicit instruction regarding the discourse of power (Standard American English). In like manner, these teachers teach their students to use their own discourse patterns (specific to students' language and culture) to convey meaning in powerful ways: through questioning, writing their experiences, and negotiating the world around them.

As a teacher on the border of Mexico, I recognized many differences in the ways my Spanish-dominant students expressed themselves orally and in writing as compared to their native English-speaking counterparts. As we moved through different writing genres, it occurred to me that my students would be at a disadvantage if I didn't address differences in discourse patterns with them. We talked about the discourse patterns that are used in songs and poetry and looked at various linguistic styles as they relate to culture and language. Next, we looked at our own personal narratives and analyzed our writing to see what discourse patterns we were using. We found that most of the children in our classroom (third graders at the time) were using digressions in their narratives, but eventually made their way back to the central theme. That is, they were using a "topic-associating" communicative style that is similar to what Michaels (1981) found in her work with African American children's oral narratives. A few others wrote their narratives with an easy-to-follow beginning, middle, and end, the way our storybooks looked.

We discussed the rich ideas and content in all of their narratives and what was special about each of them. As a class, we talked about whether or not we were writing our narratives the way in which we would have told our personal experience narratives aloud. This was a wonderful way to see how our writing matched our oral storytelling, which was always connected to our language and our cultures. What a great discovery that was for the students! The study of other linguistic styles brought us to the conclusion that there were times when we could use our rich and beautiful discourses to communicate in specific contexts and for specific audiences. Learning about other ways of communicating also helped us to have in-depth discussions about the more linear and formal discourse style found in essays, reports, and responses to literary selections. The importance of acquiring knowledge about discourse patterns, how they relate to language and culture, and when and how to use them, were immeasurable for my students. In turn, it was a wonderful reminder for me as an educator to be consistent in explaining the "why" as we moved in and out of learning with one another each day.

In examining various discourse patterns, it is important to recognize that linguistic competence is a source of power. As was noted in the previous chapter,

Gee (1996) defines literacy as acquiring and gaining control over "secondary discourses"—those specific ways of thinking, acting, and using language in institutions outside of our home community. That is, students are empowered when they develop the ability to be flexible in their language use so as to be able to use language appropriately in various social contexts. Hence, students need to have opportunities to examine language differences and to learn how to use different linguistic forms for their own purposes and intentions. Studying language differences and expanding students' linguistic repertoires while simultaneously celebrating the rich linguistic traditions of their families and communities can provide students with the linguistic knowledge they need to negotiate power in diverse social situations.

To acquire secondary discourses, however, students need to actually practice using them in authentic social contexts. Thus, teachers who recognize the power of language will engage students in genuine debate and will provide opportunities for students to use language for a variety of purposes and with a variety of audiences. For instance, in the Saving Black Mountain project (Powell, Cantrell, & Adams, 2001), students made oral presentations to coal operators and the state legislature on the ecological impact of strip mining. They also wrote comprehensive proposals arguing for alternative solutions. Their teacher, Sandy Adams, was intentional in explicitly teaching students the linguistic forms that were required for presenting their ideas to those who hold positions of power, including how to write a persuasive text that includes facts gathered from internet research and interviews. Similarly, Mr. Ledesma provided numerous lessons on the appropriate linguistic forms to use when writing letters to those in authority so that they could persuade city officials to install a stoplight. Through explicitly teaching the discourse forms necessary for tackling these real-world issues, these teachers were helping their students to develop the linguistic competence necessary for social transformation.

Praxis: A Pedagogy of Hope

Ultimately, a literacy that is grounded in sociopolitical consciousness is one that engenders agency, empowerment, and hope. It is a literacy that encourages students to critique the way things are and to work for change. It is a "literacy of promise"—one that "seeks wisdom and truth . . . [that] gives rise to social consciousness and transcends the boundaries of class, race, gender, ignorance, hopelessness, and learned helplessness" (Spears-Bunton & Powell, 2009, p. 37).

I conclude this chapter with a story that shows how literacy can lead to *praxis*. It is a personal story that illustrates how students, teachers, parents, and the community can come together to affect change. As noted previously, the

251

ultimate goal of a critical *praxis* is to question the way things are and to act in transformative ways in order to realize a more just and compassionate society. Critical theorists step out into the world with their students, critically examining language and cultural practices and the material forms and structures of society for their inherent ideological perspectives. As a bilingual educator, I was forced to acknowledge the ways in which dominant perspectives of language can negatively impact the lives of teachers, students, and communities.

As an elementary bilingual/biliterate educator on the border of Mexico, I had the rare opportunity to help start a bilingual program. This dual language program benefited Spanish-dominant students and English-dominant students who, by the time they reached third grade, were well on their way to bilingualism and biliteracy in Spanish and English. The research-based program functioned beautifully and had the full support of administration at the school and district level. After a few years of strong success, a change in administration led to a hegemonic, subtractive ideology that threatened bilingual education for the culturally and linguistically diverse learners at our school. Slowly, the bilingual program that had shown such promise and success was dismantled due to political forces that were bent on eradicating students' native language as they acquired English, while at the same time, taking away native English-speaking students' opportunity to become bilingual and biliterate in two languages.

In response to this situation, I joined two other teachers from that school district and a pre-service teacher, and embarked on a grassroots effort that resulted in our own bilingual, bicultural school completely apart from the school district. We were all trained and certified to teach in a bilingual/bicultural setting, but our project needed more: It was necessary for us to include the voices of the people we were interested in serving. We went door-to-door talking to parents and students about our dream of providing a school where research-based practices empowered the educational community—where we would all have a voice together in educating our children. Little by little, we gathered our numbers. We held cafés (gatherings that included coffee, sweetbread, and conversation) in homes, the nearby Boys and Girls Club building, and any other place that offered a venue where we could all meet and discuss our dream. We talked about what bilingual education meant to all of us in that social location. We shared what studies have taught us about this kind of learning and what all of us could contribute to that body of knowledge. We took a stance of reciprocity in this area, knowing that research was important to consider, but acutely aware that we could, in turn, inform the research. This kind of conversation was held *with* the parents and prospective students of our dream school. Together, we met with city officials to acquire land, looked at how to present curriculum, researched food service programs, and studied materials we thought were adequate for our students. We learned not only how to put together a school and about the politics that surrounded that endeavor, but more importantly, we learned how to connect our life stories.

Through this process, I realized that my own biography was intricately connected to the people I served. In fact, it wasn't that I served them; it was that we served one another through a shared and meaningful vision that sought to bring language, power, and pedagogy to each and every one of us regardless of our station in life. This was *real* power. By working together and questioning the dominant ideology, we created a school that has been serving culturally and linguistically diverse students, families, and educators for well over a decade.

Freire (2007) refers to "educative gatherings" where people get together and confront the obstacles they face in reaching their goals with hope. This is exactly what happened as we worked toward creating our school. *Praxis* engenders hope. Culturally responsive instruction cannot be carried out in classrooms and schools without including these types of "educative gatherings," whether they are held in the classroom or the community. As students are encouraged to use inquiry, they must be given hope that transformative change is possible!

Table 9.1 Summary of CRIOP Component: Sociopolitical Consciousness/Multiple Perspectives

Element	What you would expect to see in a classroom where CRI practices are occurring	What you would expect to see in a classroom where CRI practices are not occurring
Students are allowed to question the way things are.	Teacher helps students identify important social issues and facilitates students' investigation of the status quo and how to challenge it. Students may identify issues within their own school or texts to investigate and question.	Teacher teaches to the "norm" by using standard textbooks and curriculum. Teacher discourages critical thought or questioning of instructional materials or social issues.
Students take action on real world problems.	Teacher and students identify and discuss issues within the community that are of relevance to their lives. Teacher facilitates student advocacy for their communities.	Teacher does not bring community and social issues into the classroom. Learning occurs only as it relates to the standard curriculum.
Instructional materials that demonstrate negative stereotypes are deconstructed.	Teacher facilitates students' understanding of stereotypes and their function in society. Teacher helps students frame differing viewpoints about accepted roles (race,	Teacher uses materials in class that perpetuate stereotypes without deconstructing their meaning for students.

253

Table 9.1 Continued

Element	What you would expect to see in a classroom where CRI practices are occurring	What you would expect to see in a classroom where CRI practices are not occurring
	gender, age, ethnicity, class, etc.) depicted in instructional materials.	
Students uncover biases in popular culture.	Teacher helps students identify bias in text and media. Teacher facilitates instruction that promotes student questioning of popular culture in various ways.	When popular culture is used in the classroom, bias is not identified or deconstructed.
Students have the opportunity to learn about differing discourse patterns in varied social contexts.	Teacher uses students' discourse in literacy instruction and facilitates students' understanding of their own rich discourses and the discourse of power. Students understand when varied discourses are appropriate when engaging in all domains of language (reading, writing, listening, speaking).	Varied home discourses of students are not validated or employed in instruction. Teacher uses and expects only the discourse of power to be used in instruction and learning.

REFLECTIVE ACTIVITIES

1 Examine the materials you are using in your instruction. Do they prompt students to question "the way things are?" Think about bringing in supplementary materials that offer different perspectives and help students question text in positive and proactive ways. Model ways to question the status quo in instructional materials and even within the school setting. What are ways that you can model questioning "the way things are" for students that help them approach issues in an informed and meaningful manner?

2 Brainstorm about current issues that are going on in the surrounding community and the world at large with students. Are there any issues that are of great importance to the students? How can literacy be used to empower students to take action on real-world problems that affect

their lives and the lives of their families (i.e. writing letters, inviting speakers, interviewing)? How can you help students identify audience, purpose, and advocacy when addressing real world issues?

3 Choose a text that would normally be used in instruction, but is rarely questioned (e.g., a book about male doctors and female nurses). Engage students in questioning among one another in small groups and then as a whole group. Who is the character/person in power? Why is that individual in power? What characteristics does that character possess? Is this scenario always accurate? What if the female was the one in power? What if the grandparent was shown as the one with strength? Allow students to tell the story in a different way, a way that counteracts the negative stereotype.

4 Prepare a lesson on bias in the media/popular culture that includes the use of magazines, YouTube, or DVDs. Allow students to identify the messages that are depicted in the "texts" that they are exposed to and to ask questions related to the text. Have students develop counter-narratives and share/discuss them with one another.

5. Take a good look at the students in your classroom. Do they use a different discourse than you in informal communication or formal learning situations? Do they use differing discourses from one another? Language and culture are represented in an individual's discourse and can bring valuable experiences to the classroom. How can you include your students' discourses in literacy? How can you teach students about the language of power in a way that validates who they are and empowers them at the same time?

REFERENCES

Alvermann, D. E., Moon, J. S., & Hagood, M. C. (1999). *Popular culture in the classroom: Teaching and researching critical media literacy*. Newark, DE: International Reading Association.

Ball, A. F. (2000). Empowering pedagogies that enhance the learning of multicultural students. *Teachers College Record, 102*, 1006–1034.

Banks, J.A. (1995). Multicultural education and curriculum transformation. *Journal of Negro Education, 64*, 390–400.

Bernhardt, E. (2003). Challenges to reading research from a multilingual world. *Reading Research Quarterly, 38*, 112–117.

Bourdieu, P. (1973). Cultural reproduction and social reproduction. In R. Brown (Ed.), *Knowledge, education and cultural change* (pp. 71–112). London: Tavistock.

Bourdieu, P. (1977). Cultural reproduction and social reproduction. In J. Karabel and A. H. Halsey (Eds.), *Power and ideology in education* (pp. 487–511). Oxford: Oxford University Press.

Bourdieu, P. (1984). *Distinction: A social critique of the judgment of taste.* Cambridge, MA: Harvard University Press.

Bourdieu, P. (1987). What makes a social class? On the theoretical and practical existence of groups. *Berkeley Journal of Sociology, 32,* 1–18.

Bourdieu, P., & Passeron, J. C. (1977). *Reproduction, education, society and culture.* Beverly Hills, CA: Sage Publications.

Cary, S. (2000). *Working with second language learners: Answers to teachers' top ten questions.* Portsmouth, NH: Heinemann.

Cortés, C. E. (2000). *The children are watching: How the media teach about diversity.* New York: Teachers College Press.

Darder, A. (1991). *Culture and power in the classroom.* Westport, CT: Bergin & Garvey.

Darder, A., Baltodamo, M. P., & Torres, R. D. (2009). *The critical pedagogy reader* (2nd ed.). New York: Routledge.

Edelsky, C. (1999). *Making justice our project: Teachers working toward critical whole language practice.* Urbana, IL: National Council of Teachers of English.

Fickel, L. H. (2009). "Unbanking" education: Exploring constructs of knowledge, teaching, learning. In L. A. Spears-Bunton & R. Powell (Eds.), *Toward a literacy of promise: Joining the African American struggle* (pp. 41–56). New York: Routledge.

Freire, P. (1970). *Pedagogy of the oppressed.* New York: Herder & Herder.

Freire, P. (1998). *Pedagogy of freedom: Ethics, democracy, and civic courage.* Lanham, MD: Rowman & Littlefield.

Freire, P. (2001). *Daring to dream: Toward a pedagogy of the unfinished.* Boulder, CO: Paradigm Publishers.

Freire, P. (2009). From a pedagogy of the oppressed. In A. Darder, M. P. Baltodano, & R. D. Torres (Eds.), *The critical pedagogy reader,* 2nd ed. (pp. 52–60). New York: Routledge.

Freire, P., & Macedo, D. (1987). *Literacy: Reading the word and the world.* South Hadley, MA: Bergin and Garvey.

Gee, J. P. (1996). *Social linguistics and literacies: Ideology in discourses.* Bristol, PA: Taylor & Francis.

Hall, S. (1981). Cultural studies: Two paradigms. In T. Bennett et al. (Eds.), *Culture, ideology and social process.* London: Batsford Academic & Educational Press.

Jones, S. (2006). *Girls, social class and literacy: What teachers can do to make a difference.* Portsmouth, NH: Heinemann.

Kress, G. (2003). *Literacy in the new media age.* New York: Routledge.

Lewison, M., Leland, C., & Harste, J. C. (2008). *Creating critical classrooms: K-8 reading and writing with an edge.* New York: Lawrence Erlbaum Associates.

Macedo, D., Dendrinos, B., & Gounari, P. (2003). *The hegemony of English.* Boulder, CO: Paradigm Publishers.

McLaren, P. (2009). Critical pedagogy: A look at the major concepts. In A. Darder, M. P. Baltodano, & R. D. Torres (Eds.), *The critical pedagogy reader* (2nd ed., pp. 52–60). New York: Routledge.

Michaels, S. (1981). "Sharing time": Children's narrative styles and differential access to literacy. *Language in society, 10,* 432–442.

Munsch, R. N., & Martchenko, M. (1999). *The paper bag princess.* New York: Scholastic.

Paul, R., & Elder, L. (2005). *The thinker's guide to the nature and functions of critical and creative thinking.* Dillon Beach, CA: Foundation for Critical Thinking.

Powell, R. (1999). *Literacy as a moral imperative.* Lanham, MD: Rowman & Littlefield

Powell, R., Cantrell, S.C., & Adams, S. (2001). Saving Black Mountain: The promise of critical literacy in a multicultural democracy. *The Reading Teacher, 54,* 772–781.

Sholle, D., & Denski, S. (1993). Reading and writing the media: Critical media literacy and postmodernism. In C. Lankshear, & P. L. McLaren (Eds.), *Critical literacy: Politics, praxis, and the postmodern* (pp. 297–321). Albany, NY: SUNY Press.

Shor, I. (1992). *Empowering education: Critical teaching for social change.* Chicago: University of Chicago Press.

Shor, I., & Freire, P. (1987). *A pedagogy for liberation: Dialogues on transforming education.* New York: Bergin & Garvey.

Spears-Bunton, L. A., & Powell, R. (2009). Along the road to social justice: A literacy of promise. In L. A. Spears-Bunton, & R. Powell (Eds.), *Toward a literacy of promise: Joining the African American struggle* (pp. 23–39). New York: Routledge.

Stevens, L. P., & Bean, T. W. (2007). *Critical literacy: Context, research, and practice in the K-1 classroom.* Thousand Oaks, CA: Sage.

Sumara, D., & Davis, B. (1999). Interrupting heteronormativity: Toward a queer curriculum theory. *Curriculum Inquiry, 29* (2), 191–208.

Tobin, J. (2000). *Good guys don't wear hats: Children's talk about the media.* New York: Teachers College Press.

van Leeuwen, T. (2005). *Introducing social semiotics.* London: Routledge.

Villegas, A. M., & Lucas, T. (2007). The culturally responsive teacher. *Educational Leadership, 64,* 28–33.

Wallowitz, L. (2008). *Critical literacy as resistance.* New York: Peter Lang Publishers.

Notes on Contributors

Susan Chambers Cantrell is an Assistant Professor in the Department of Curriculum and Instruction at the University of Kentucky and is Director of Research for the Collaborative Center for Literacy Development. Her research focuses on teachers' efficacy and development and instructional practices for improving children's and adolescents' reading comprehension.

Yolanda Gallardo Carter is Dean of Undergraduate Education at Georgetown College in Georgetown, Kentucky. Her areas of interest are second language acquisition, critical pedagogy, culturally responsive instruction, and the sociology of education. Currently, she is involved in second language acquisition and literacy research.

Angela Cox is an Assistant Professor of Education at Georgetown College in Georgetown, Kentucky. She teaches reading methods, literacy for elementary teachers and clinical literacy courses for graduate candidates. Her research interests include teacher beliefs and efficacy, critical literacy, and culturally responsive instruction.

Rebecca Powell holds the Majorie Bauer Stafford Professorship of Education at Georgetown College in Georgetown, Kentucky. She directs the Center for Culturally Relevant Pedagogy and is the author of three books: *Literacy as a Moral Imperative: Facing the Challenges of a Pluralistic Society*; *Straight Talk: Growing as Multicultural Educators;* and *Toward a Literacy of Promise: Joining the African American Struggle* (with Linda Spears-Bunton).

Sherry Wilson Powers is a Professor of Literacy Education, the Director of the School of Teacher Education, and Associate Dean in the College of Education and Behavioral Sciences at Western Kentucky University. Her research focuses on teacher discourse, equity pedagogy, and culturally responsive instruction. Currently, she is involved in critical race theory research.

Elizabeth Campbell Rightmyer is an education/research consultant whose interest in culturally responsive instruction stems from her research on effective intervention for struggling primary school readers. Also interested in curricula based on children's interests and abilities and democratic classroom management, she is currently Head of Lower School at Louisville Collegiate School.

Kelly A. Seitz joined the educational field as a second career, earning a post-baccalaureate degree in Elementary Education from the University of Kentucky and a Master's in Elementary Education at Georgetown College. Through her work with the Center for Culturally Relevant Pedagogy, she has developed a passion for assisting educational professionals in developing genuine educator–parent partnerships and has made it the theme of her doctoral research.

Tiffany Wheeler is an Assistant Professor of Education at Transylvania University in Lexington, Kentucky. Her teaching and research interests include culturally responsive pedagogy, sociocultural perspectives of literacy instruction, race and ethnicity issues in education, and immigrant children. She is a former elementary classroom teacher and is a National Board Certified Teacher.

Index

Note: 't' after a page number denotes a table.

achievement gap: and CRI
   (culturally relevant instruction) 7,
   126; and cultural data sets
   127–128; and deficit perspective
   3, 8; and explicit instruction
   158–161; and standardized
   testing 90
Ada, A. F. 57, 74
Adams, S. 177, 243, 251
African American Adolescent Male
   Summer Literacy Institute
   (AAAMSLI) 176
African Americans: call and
   response 194, 204, 208–209;
   and codeswitching 206;
   collaborative learning 176; and
   cultural modeling/cultural data
   sets 128; and Culture and
   Language Academy for Success
   (CLAS) 35–36, 206, 208–209;
   and distrust of school system 67;
   effect of social context on
   107–108; and funds of knowledge
   169–170; "signifying" language
   157, 208; and "stage setting"
   classroom behavior 193–194

African American Vernacular
   English (AAVE) 171, 206–207
Allen, J. 133–134
Alvermann, D. E. 213, 248–249
Amanti, C. 7, 76–77, 129
Appalachia 50, 190–192
Apple, M. W. 125
Arter, J. 90–91
Asanto, J. 197
Ashton-Warner, S. 146
Asian Americans 41, 194
assessment practices: and
   collaborative learning 110–111;
   CRIOP (Culturally Responsive
   Instruction Observation Protocol)
   components 113–114t; dynamic
   assessments 97–98, 101–102;
   effective 90–92, 97–99; for
   English language learners (ELLs)
   105–107; example of 102–105;
   formative assessments 91–92,
   110; ineffective 91–92;
   Initiation-Response-Evaluation
   (IRE) 91, 202; and learner self-
   assessment 108–110; in Nunavut,
   Canada 111–112; practical

applications of 99–111; reflective activities 114–115; social context of 107–111; standardized testing 15, 89–90, 92, 93–97; student-parent conferences 109; summative assessments 92; "talking partners" strategy 100–101, 110–111
Au, K. H. 44, 121, 124, 194
August, D. L. 95, 199
Avalos, M. A. 175

Baber, C. R. 67
Bailey, J. 110
Baker, A. 17–19, 215–216
balanced instruction 161–163
Ball, A. F. 236
Ballenger, C. 22–23, 29
Baltodano, M. P. 235
Banda, D. R. 62
banking model of education 235–236, 238
Banks, C. M. 138
Banks, J. A. 24, 126, 127, 138
Baquedano-Lopez, P. 131, 197
Barrie, J. 247
Barton, D. 76
Bean, T. W. 249
Bechard, M. 216–217, 218
Becoming Teammates (Endrizzi) 59
Beltrán, A. 106
Berry, R. A. W. 38
best practices. *See* literacy instruction
bias. *See* educator bias
Bilingual Cooperative Integrated Reading and Composition program (BCIRC) 156
Blachowicz, C. L. Z. 160
Bode, P. 119, 122, 152
Bondy, E. 21, 23
Bourdieu, P. 248
Boykin, A. W. 156
Bridges, E. M. 62
Brock, C. H. 98, 211
Brooks, J. L. 14
Brown, D. F. 21–22

Browning-Aiken, A. 77
Buhrow, B. 178

Calderón, M. 156
call and response 194, 204, 208–209
Campano, G. 48, 130–131
Campoy, F. I. 57, 74
Cantrell, S. C. 177, 243
care: as compassion/empathy 24–26, 30t; definition of 17; as ethic of helping 26–28, 30t; example of 17–19; and high expectations 28–30, 31t; as instructional strategy 13–14; reflective activities 31–32; as respect for all 20–23, 30t; six themes of 16
Carroll, J. H. 44
Carter, Debbie 71–72
Cary, S. 244
Center for Culturally Relevant Pedagogy 245–246
Center for Research on Education, Diversity, and Excellence (CREDE) 28
Chappuis, J. 90–91
Chappuis, S. 90–91
Charlotte's Web (White) 208
Chavez, C. 175
Chen, C. 198
Chinn, P. C. 121
Christenson, S. L. 63, 211–212
Christian, S. 176
citizenship 119–120, 145–146
Clarke, S. 100, 109, 110
CLAS (Culture and Language Academy for Success) 35–36, 206, 208–209
classroom climate/physical environment: CRIOP (Culturally Responsive Instruction Observation Protocol) components 52–53t, 168–169; and dominant culture 36–37; and educator-family partnerships 68; example of 48–49; practical applications 44–48; "print-rich" 43–44; reflective activities 53;

research on 38–44; seating arrangements 43, 45–46. *See also* collaborative learning

classroom discourse practices: and contrastive analysis 206–207; CRIOP (Culturally Responsive Instruction Observation Protocol) components 221–223t; and cultural congruity 193–194; English-only policies 196–198; examples of 215–220; Initiation-Response-Evaluation (IRE) 91, 202; instructional conversation 199–200, 210–220; and learners' home languages 194–196, 202; practical applications of 202–220; reflective activities 224; research on 192–201; situational appropriateness of language 196, 206; and social context 249–251; Standard English 170–172, 200–201, 202–203, 237, 250; and student talk 198–200

Cleary, M. 63

coal mining 177, 243–244, 251

codeswitching 206

Coleman, T. J. 62

collaborative learning 52–53t; African Americans 176; as assessment practice 110–111; classroom activities 45–46; effects on learning 40–41; and English language learners (ELLs) 98–99, 156, 176; vs. individualistic learning 38; and instructional conversation 210–211; as instructional practice 155–157; obstacles to 157; and racial/ethnic identity 41; and respect 46–48; seating arrangements for 43, 45–46; and social change 39–40; and social skills instruction 46–47; and student talk 198–200

collective learning. *See* collaborative learning

Collins, M. 27, 30

commodification of literacy instruction 1–2, 8

compassion/empathy 24–26, 30t

Compton-Lilly, C. 77–78, 134, 164

constructivist model of literacy instruction 124, 125t, 145

contrastive analysis 170–172, 206–207

Costello, P. 101–102, 105

counter-narratives 247–248

CREDE (Center for Research on Education, Diversity, and Excellence) 28

CRI (culturally responsive instruction): compared to traditional practices 9; definition of 7, 154; pedagogy 126–127; premise of 4

CRIOP (Culturally Responsive Instruction Observation Protocol), components of 8

critical literacy 239–240, 241, 244, 248–249. *See also* sociopolitical consciousness

critical thinking 143–145. *See also* critical literacy

Crowe, C. 14

cultural congruity 154–158, 193–194

cultural data sets 127–128, 134

culturally responsive instruction. *See* CRI (culturally responsive instruction)

cultural mismatch 29, 124

cultural modeling 128, 157

Culture and Language Academy for Success (CLAS) 35–36, 206, 208–209

curriculum: and affirmation of learners' identities 138–139; and alternate perspectives 142–143; CRIOP (Culturally Responsive Instruction Observation Protocol) components 147t; and cultural data sets 127–128; and culturally responsive pedagogy 126–127; example of culturally responsive 135–137, 139–142; and funds of knowledge 129; multicultural 121; and No Child Left Behind (NCLB) 120–121; as political 131; practical applications for 132–145; prescribed 121; and real-world issues 143–145; reflective activities 148; research on 122–132; and sociocultural theory 122–124; and structural inequality theory 124–126

Darder, A. 235, 238
Davidson, N. 177–178
Davis, S. 23
"deficit model": and achievement gap 126; countered by educator-learner relationships 4; and educator bias 3, 65
Delpit, L. 200
Dendrinos, B. 236
Denski, S. 248
Denton, P. 22
Deuel, A. 109
Dewey, J. 127
Dill, E. 156
discourse practices. See classroom discourse practices
discussion web activity 213–214
Disney movies 248
diversity: and classroom environment 47–48; vs. ethnic encapsulation 138; importance of reflecting learners' 35–37; and structural inequality theory 124–126
Dixon-Krauss, L. 97
dominant culture: bias in 248–249; and classroom environment 36–37; and cultural mismatch 29; and education 237; and marginalized populations 237–238; recognition of 24; Standard English 170–172, 200–201, 202–203, 237, 250
Dowdy, J. K. 190
The Dreamkeepers: Successful Teachers of African American Children (Ladson-Billings) 38–39, 133

Dudley-Maring, C. 139
Duffy, G. 123–124
dynamic assessments 97–98, 101–102

Eastern Kentucky Teachers' Network 50
Edelsky, C. 121, 244
education: banking model of 235–236, 238; bias in 246–248; and dominant culture 237; as political 237, 244. See also literacy instruction
educator bias 2–3, 36–37, 42, 65
educator-family partnerships: benefits of 61–63; challenges to 64–67; and classroom climate/physical environment 68; CRIOP (Culturally Responsive Instruction Observation Protocol) components 80–81t; definition of 61; example of 71–72; and families' "funds of knowledge" 76–79; and home visits 74–75; and open communication 68–70; vs. parent involvement 59–60; practical applications for 68–79; reflective activities 81; research on 59–67
Eller, R. G. 191
Elliott, J. 29
Ellis, S. 218–219
Endrizzi, C. K. 73, 105–107
English language learners (ELLs): affirming identities of 201, 205; assessment practices for 105–107; and collaborative learning 98–99, 156, 176, 211; and English-only policies 196–198; expanding level of talk for 198; and explicit instruction 160–161, 175–176; and home language 199–200; and inquiry-based learning 178–179; and literacy curriculum 130–132; and standardized testing 95–97; and vocabulary development 161, 165. See also learners

English-only policies 196–198
Enriquez, G. 109
Epstein, J. L. 60
Eskimo dance 139–142
explicit instruction 158–161, 160–161, 172, 175–176

Fabregas, V. 133–134
fairness 20–21
families 63–64. *See also* educator-family partnerships
Fickel, L. H. 240
Fine, M. J. 63
Fisher, D. 100, 105
Fisher, P. J. 160
Fitzgerald, J. 161–162
Flood, J. 105
fluency rubrics 105
Ford, D. Y. 28
Formative Assessment in Action (Clarke) 100
formative assessments. *See* assessment practices
Frasier, M. M. 62
Freire, P.: on banking model of education 235–236, 238; education as empowering 244; on educative gatherings 253; on engaging in learning 240, 241; on inequality 233; on *praxis* 235; teaching as political act 237
Frey, N. 100
funds of knowledge: integrating into curricula 129, 157–158; practical applications of 76–79, 133–134, 169–170
Funds of Knowledge: Theorizing Practices in Households, Communities, and Classrooms (González, Moll, and Amanti) 76–77, 129

Gallimore, R. 199
Gándara, P. 197
Garcia, A. U. 178
García, G. E. 95
Garza, C. L. 102–103
Gay, G.: on caring for learners 20; on classroom environments 168; on collaborative learning 27, 39–40, 52; on culturally responsive teaching 127; and curricula 125; on relational competencies 126–127; on "stage setting" classroom behavior 193–194; on uncaring learning environments 28
Gee, J. P. 202, 251
Gersten, R. 160
Ginsberg, M. B. 164, 176–177
Giroux, H. 120
Goble, P. 79
Goldenberg, C. 210
Gollnick, D. M. 121
González, N. 7, 76–77, 125, 129
Gounari, P. 236
Grantham, T. C. 62
Greenfield, E. 171
Guskey, T. 110
Guthrie, W. 245–246
Gutiérrez, K. 130, 131, 158, 197
Gutiérrez, K. D. 52

Hagood, M. C. 248–249
Haitian students 22–23, 209
Hall, S. 236
Halo (video game) 136
Hamlyn, H. 48–49
Hampton, L. 102–105, 218
Hankins, K. 133–134
Hansen, J. 43
"Harriet Tubman" (Greenfield) 171
Harry, B. 62, 68
Harste, J. 145, 241, 242–243, 247
Hawaiian students 155, 194, 210
Heath, S. B. 171, 193, 207
"helping" classroom environment 26–28, 30t, 38
Hensley, M. 75
Hertz-Lazarowitz, R. 156
high expectations 28–30, 31t, 168
Hispanic Americans 41–42, 98, 106–107, 193–194, 233–234. *See also* English language learners (ELLs)

history 242–243
Holubec, E. J. 157
homelessness 145
Homer 136
home visits 74–75, 129, 133
hooks, bell 35
Howard, A. 217
How Sweet the Sound (Hudson and Hudson) 79
Hudson, C. 79
Hudson, W. 79
Hurley, S. R. 105

Ice Cube 135
ideology: definition of 236–237; and dominant culture 238
Igus, T. 79
Implementing Student-Led Conferences (Bailey and Guskey) 110
information reading inventory (IRI) 97
Initiation-Response-Evaluation (IRE) 91, 202
In my family/En mi familia (Garza) 102–103
inquiry-based learning 164, 176–179
instructional conversation 199–200, 210–220
instructional practices. *See* literacy instruction
Irvine, J. J. 14
I See the Rhythm (Igus) 79

Jackson, O. 135
Jacob, E. 156
jargon 66, 69
Jerry Maguire (film) 14
Jimenez, F. 79
Jiménez, R. T. 160
Johnson, D. W. 157
Johnson, T. R. 157
Johnston, P. 93–94, 101–102
Jones, S. 109
journaling 106
Julius Caesar (Shakespeare) 136

Kamehameha Early Education Program (KEEP) 155–156
KEEP (Kamehameha Early Education Program) 155–156
Kelly, T. E. 120
Kennedy, A. 109
Kohl, H. 25
Kohn, A. 146
Kraemer, J. 198
Kruse, M. 138
Kuhn, M. R. 198
Kyle, D. W. 198

Labov, W. 107
Ladson-Billings, G.: on culturally responsive teachers 38–40, 127; on culturally responsive teaching 3–4, 9, 133; on learners' funds of knowledge 158
Ladybugs, Tornadoes, and Swirling Galaxies: English Language Learners Discover Their World through Inquiry (Buhrow and Garcia) 178
The Lady in the Box (McGovern) 145
Landsman, J. 50–51, 65
language: codeswitching 206; of home vs. school 194–196, 220–221; of power 200–201; situational appropriateness of 196, 206. *See also* Standard English
Language Assessment Scales (LAS) 96
Lapp, D. 105, 211
learners: affirming identities of 50–51, 138–139, 201, 203–205; expanding level of talk for 198–200; home languages of 194–196, 200–201; male 43; motivations of 163–167, 176–179; as objects 25, 121, 239; passive/apathetic 123; racially/ethnically diverse 35–36, 39, 41–42; relevancy of instruction to 143–145, 157, 163–167; resistant 40; self

assessments 108–110; and student-parent conferences 109; as teachers 27–28. *See also* English language learners (ELLs)

learning as social activity 1–2, 7–8, 15, 39, 97–99, 124, 153–154, 162–163. *See also* collaborative learning

Lee, C. 128, 134, 157, 208

Leland, C. 145, 241, 242–243, 247

Levine, D. U. 62

Lewis, C. W. 65

Lewison, M. 145, 241, 242–243, 247

Lezotte, L. W. 62

Li, G. 42

Lipson, M. Y. 122

Lipton, M. 122–123

listening: in educator-family partnerships 75; as form of respect 23–24, 69

literacy instruction: balanced instruction 161–163; best practices 153–154; commodification of 1–2, 8; constructivist model of 124, 125t, 145; and contrastive analysis 170–172; CRIOP (Culturally Responsive Instruction Observation Protocol) components 181–182t; and cultural congruity 154–158; and English language learners (ELLs) 130–132; and explicit instruction 158–161, 172, 175–176; and families' "funds of knowledge" 76–79, 157–158; inquiry-based learning 164, 176–179; modified guided reading (MGR) 175–176; multicultural 121; practical applications for 167–179; as preparation for citizenship 120, 145–146; and prescribed curricula 121; and reading compacts 70; reductionist view of 8, 93–94; reflective activities 182; and relevancy to learners 143–145, 157, 163–167;

research on 153–167; sociocultural context of 97–99, 122–124, 153–154, 162–163; and strategy instruction 159–160; vocabulary development 160–161, 165, 172–175. *See also* assessment practices; curriculum; education

Lord of the Flies (Golding) 136

Lost (TV series) 136

Louie, Belinda 138

Lynn, M. 158

Lyon, G. E. 205

Macedo, D. 236

Malo-juvera, V. 135–137, 173–175

Maori people 146

Marshall, K. 25

Martchenko, M. 247

Martinez-Roldan, C. 199

Matuszny, R. M. 62

McGinnis, T. A. 178–179

McGovern, A. 145

McIntyre, E. 124–125, 198

McKoon, G. 95

McLaren, P. 241

Messing, J. 77

Meyer, R. 4–5

Meyer, S. 136

MGR (modified guided reading) 175–176

Michaels, S. 250

modified guided reading (MGR) 175–176

Mohr, K. A. J. 44

Moll, L. 7, 26, 76–77, 129

Montero, M. K. 198

Moon, J. S. 248–249

multicultural education: and cultural data sets 127–128; curriculum 121; goals of 122; literature 138–139

multiculturalism. *See* diversity

Munsch, R. N. 247

Murphy, S. 93

mutualism. *See* educator-family partnerships

National Literacy Panel on
  Language-Minority Children and
  Youth 95, 199
National Reading Panel 159
Navajo students 209–210
NCLB (No Child Left Behind)
  120–121
Neff, D. 7
Nelson, T. H. 109
Nieto, Sonia 15, 17, 119, 122, 152
No Child Left Behind (NCLB)
  120–121
Noddings, N. 16–17
Nunavut, Canada 111–112
NWA 135

Oakes, J. 122–123
October Sky (film) 134
The Odyssey (Homer) 136
Ogbu, J. U. 40
100% Club program 70
On Solid Ground (Taberski) 46
oppositional identity theory 40
Optimal Learning Environment
  (OLE) Project 106–107

Paley, Vivian Gussin 24
Pang, V. O. 194
The Paper Bag Princess (Munsch
  and Martchenko) 247
parent collaboration. See educator-
  family partnerships
parent involvement 59–60
Parr, J. 198
partnerships. See educator-family
  partnerships
Pascucci, R. 216
Peck, S. M. 179
Peter Pan (Barrie) 247
Peterson, B. 142
Photographs of Local Knowledge
  Sources (phOLKS) project
  133–134
physical environment. See classroom
  climate/physical environment
Pirates of the Caribbean (film) 136
Plasencia, A. 175
Pops on Patrol program 70

popular culture 248–249
Powell, R. 44, 123, 125, 177, 243,
  251
Powerful Reading Plans (PRPs) 109
praxis 235–236, 251–253
"print-rich" classrooms 43–44
PRPs (Powerful Reading Plans)
  109
Public Enemy 135
Push (Sapphire) 13, 14–15, 20, 24,
  26–27, 28, 29–30
Pygmalion study 28–29

racial/ethnic identities 41, 44,
  47–48, 50–51
Raphael, T. 98
Rascon, J. 175
Reaching Out (Jimenez) 79
read-around activity 212–213
Reading First Impact Study 7
The Reading Turn-Around (Jones,
  Clarke, and Enriquez) 109
relationships. See care
respect: as active listening 23–24,
  69; and collaborative learning
  46–48; as cultural concept 22;
  for diversity 47–48; as form of
  caring 20–23, 30t
Results Now: How We Can Achieve
  Unprecedented Improvements in
  Teaching and Learning
  (Schmoker) 165–166
retrospective miscue analysis
  108–109
Reyes, P. 39
Rickmers, D. 215, 219–220
Risko, R. J. 128
Roberts, A. C. 62
Robinson, E. L. 63
Roseberry, A. 124–125
Ross, D. D. 21
Ruiz, N. T. 106

Salas, R. 211
Samson, S. 139–142
Sanders, M. 61, 70
Sapphire 13, 14–15, 20, 24, 26–27,
  28, 29–30

Saving Black Mountain project 177, 243–244, 251
Scheu, J. A. 44
Schmidt, P. R. 73–74
Schmoker, M. 165–166
Scott, J. 234
Scribner, A. P. 39
Scribner, J. D. 39
seating arrangements 43, 45–46
second language learners (SLLs). See English language learners (ELLs)
self-assessments 108–110
Shade, B. J. 155
Shakespeare, W. 136
Shanahan, T. 199
Shannon, P. 89–90
Shobe, R. 16
Sholle, D. 248
Shor, I. 238
Short, D. J. 165
"signifying" language of African Americans 157, 208
Slavin, R. E. 156
Slavit, D. 109
Smith, B. 192
Smith, M. W. 43
social action 243–244
social change 39–40
social context: of assessment practices 107–111; of discourse patterns 249–251; of learning 1–2, 7–8, 15, 39, 97–99, 124, 153–154
social skills instruction 46–47
sociocultural theory 122–124. See also social context
sociopolitical consciousness: countering stereotypes 246–249; CRIOP (Culturally Responsive Instruction Observation Protocol) components 253–254; and critical literacy 239–240; and discourse patterns 249–251; practical applications of 240–253; and praxis 235–236, 251–253; questioning received knowledge 241–243; reflective

activities 254–255; research on 235–240; and social action 243–244; as transformational 235
Sparks, D. 108, 110
Spears-Bunton, L. A. 251
SpongeBob: The Movie (film) 136
Standard English 170–172, 200–201, 202–203, 237, 250
standardized testing: and achievement gap 89–90; and English language learners (ELLs) 95–97; limitations of 15, 92, 93–95, 239; and No Child Left Behind (NCLB) 120–121
Standards for Educational and Psychological Testing 96
Stanley, N. V. 97–98, 101
Star Boy (Goble) 79
Star Wars: Revenge of the Sith (film) 136
Steele, C. 107–108
stereotypes, negative 246–248
stereotype threat 95, 107–108, 110
Stevens, L. P. 249
Stiggins, R. 90–91, 108, 110
Stories from the Heart (Meyer) 4
strategy instruction 159–160
strip mining 177, 243–244, 251
structural inequality theory 124–126
Stubbs, Michael 195–196, 206
student-parent conferences 109
summative assessments. See assessment practices; standardized testing
Swords, R. 171, 206

Taberski, S. 46
Taffe, S. W. 160
"talking partners" strategy 100–101, 110–111
Tatum, B. D. 40, 169–170, 176
Taylor, B. M. 159
teacher care. See care
Teaching Other People's Children (Ballenger) 209
tea party activity 211–212

Tejada, C. 131
Tellez, K. 198
Thanksgiving 242
Tharp, R. G. 199
"third space" hybrid literacy
    practices 131, 158
"This Land Is Your Land" (Guthrie)
    245–246
Thompson, G. L. 16
Thorndike, E. L. 89
Tinajero, J. V. 105
Todd, M. 219
Torres, R. D. 235
Townsend, D. 211
transmission model of literacy
    instruction 124, 125t
Treisman, P. U. 41
Turner, J. C. 164–165
Twilight (Meyer) 136

U.S. Department of Education 7

Valenzuela, A. 41–42
Vargas, E. 106
vocabulary development 160–161,
    165, 172–175
Vocabulary Self-Collection Strategy
    (VSS) 165
Voltz, D. 67
Vygotsky, L. S. 1, 192
Vygotsky in the Classroom
    (Dixon-Krauss) 97

Walker-Dalhouse 128
Wallowitz, L. 239
warm demanders 21
Waxman, H. C. 199
What Can I Do? (Jackson) 135
Wheeler, R. S. 171
Wheeler, T. R. 168–169, 206
Where I'm From (Lyon) 205
White, E. B. 208
White privilege 40, 167. See
    also dominant culture; educator
    bias
White Teachers/Diverse Classrooms
    (Landsman and Lewis) 65
A White Teacher Talks About Race
    (Landsman) 50–51
Why Are All the Black Kids Sitting
    Together in the Cafeteria?
    (Tatum) 40
Wilhelm, J. D. 43
Williams, E. R. 67
Williams, W. 206
Wilson, P. 43
Wilson, S. 43
Wixson, K. K. 122
Wlodkowski, R. J. 164, 176–177

Yuraq (Eskimo Dance) 139–142

zone of proximal development 1,
    153
Zubizarreta, R. 57, 74